Charles P. Meehan

The Confederation of Kilkenny

Charles P. Meehan

The Confederation of Kilkenny

ISBN/EAN: 9783337180621

Printed in Europe, USA, Canada, Australia, Japan

Cover: Foto ©Andreas Hilbeck / pixelio.de

More available books at **www.hansebooks.com**

THE

CONFEDERATION

OF

KILKENNY.

BY THE REV. C. P. MEEHAN.

"Hapless nation—hapless land—
Heap of uncementing sand!
Crumbled by a foreign weight,
And, by worse, domestic hate."
DR. DRENNAN.

NEW YORK:
FELIX E. O'ROURKE,
9 BARCLAY STREET.
1873.

TO

CHARLES GAVAN DUFFY,

EDITOR OF THE NATION,

THE MAN WEO HAS ACHIEVED SO MUCH FOR THE
LITERATURE OF HIS NATIVE LAND,

THIS VOLUME,

UNDERTAKEN AT HIS DESIRE,

IS INSCRIBED,

BY ONE WHO IS PROUD OF HIS PERSONAL FRIENDSHIP

AND A SINCERE ADMIRER OF HIS PUBLIC

AND PRIVATE WORTH.

88. Michael and John's,
Dublin, July 28, 1846.

TO THE READERS OF THE LIBRARY OF IRELAND.

IT was my most anxious desire that this Volume might come from the Press without a single line of Preface or Introduction. I feel, however, constrained to relinquish my original intention; but the observations I have to make shall be few, and, I trust, satisfactory.

This volume, instead of preceding should have followed, the "Rising of the North," commonly called the "Great Popish Rebellion;" but as the writer who is to treat that important subject, has been prevented by urgent public duties, from completing it, I exerted whatever power in me lay to have the CONFEDERATION ready for the month of August.

All the incidents which I have endeavoured to narrate had their origin in two sources—one remote, the other proximate; the former is to be found in the "History of the Confiscations during the reign of James I." and it is presumed, that the readers of the "Library of Ireland" are already acquainted with that unparalleled system of fraud and rapine so ably depicted by Mr. Mac Nevin. The latter or proximate source is to be discovered in the history of 1641; for out of the events of that year sprang the remarkable Confederation, whose prelates and military leaders shone out like stars in one of the darkest and stormiest periods of our history. It is not my province to vindicate the men who originated that extraordinary movement, so grossly misrepresented by Warner, Temple, Borlase and others; that duty rests with the man to whom this Volume is dedicated, and it would be difficult to find one more able or willing to rescue the transaction of that period from the calumnies in which interested parties have laboured to involve it. I, therefore, will hasten to lay before the reader a brief sketch of the events which have immediate reference to the subject matter of this volume.

The accession of Charles I. was hailed by the Catholics
of Ireland as the dawning of hope and tranquillity,
after the terrific persecutions and rapacity of his predecessor. They fondly indulged the belief that the rack
and the thumb-screw would fall into disuse, and that
their religion would no longer be a pretext for sacrificing
their lives, and stripping them of the remnant of property which a crowned and disgusting pedant suffered
them to retain. With a fatal confidence in Charles I.
they imagined that he would cause measures to be enacted
which would supersede that infamous penal code which
has no parallel in the history of any other country.
But in reality they hoped against hope. Ussher, whose
character for erudition none may gainsay, was a rabid
bigot, and the representative of a class who held it to
be " a grievous sin to give toleration to the Catholics,
or to consent that they should freely exercise their
religion."—Ussher, as well as the other bishops who made
this avowal, spoke the sentiments of the Puritans in
England and in Ireland. Yet, with this declaration in
their ears, the infatuated Catholics dreamed that the
good-will and kind intentions of the monarch would come
between them and their implacable persecutors. Promises, it is true, were plenty, but they produced no
beneficial measures. Long-sufferings and passive obedience under the most withering oppression, brought no
redress. The monarch who could so freely promise
concessions, had not the remotest idea of realizing them.
One hundred and twenty thousand pounds sterling,
were subscribed by the Catholics as the price of the
concessions, known as " graces." Such an enormous
sum from a people so grossly robbed by James I. must
have well nigh ruined their resources. Charles took it,
and with that perfidy which characterized all his acts,
gave himself no concern to alleviate their sufferings or
ameliorate their condition.

In 1633 he commissioned Strafford to proceed to

Ireland as Lord Deputy; not indeed with the design of removing abuses, but of perpetuating them. This man, whose name is, even now, a sound of dread and terror, entertained an abhorence of the puritanic spirit so boldly manifested by the Primate Ussher, and Bedel, Bishop of Kilmore. It was his ambition to extinguish it, but his cherished project was to carry out the schemes of James I., and a more terrible agent could not have been found for the purpose. An exhaustless store for the lovers of the marvellous and cruel, is to be found in the history of the Spanish Inquisition; but, disgusting and terrific as its acts may have been, they furnish no record of blacker guilt or more flagrant profligacy than what may be collected from the history of Strafford's administration in Ireland. The promises of the King, so often given to the Catholics, and so warmly welcomed by them, were all violated on his responsibility. The Commission of Defective Titles was only another name for systematic plunder. The School of Wards, with its insidious scheme for sapping the faith of Catholics, was an apt instrument in the hands of this unscrupulous Deputy, who hated the Irish as much as he lusted after their substance. Nevertheless, grant after grant was generously given, amounting in all to three hundred and ten thousand pounds, in the hope of securing themselves against persecution on the score of religion, and having confirmed to them the possession of their estates. But all in vain; the statutes known as those of "Uses" and "Wills" were passed in the Irish parliament, and the religion of all Catholic minors was left to the guidance of those who preached extirpation of Popery as Gospel.

To suppose that Strafford's conduct elicited the displeasure of Charles I. would be a presumption not warranted by history. On the contrary, the king who participated in his guilt could not but applaud it. The Commission of Defective Titles contemplated the

viii

confiscation of the entire of Connaught—its object was to subvert the title to every estate in the
whole province, and to establish a new plantation.
Compliant jurors were easily found, and where they
were not, the Star Chamber, with its horrid engines,
was speedily resorted to. The Lord Deputy Chichester,
in 1613, claimed the honor of this device, and it
succeeded, to Strafford's most sanguine wishes, in
plundering the rightful possessors, and finding for the
crown. Nor did Strafford limit his sphere of evil action
to subverting the religion of the Irish Catholics and
divesting them of their patrimonial inheritance. The
Woollen Manufactures of Ireland were not suffered to
escape; they were pronounced injurious to English
speculation, and were consequently annihilated; even
salt was adjudged a monopoly to the king, and the Lord
Deputy consoled himself with having sought to bring the
people to a conformity in religion, but above all, on hav
ing raised a good revenue for the crown. Hence, when
ne returned to England, and made a report of his conduct to the council, he was gratefully informed by the
king, that "if he had served him otherwise, he would
not have served him as he expected."

Strafford, or as he is yet known to the Irish peasantry
by the epithet of "Black Tom," was succeeded by Wandesford, whose administration was too short-lived to be of any
benefit to the Catholics, if he ever contemplated such, or
of greater misery, which it is likely he meant to inflict.
Tyranny, less vexatious than this which we have glanced
at, would have driven any other people to madness.
In fact, the Scotch Covenanters had no such provoca-
tion to rebellion, and yet they rose in might and
strength, and, in a great measure, brought about that
terrible tragedy which commenced with the execution ot
Strafford and terminated in the overthrow of the monarchy:
yet, withal, the Irish Catholics clung to the throne, as
if they had been its cherished objects; and, although it

has been the wont of others to applaud them for raising men and money to aid the king in his efforts to crush the Scotch, our habits of thought, at the present day, must be far from justifying that over-weening loyalty which induced them to arm in the cause of despotism.

Wandesford was succeeded by Sir William Parsons and Sir John Borlase, two Puritans, who seem to have thought of nothing save pillaging the Catholics and anathematizing their religion. The odious tyranny of these men—their wanton invasion of the most sacred rights, and the utter disregard of all the obligations of oaths and conscience, find no counterpart, even in the terrible time of Strafford. Human patience had reached its limit—the people goaded to desperation, prepared to fling off the yoke—a plot for seizing the Castle of Dublin was laid—treachery was at work—the conspiracy failed, but a revolution speedily followed. From north to south the masses rose, headed by Sir Phelim O'Neill and other chiefs of the old nobility. In the December of 1641, a coalition took place between the Anglo-Irish Catholics of the Pale, and the "ancient Irish." Out of hat coalition sprung the Confederation, the avowed object of which was, to assert by force of arms the free and independent exercise of the Catholic religion, and the restoration of the churches to their rightful inheritors. Of course, both parties, "the Catholics of the Pale" and the "Celtic tribes," were solemnly pledged to win back their estates and homesteads, or perish in the struggle. They were glorious objects and well worth fighting for. A congregation of bishops pronounced the war to be "lawful and pious;" and the men who were engaged in it must have triumphed had they been true to themselves and firmly banded together; but they were not. Mutual jealousies, distrusts, temporizing expediency, and wily diplomacy broke their compact array, and left them victims to the horrors which subsequently desolated the land. But

even so; in the annals of Europe it would be difficult
to find nobler devotion or more brilliant chivalry than
that which may be learned from this period of our
history. Could there have been a more spirit-stirring
motive for gallant achievements? The faith, for whose
independence those men drew their swords, was that
which our Apostle preached on the heights of Slane,
and in the presence of the great assembly of Tara. The
lands of which the Catholics had been plundered were
theirs before the Norman set foot on our shores. The
descendants of the invaders who remained true to their
religion, were robbed and tortured for their martyr-like
attachment to the ancient creed. The churches which
the piety of Irish princes and Norman barons had erected
were in the gripe of usurpers, and were not the Irish
Catholics justified before God and man in seeking to
expel them by force of arms? In a country like Ireland,
at all times so fondly devoted to the Chair of St. Peter,
such events as these could not have been unaccompanied
by deeds of heroism which may have been equalled, but
certainly cannot be surpassed in the history of any
other country. Even now, after centuries of degradation and sufferings, are not the religious characteristics
of the Irish people still the same? The love of their
religion, like that of Francesca, so thrillingly described
by Dante,* has endured and outlived bitter trial and
agonizing torment; even now it does not abandon them,
but seems to have been more closely wedded to their
hearts by the recollection of all the blood and tears it
cost them. That sublime passion brought death to the
lover and the loved; but a resurrection has followed,
and Ireland is now the wonder and the admiration of
the world. Go where we will, we cannot meet any
section of the human race braver, purer, or more
generous; their love of fatherland is only equalled by
their attachment to the ancient creed. Would you ask

* Inferno. Canto V.

the Irish peasant, whether toiling for a livelihood "beyond the Atlantic foam," or brooding in sullen silence over his miseries in his own land, what hope is nearest to his heart, he will tell you, it is that of laying his bones within these grey old ruins which chronicle the rise and fall of his country?

But, heaven forbid that it should be inferred from these reflections that I or any one else designed to stir an angry passion, or shadow forth a desire of resorting to violence for the possession of these grand old temples, now no longer ours. Too much blood has been already shed in the struggle to win them back. Who would strike a blow for the casket while the gem is in our hands? Enough for us that these majestic monuments still remain indisputable evidences of our former greatness and the antiquity of our faith. It is not by armed violence that they will ever revert to us ;—no, that consummation is only to be hoped for when

    " Europe, repentant of her parricide,

    Shall . . . sue to be forgiven." *

But the age of the Confederation has gone by, and extraordinary events have succeeded it. A Confederation of another order has sprung up, and done much more for the "dear old land" than all that the sword of Owen Roe was able to accomplish ;—" the voice and the pen" are more potent weapons in the nineteenth century. Yet, whilst we gladly acknowledge their efficiency, let us not befool ourselves by seeking to disparage those who, in the battle for liberty, resorted to the sword. The idea of casting censure on Tell, or Hofer, or Hugh O'Neill, is unworthy of a brave and generous people. In a country like this it would be dishonoring the memories of our illustrious dead were we to depreciate that heroism which held life not worth possessing when deprived of the incomparable blessings of freedom. All our hopes are now

    * Childe Harold. Canto IV.

linked with the great unarmed Confederacy which has
brought mind and argument to combat injustice; but
that Confederacy has reason to be guarded against the
weapons which ruined its martial predecessor. Even
now there is a Pale, the foundations of which are laid in
inveterate prejudices and hostile feelings. It is necessary that it should disappear, and that all of us, of every
creed, be banded together in the peaceful determination
to "have our own again." The fatalities which destroyed the men of another period originated in crafty
diplomacy, soothing promises, and flattering expediency.
Heaven guard us against a recurrence of similar evils!
Unity and untiring exertion are our only means of establishing our legislative independence. To use the lan
guage of an eloquent writer—"There is now no statute
of Kilkenny—no Catholic Confederacy—no Protestant
Ascendancy, to keep us from entire nationhood. The
religion of each is free,—the golden gates of prosperity
open in the vista of our predestined path; we must
enter them hand-in-hand, or not at all." *

One word more, and I have done. I know full well
how unequal I have been to treat this momentous subject; but, if I lacked the necessary ability, no one
can accuse me of want of industry. The volume which
will describe the wars of Cromwell is yet to be written, and it will be the duty of the individual whose
province that is, to commence where I left off. The
congregation of the Prelates at Jamestown and Loughrea, as well as the Lorrain embassy, are intimately connected with all that I have left untouched, and will be
fully developed in a subsequent volume.   C. P. M.

* *Nation* newspaper, June 27th, 1846.

CONFEDERATION OF KILKENNY.

CHAPTER I.

THE twenty-third of October, 1642, is a memorable epoch in the annals of Ireland. On that day, the representatives of the Irish Catholics, deputed by the cities, counties, and towns, were assembling in the city of Kilkenny, to deliberate on their actual position, and organise a confederacy, the foundations of which had been already laid.

It was a grand and solemn spectacle—nor does the history of any country record a more spirit-stirring scene than that which was witnessed in the old city of St. Canice,* at this momentous period. The rapid transition from heart-breaking thraldom to bold and armed independence, was never more convincingly manifest. Ireland, hitherto chained, and tortured by the most inhuman enactments, beheld her sons, clergy and laity, repudiating the despotism of Parsons and Borlase, who, in the absence of Lord Leicester, held the reins of government, and resorting to the only means left them for the redress of their grievances—self-legislation and an appeal to arms.

Who can adequately describe the feelings which, at this moment, must have thrilled the hearts of the Irish Catholics? But thirty-nine years before, the Lord Deputy Mountjoy, from the Castle of Dublin, sent an insolent letter to the mayor of Kilkenny, reprimanding him for allowing the old abbey church of St. Francis to be used for the celebration of the mass. His orders to

* /.t. plerisque vero Canicopolis nuncupatur."—Hib. Dom. 204.

close its gates were promptly obeyed, and the frightened
worshippers were obliged to betake themselves to some
obscure spot in the dingy lanes of the city, to celebrate
the mysteries of their religion. The sanguinary edicts
of the times caused men to pray after the manner of their
forefathers, as though the moments of their existence
were to be counted by the duration of the sacrifice—for
that one act, life and property might be said to be at stake ;
for, in the unscrupulous calculations of such men as Mountjoy, Parsons, and Borlase, it was deemed no sin to perse-
cute and plunder, in this world, those whom their gloomy
fanaticism excluded from all participation in the happiness of the next. But what an extraordinary contrast
now presented itself—in less than one year how much had
been done to exalt the condition of the Catholic people of
Ireland ! Men, who were hitherto impatient of the yoke,
now bravely flung it off. Mountjoy's malevolence, and the
intolerable dictation of the justices were treated with
scorn and contempt. Those who commenced the
struggle in the preceding October, knew well that
they had been driven from their sanctuaries and homesteads, by fraud and violence, and were now determined to assert their rightful claims, even at the
sword's point. The struggle for independence was to be
resumed in a more formidable and combined manner ;
and, even now, they might behold some glorious results
from a warfare which had all the appearances of a
sudden onfall without any characteristic of well ordered
arrangement. On such an occasion, what heart could
have been indifferent to the exciting circumstances of the
time and place. From the towers of St. Canice and the
black abbey the gladsome pealing of the bells proclaimed
a new era. David Roth, bishop of Ossory, ascended the
episcopal throne in the cathedral. The altars, which were
sacrilegiously overthrown, were re-erected, and the
shrine of the saint was restored. A monument was set
up to record the fact, and the splendid old fane was once
more devoted to the ancient worship*—nor was this all—

* " Memoriæ David Roth
Qui hanc eccl. cathed.
S. Canicio sacram
Pristino restituit cultui."
          O'PHELAN'S

some of the monasteries which had been used for profane purposes were again occupied by the religious bodies, and the friar walked abroad in the habit of his order. Never, in the history of any country, was there wrought so wondrous a change in so short a time, and against such fearful odds.

Nor are we to suppose that the joy created by these extraordinary events was confined to those who witnessed them at home. Some of the most chivalrous men who had served in continental armies, were born in Ireland. Religious persecution had driven them from their homes, and they eagerly watched the moment when they might return, and be useful to their own land. That moment had come, nor were they slow in sympathising with their kinsmen and friends. Owen Roe O'Neill, who had distinguished himself in the Spanish armies, relinquished his command, and was warmly commended by the Pope for that zeal and love of fatherland, which prompted him to peril all he held dear for the emancipation of his country and religion. Preston, too, of the house of Gormanstown, who had won his laurels in 1636, under the walls of Louvain, apparently actuated by the same feelings, and at the expense of Cardinal Richlieu, sailed with a considerable number of officers for the coast of Wexford, where he landed arms and ammunition. From the banks of the Seine to the Tagus, and thence to the Vatican, beyond the Tiber, the news of the Irish rising had travelled with rapidity. Philip IV., of Spain, extolled the boldness of his co-religionists. France, chivalrous France, applauded the bravery of the men who had arisen to smite oppression; and Urban VIII., at the tomb of the apostles, invoked blessings on the arms of his faithful Irish children.

But if anything could add to the joy of those who beheld these occurrences from a distance, or raise still higher the enthusiasm which reigned at home, it was an event which had recently occurred: that event was the coalition of the Catholic nobility and gentry of the Pale with the Celtic or "old Irish." Let us pause to examine the characteristics of both, ere we describe the causes which brought them to struggle in the same cause, and march under the same standard.

" From time immemorial," says an accurate observer, "there always existed among the Irish two adverse parties, 'the ancient and the modern;' the former was ever opposed to the dominion of England, and, generally speaking, refused the investiture of church property; the latter, on the contrary, aggrandised by the spoils of the religious houses and cathedrals, and bound to the King of England by obligation no less than interest, neither sought nor desired anything but the exaltation of the Crown."

In fact, the Catholics of the Pale were thoroughly English in all their sympathies, if we except those which regarded religion; they were strongly contrasted with the ancient Celtic tribes, who had been plundered, even with the connivance of their new allies; nor did the two races differ as to feelings and predilection only : the superiority of the " old Irish," in the year 1641, was not less striking, as to outward appearances, than in the days of Hollinshed; for, while the " Anglo-Irish" are described as " weak and low of stature," the " old Irish" we are told, " were tall, and of huge frame."[*] Well may we wonder, that men of such different views and predilections could be brought together within the walls of Kilkenny. Verily it must have been some irresistible motive which could induce the two parties to bury in oblivion the antagonism and mortal enmity of 400 years. No matter how ardently the mendacious publications of the times sought to identify them with the men who originated the rising of 1641, they did not succeed in convincing any unbiassed mind. One who was a conspicuous actor in these varied scenes, so often bright with hope, and darkened by reverses, has triumphantly proved that the Irish rising, so far from being countenanced by the nobility and gentry of the Pale, had not a single individual of English extraction concerned or implicated in it.[†] On the contrary, when the " old Irish" took up arms to resist the Puritans, " who were bent on extinguishing the Catholic faith, and plucking up the Irish nation, root and branch,"[‡] their brethren of the Pale earnestly besought the justices to put them in possession of arms, that they might march against them, and, if possible, crush them.[§] Sir Robert Talbot, a Catholic, was ready, in

* Rinuccini.   † Castlehaven's Mem.
‡ Declaration of the Prelates at Jamestown.   § Carte's Orm.

His hasty zeal, to proceed to the county Wicklow, and outroot the septs of the O'Byrnes and O'Tooles, who had been plundered by Sir William Parsons, and driven to madness by the savage Coote. Lord Gormanstown, and others of his order, such as Dunsany and Netterville, burned for an opportunity in which they might prove their loyalty, by persecuting the men who had arisen to beat down the most intolerable despotism—they sought arms, but were denied them,—they were treated with the contempt which they merited, nor did they repent them of their bloody purpose, till they found themselves involved in the damnatory edicts which the justices published against "all Papists without distinction of any." Yet did they still indulge a hope that these denunciations might be mitigated in their behalf, but the hope soon vanished. Their religion was a plausible pretext for robbing them; their estates were worth having, and had long tempted the cupidity of Parsons and Borlase. Indeed the sordid griping of those men stands without parallel. Perfectly unscrupulous as to the means of acquiring wealth, they hesitated not to smite, with "axe and oath," all who stood between them and their object; nor can we find the counterpart of such unblushing plunderers, save amongst those whom Dante describes in the eighth circle of the Inferno.*

But a new light began to break in on them, and they were soon made aware of the danger which beset them. A letter from the Earl of Essex to the justices, suggesting the expediency of banishing the lords and gentry of the Pale to the West Indies, was sufficient to alarm and teach them to provide for their safety. They had no alternative; to stay any longer separated from the national movement, perilled their lives and fortunes. The rackings and torturings of their own kinsmen, and the cruelties and the atrocities which they were forced to endure in the Castle of Dublin, gave fearful warning that a similar course of treatment was in reserve for themselves. Remonstrances were vain, for they were unheeded,—loyalty, and hoary age, were but "scurvy pleas" at such a moment. Patrick Barnwell† of Killbrew, and Sir John Read, were living witnesses

* Inferno, Canto xxviii.   † Carte's Ormond.

of the inhumanity of the executive: without the shadow
of a charge against their devotion to the Crown, they
had their sinews stretched, and their bones broken
in the torture-chamber of Dublin Castle. Their crime
was, that they were Papists, and, consequently, fit
objects for the vengeance of Parsons and Borlase. No
matter how reluctant they might have been, the nobility
and gentry of the Pale had no other course open to
them, save that of joining with those who, in the
hypocritical slang of the times, were denominated
"rebels." Naturally enough, they dreaded to encounter
the pains and penalties to which their religion consigned
them, and they determined to abandon their vacillation,
and seek protection in the patriot ranks. Thus were the
lords of the Pale at length convinced that their kindly
feelings to England could not protect them when the
rack might be called in to support the suspicions and
confirm the jealousies of the justices, who had an interest
in their destruction.* Their tenants on their own
estates had been wantonly pillaged, and their persons
wounded. Coote's thirst for blood was insatiable, and
his threat of not leaving a Catholic in Ireland began to
gain some truth, from the recollection of his barbarities
in Wicklow. Was the man who could smile and become
facetious when an infant was writhing on the pike of one
of his soldiers, incapable of any deed which diabolical
ingenuity could suggest?

Finglas, Clontarf, and Santry, were the scenes of the
most wanton murders, perpetrated by this man on people
whose proximity to the capital might have been sufficient
guarantee for their loyalty, or, at least, for their inability
to do the state any mischief. When the humbler classes
of the Catholics were thus persecuted, what could their
lords expect by tame acquiescence, or what solace could
they borrow from delusive hope? But, above all, what
good could accrue to them from perpetuating the antagonism which, alas! had too long divided "the modern"
and the "old Irish." It was madness to continue it,
and the meeting on the Hill of Crofty, in the county
Meath, was the result of their reflections. There, as on
an altar, Roger O'Moore and Lord Gormanstown, the

* Carte's Orm., p. 259.

representatives of the two parties, plighted a solemn
vow, and swore to bury in oblivion the feuds and dissensions which had long wasted their strength and now left
them a prey to the designs and hatred of the common
enemy.

Lord Gormanstown, and the other lords of the Pale
proceeded, soon after, to take measures which the
exigencies of the times necessarily demanded. Some
levies of men, badly equipped, and hastily disciplined,
were made in the various baronies. Commanders were
appointed, and orders were issued to raise such means
as were necessary for their support. The meeting on
Knockcrofty, and its immediate results, had two very
natural consequences : all hope of reconciliation with
'the justices was henceforth abandoned, and the " old
Irish," who had commenced the struggle in the north
and south, determined to persevere with redoubled
energy, now that they were joined by the men of the
Pale. Willing or unwilling, they were driven into a
position from which they could not recede. No matter
what their sympathy might have been for English domi-
nation, their religion was the grand plea for their
destruction : that they held in common with the "old
Irish," and in defence of the ancient creed they were
solemnly pledged to stand or fall. The objects of the two
parties now united were grand, and well worth a combined effort. The Puritans of England meditated the
ruin of the monarchy : they were assisted in Ireland by
the machinations of the justices. Next to the ruin of
royalty, they ambitioned nothing so much as the extirpation of the Catholics. The preservation of the regal
power was an object dear to the ancient and modern
Irish, but in every thing pertaining to religion, the Celt
knew no compromise, while his ally on the other hand
would be satisfied with mere toleration. Manifestoes,
calling on the leaders to arm in the common cause, were
forwarded to the principal towns; a great portion of
Ulster had been already won back by Sir Phelim O'Neill;
Lord Mountgarret captured Kilkenny; Waterford opened
its gates to his son, Colonel Edmund Butler ; Ross and
Wexford declared for the national cause ; the O'Briens
were almost masters of Clare ; and, in the fastnesses of
far-Connaught, there was a steady organisation in pro-

gress, which alarmed the Earl of Clanricarde, who, wishing to preserve the good opinion of the justices, stood aloof from the general movement.

But it was not till the 22d of March 1642, that the Catholic prelates took any part in these momentous proceedings. Of course their influence had been employed to exhort and encourage their flocks in fighting the battle of the faith; but, previous to that period, it was quite impossible that they could have been synodically convened. Their presence was required in many a hard fought field, to console and comfort those who had fallen in the struggle; nor had they time or opportunity to assemble and deliberate in councils.

The provincial synod at Kells, convened by Hugh O'Reilly, archbishop of Armagh, was attended by all the bishops of the province, with the exception of Thomas Dease, bishop of Meath, who, like Lord Clanricarde, sought to extinguish the spirit of patriotism in the hearts of his people. Dease, who was evidently influenced by the Earl of Westmeath, had already done serious evil to the Catholic forces besieging Drogheda, by preventing supplies from reaching them; his presence, therefore, must have been anything but agreeable to the patriotic primate and other prelates. Their meeting was brief, but of great moment; after mature deliberation, they pronounced the war undertaken by the Catholics to be lawful and pious, and issued a spirited address to their flocks, exhorting them to take up arms for their religion, country, and king. A series of decrees against murderers and usurpers of other men's estates, was published by this synod, and the pains and penalties which the bishops pronounced against all evil doers, fully cleared them from the foul aspersions of the justices, who, in their puritanical cant, declared that "*they had walked invisibly in works of darkness.*"* Before the prelates retired to their respective sees, they sent a manifesto to those bishops who had not been present, advertising them of a national synod to be held at Kilkenny, on the 10th of May following. The meeting of the prelates had scarcely terminated, when two events occurred which were calculated to depress the hearts of men with loss

* Carte's Orm. p. 326.

holy and inspiriting objects than those of the Irish Catholics.

The civil war had not, as yet, broken out in England ; the fire of revolution was still smouldering, and only required the breath of popular excitement to fan it into flame. The hatred which the factions on the other side of the channel entertained for the Irish Papists, was fed and invigorated by printed catalogues of forged murders and shocking atrocities, sworn by corrupt witnesses to have been committed on the Protestants in Ulster, and the other provinces. If anything could add to that deadly hatred, it was the event known as the *"defection of the Pale."* Charles I. gladly seized an opportunity of turning the attention of the English parties to the state of Ireland ; and, in a message to the House of Commons, on the 8th of April, he signified his desire of crossing the channel, to chastise the *detestable rebels*, and settle the peace of the kingdom ; protesting, at the same time " that he would never consent to *the toleration of the Popish profession, or the abolition of the laws then in force against Popish recusants.* The parliament, however, demurred, and the justices in Ireland made such a representation of the state of the kingdom, as was calculated to change his Majesty's design of visiting it. A proposition, however, was submitted to the king, of which he approved ; 2,500,000 acres were declared forfeited to the Crown, by the men engaged in *rebellion ;* and in order to raise money for prosecuting a war against the Irish on their own soil, and against the king in England, the public credit was pledged that for every sum advanced they should receive a proportionate return of forfeited property.* This, however, was one of the many acts of English despotism which might have been turned to a good account—for, by it, the Irish people were reduced to the alternative of crushing their tyrants, or perishing in the ruins of their proscribed religion, and forfeited homesteads.

Cooped up within the walls of Dublin, the justices vainly represented to the English people the wretched state of their troops, and the formidable array of the *rebels.* Petition after petition was sent to England,

* Lingard, vo. x.

and many a supplication for supplies of old *clothing*
and arms, pathetically headed "*an affair of bowels,*"*
was passed over unheeded. But in keeping the king
from the Irish shores, they had accomplished their
purpose, for they dreaded nothing so much as any
investigation of their cruel and perfidious acts.

The second of the events alluded to, was the arrival
of Munroe, who, with 2,500 men, landed at Carrickfergus on the 15th of April, where he was soon after
joined by Lord Conway, and Sir Arthur Chichester,
with a large supply of arms and ammunition.

But neither the king's insolent declaration, nor the
arrival of the Scotch troops in Ulster, had power to
turn the Irish from their purpose.

In the south and west the people were everywhere
crowding round the popular leaders. Clanricarde's
dictation could not restrain the enthusiasm of his province. He had no hold on the affections of his people,
and as they knew that he was in correspondence with
the justices, they had little confidence in him. They
therefore thought it advisable to stand prepared against
such horrors as Sir William St. Leger, the president of
Munster, was inflicting on the Catholics in his province.
That man, whose barbarities equalled those of Sir Charles
Coote, was supplied by the justices with money and
provisions, and ordered to execute martial law on those
who fell into his hands. Early in March he entered
"Condon's Country," and having massacred the inhabitants, continued his march into the county of Wexford; nor did he return till he had burned the country
from Lismore to Dungarvan. In this work of devastation he was ably assisted by the Earl of Cork and his
sons, one of whom, Lord Kinalmeaky, is thus eulogised in
a letter from his father to the Earl of Warwick :—"*And*
now that the boy has blooded himself upon them, I
hope that God will bless him; that as I now write but
of the killing of an hundred, I shall shortly write of
the killing *of thousands.*"† Nevertheless, St. Leger and
the Earl of Cork could not have withstood the frequent
assaults of the masses, *one-half* of whom *were not
armed*, had there been unanimity amongst the leaders.

* Thorpe's Collect., R. D. S.   † Smith's History of Cork.

The appointment of generals was a never-ending subject of controversy. Undisciplined and badly equipped, they divided their strength and made a simultaneous attack on Youghal, Bandon, and Kinsale. Failure was the result. Mountgarret and Barry invested Cork, but were successfully resisted by St. Leger and Inchiquin, and were finally obliged to retire into Leinster.

Notwithstanding these reverses, the natural result of want of plan and well-combined arrangements, almost every town in Munster was in the hands of the Irish. The justices, however, were determined on crushing the unorganised levies in the province of Leinster, and Lord Ormond was deputed to command their troops. This nobleman, though of Irish origin, was born in England. At a very early age he was removed from the Catholic school of Finchley, near Barnet, to the tutelage of the Archbishop of Canterbury, under whom he soon abjured the faith of his fathers. He tells us himself that he was, not only by birth, extraction, and alliance, but likewise in his affections, wholly and entirely an Englishman.* With military talents of a superior order, he was in every respect equal to many of the generals of his time. In diplomacy, however, he excelled them all. With the most fascinating and artful address, he easily worked himself into the confidence of friends and foes; but under the guise of simplicity and candour he covered a heart which was full of treachery and craft. The justices had unbounded confidence in him, and he in return made no secret of his love and honour for them. He was the hope of that faction which desired nothing so much as the ruin of the Irish Catholics, and it mattered very little how many perished, provided Ormond was spared to carry out the designs of his patrons. In the opinion of the men whom he served, he is described by a writer at the period of which we treat as " *The Jewell of the Kingdom; not greater in name than rare abilities.*" †

The justices were now aware that the time appointed by the prelates for the national synod was nigh at hand; and, as it were anticipating the order and organization which they expected to result from the congregated pre-

* Carte's Orm., v Ormond's Letters. ¡ Thorpe Papers, R.D. S.

lacy and lay lords, they determined to strike a blow
which would leave the leaders comparatively powerless.
One, whose name and influence might have been considerable, did not live to witness the new era which was
about to dawn.   Lord Gormanstown, the chief of the
Catholic nobility of Leinster, a prey to grief and vexa-
tion of spirit, died, and the command of the Leinster
levies devolved on Lord Mountgarret.   This nobleman,
who was married to a daughter of Hugh, Earl of Tyrone,
had early distinguished himself in the wars of Queen
Elizabeth; in 1559, he successfully maintained the castles of Ballyragget and Coleshill against her Majesty's
forces.   In the parliament of 1613 and 1615 he was
fortunate enough to win the good will of James; and in
1619 he got a confirmation of all his estates with the
creation of several manors and various lucrative privileges.* He had not, however, the talents which were
necessary for a great military leader; and, like the other
lords who had lately joined the "old Irish," "he was
forced," according to his own confession, "into the general cause by the example of those, who, as innocent
and free from infringing his majesty's laws as himself,
had been used in the nature of traitors."†
On the 2nd of April, Ormond marched out of Dublin
with 300 foot, 500 horse, and five field pieces. It was on
this day that his castle of Carrick had been taken by
Colonel Edmund Butler, who caused all the prisoners,
including the Countess of Ormond, with her children,
and about a hundred Protestants, to be safely conveyed
to Dublin.   Ormond's object was to victual several detached garrisons, which were still held by the lords
justices. He went forth with the usual commission to
pillage, burn, and kill; and notwithstanding the humanity and forbearance with which his own people
had been treated, he did not fail to execute his orders to the very letter. He advanced to Carlow, Stradbally, and Maryborough; from the latter place he sent
Sir Charles Coote to reinforce the garrisons in Burris-
Knockmenease, and Birr; which service having been
performed, Coote rejoined him at Athy on the 13th.

* Lodge, iv. p. 52.
† Mountgarret's letter to Ormond, March 25, 1642.

Queen Henrietta Maria, princess of France, was represented by the growing party as inimical to the liberty of the subject, and bent on some contrivance for the introduction of Popery. Reared in the heart of a despotic court, her religion and pretended ascendancy over the king, furnished ample themes for the mal-contents, who argued that the marriage of Charles was far from being sanctified by his Popish queen. Her confessor was arrested, the service of her chapel was dissolved, and she herself had retired to Holland with a view of soliciting such means from foreign princes, as would render her husband equal to the exigencies which beset him.[*]

But in Ireland the success of the Catholics might have been far more signal, had there been a combined system between the leaders. There lacked not energy nor motive to unite them. The views of the Puritan faction, represented by Parsons and Borlase, were unmasked, and the opinion which had already seized the minds of the Catholics, grew stronger, and struck its roots more deeply day by day. There was now but one conviction on their minds, and that was, that the faction who were levying war against the throne, had set their hearts on the extirpation of the Papists, and the confiscation of whatever property they still retained.

It has been already stated that the provincial synod of Kells had declared the war against the Puritans to be " pious and lawful," but it may be readily conceived what mighty advantages were to be derived from a national synod of all the bishops and clergy of Ireland.

According to arrangement, the synod met at Kilkenny, on the 10th of May. The Archbishops of Armagh, Cashel, and Tuam, with six other bishops, and the proxies of five more, besides vicars-general and other dignitaries, were present, and the country anxiously awaited the result of their deliberations. The subjects which they had to treat were of a momentous nature. They regarded war as well as peace, and we may easily imagine that they would have stood aloof from all matters regarding bloodshed, if the circumstances

- * Lingard's History of England, vol. x. pp. 172, 138.

of the times did not imperatively demand their interference. Their flocks were exposed to the hate and
rapacity of unrelenting enemies; nor could the episcopal character be compromised, if the hierarchy, under
such circumstances, laid aside the crozier for the sword.
The prelate does not give up the man, when the act of
consecration appoints him to watch over his people,
and an authority of great weight has decided, that
when the rights and liberties of one's country are
invaded, it is the duty of every man to gird on the
sword.* But it is worth remark, that the acts of
this synod were couched in a spirit of mildness which
does honour to the patriot prelates, and contrasts
with the edicts of Parsons and Borlase, as day does with
night. Before we transcribe that portion of them
which has immediate reference to our subject, it is
necessary to premise, that the lay-lords and prelates
drew up an oath of association which was to be taken by
all the Catholics throughout the land. Without this
bond of union it was utterly hopeless to expect that the
Catholics of the Pale would cordially coalesce with the
"old Irish;" and in fact, as the sequel will prove, the oath
of association was "the only essential tie"† between
the two parties. The oath itself was at once grand
and simple, nor did it oblige those who took it, to any
act incompatible with the Christian precept which
ordains, that we are to give to God the things that
are of God, and unto Cæsar the things that are
Cæsar's. But it is necessary that we submit it to the
reader.

THE OATH OF ASSOCIATION.

"I, A.B., do profess, swear, and protest before God, and his saints
and angels, that I will, during my life, bear true faith and allegiance
to my Sovereign Lord, Charles, by the grace of God, King of Great
Britain, France, and Ireland, and to his heirs and lawful successors;
and that I will, to my power, during my life, defend, uphold, and maintain, all his and their just prerogatives, estates, and rights, the power
and privilege of the Parliament of this realm, the fundamental laws of
Ireland, the free exercise of the Roman Catholic faith and religion
throughout this land; and the lives, just liberties, possessions, estates,
and rights of all those that have taken, or that shall take this oath, and
perform the contents thereof; and that I will obey and ratify all the
orders and decrees-made and to be made by the Supreme Council of

* "In hostem Patriæ omnis homo miles."—Tertullian : quoted by
Dr. French in the bleeding Iphigenia.
† Hist. of the Rem.

the Confederate Catholics of this kingdom, concerning the said public cause ; and I will not seek, directly or indirectly, any pardon or protection for any act done, or to be done, touching this general cause, without the consent of the major part of the said council; and that I will not, directly or indirectly, do any act or acts that shall prejudice the said cause, but will, to the hazard of my life and estate, assist, prosecute, and maintain the same.

" Moreover, I do further swear, that I will not accept of, or submit unto any peace, made, or to be made, with the said Confederate Catholics, without the consent and approbation of the general assembly of the said Confederate Catholics, and for the preservation and strengthening of the association and union of the kingdom. That upon any peace or accommodation to be made or concluded with the said Confederate Catholics as aforesaid, I will, to the utmost of my power, insist upon and maintain the ensuing propositions, until a peace, as aforesaid, be made, and the matters to be agreed upon in the articles of peace be established and secured by Parliament.   So help me, God, and his holy gospel.

Such was this solemn oath, or " fædus," which gave a distinct appellation to those who bound themselves by it, and whom we are henceforth to know as the Confederate Catholics of Ireland.

Having issued a manifesto calling on all the Catholics of the country to take the oath, in order that all " Irish peers, magistrates, noblemen, cities, and provinces may be tied together with the holy bond of union and concord, and for the conservation and exercise of this union," they ordained the following points :—

" I.—Whereas, the war which now in Ireland the Catholics do maintain against sectaries, and chiefly against Puritans, for the defence of the Catholic religion,—for the maintenance of the prerogative and royal rights of our gracious King Charles,—for our gracious Queen, so unworthily abused by the Puritans,—for the honor, safety, and health of their royal issue,—for to avert and repair the injuries done to them,—for the conversion of the just and lawful safeguard, liberties, and rights of Ireland,—and, lastly, for the defence of their own lives, fortunes, lands, and possessions;—whereas this war is undertaken for the foresaid causes against unlawful usurpers, oppressors, and the enemies of the Catholics, chiefly Puritans, and that hereof we are informed, as well by divers and true remonstrances of divers provinces, counties, and noblemen, as also by the unanimous consent and agreement of almost the whole kingdom in this war and union,—we, therefore, declare that war, openly Catholic, to be lawful and just; in which war, if some of the Catholics be found to proceed out of some particular and unjust title—covetousness, cruelty, revenge, or hatred, or any such unlawful private intentions—we declare them therein grievously to sin, and therefore worthy to be punished and restrained with ecclesiastical censures if, advised thereof, they do not amend.

" II.—Whereas the adversaries do spread divers rumours, do write divers letters, and, under the King's name, do print proclamations which are not the King's, by which means divers plots and dangers may ensue unto our nation; we, therefore, to stop the way of untruth, and forgeries of political adversaries, do will and command that no such rumours, letters, or proclamations may have place or belief until it be known in a national council, whether they truly proceed from the King, left to his own freedom, and until agents of this kingdom, hereafter to be appointed by the *National Council,* have free passage to his Majesty, whereby the kingdom may be certainly informed of his Majesty's intention and will.

" III.—We straightly command all our inferiors, as well churchmen as laymen, to make no alienation, comparison, or difference between provinces, cities, towns, or families; and lastly, not to begin or forward any emulations or comparisons whatsoever.

" IV.—That in every province of Ireland there be a council made up, both of clergy and nobility, in which council shall be so many persons, at least, as are counties in the province, and out of every city or notable town, two persons.

" V.—Let one general council of the whole kingdom be made, both of the clergy, nobility, cities, and notable towns, in which council there shall be three out of every province, and out of every city, one; or where cities are not, out of the chiefest towns.   To this council the provincial councils shall have subordination, and from thence to it may be appealed, until this National Council shall have opportunity to sit together.

" VI.—Let a faithful inventory be made, in every province, of the murders, burnings, and other cruelties which are permitted by the Puritan enemies, with a quotation of the place, day, cause, manner, and persons, and other circumstances, subscribed by one of public authority.

" VII.—We do declare and judge all and every such as do forsake this union, fight for our enemies, accompany them in their war, defend or in any way assist them, to be excommunicated, and, by these presents, do excommunicate them.

" VIII.—We will and declare all those that murder, dismember, or grievously strike, all thieves, unlawful spoilers, robbers of any goods, to be excommunicated, and so to remain till they completely amend and satisfy, no less than if they were namely proclaimed excommunicated."

The national synod did not break up till about the end of May, and long before that period the proclamations, issued by the prelates and lay-lords, calling on the people to take the oath of association, had the happiest results. Agents from the synod crossed over into France, Spain, and Italy, to solicit support and sympathy from the Catholic princes. Father Luke Wadding was indefatigably employed collecting monies, and inciting the Irish officers serving in the continental armies to return, and give their services to their own land.   Nor was this all.   The most favourable terms were offered to foreign merchants, who would undertake to land munitions of war on the Irish shores; men skilled in the manufacture of arms were invited to come and reside amongst the Catholics.

and to carry on their trade with exemption from taxes, and other lucrative advantages to themselves and families. Lord Mountgarret was appointed President of the Council, and the October following was fixed for a general assembly of the whole kingdom.

Soon after the battle of Kilrush, Lord Lisle landed at Dublin, with his own regiment of 600 horse carbiniers, and another of 300 dragoons. A portion of these troops was distributed between Drogheda and Dundalk, and Lord Lisle lingered at Dublin awaiting orders from the justices. At this time Letitia, Baroness Ophaly, grand-daughter to Gerald, eleventh earl of Kildare, was besieged in her castle of Geashill, in the King's County, by the O'Dempsies, under the command of Lewis, lord Clanmalier. This heroine, who inherited the chivalrous spirit of the Geraldines, boldly resisted the overtures and menaces of the besiegers, and finally contrived to send a messenger to Sir Charles Coote, then at Naas, soliciting him to come to her aid. Her request was granted ; and Lord Lisle was appointed to command the expedition. He proceeded with Coote and a force of 600 men to Philipstown, and thence to the residence of the baroness, from before which the O'Dempsies retired on their approach. On their return they rendered assistance to Sir John Giffard, at Castlejordan, "and burning the country all the way as they marched,"* took the castle of Trim, which had been abandoned by the Lords Fingall, Gormanstown, Slane, and Trimbleston. When they were about to retire, they left nearly 500 men in the neighbourhood, who, rashly thinking they might recover the castle, determined to attack the troops commanded by the sanguinary Coote. Accordingly, on the 7th of May, about daybreak, they invested that old Norman stronghold, and a sally was made by the garrison, in which the besiegers were repulsed with loss. But, if they had no other success, they rid themselves of an implacable enemy. Coote was shot dead, and, in the words of his eulogist, "Trim was the tragic stage whereon he acted his last part."† His body was conveyed to Dublin, where it was buried, and as an acknowledgment of his services, the justices, with the consent of the Earl of Leicester,

---

* Carte's Ormond, 1318.   † Thorpe's Collection—R. D. S.

appointed his eldest son Provost Marshal of Connaught."*

But if the confederates had reason to regret their losses in Leinster, they had also good reason to congratulate themselves on the progress of events in the south and west. The justices were cooped up in Dublin, importuning the parliament to send them supplies of men and money. They could not carry on the war against the confederates on an extensive scale, and their expeditions from the city into the neighbouring country had more the character of border raids than a regular warfare. In fact, the want of provisions was sorely felt in the city, and it required all the dexterity of Parsons and Ormond to repress the mutinous dispositions which were every day exhibiting themselves amongst the Puritan soldiers.

The defeat which the Irish had sustained before Cork was soon succeeded by the capture of Limerick. Early in June, Pierce Butler, Viscount Skerrin, Lord Muskerry, and General Barry, with a numerous body of ill-disciplined troops, sat down before the city; the inhabitants were weary of tyranny, and longed for an opportunity of flinging off the yoke. They opened their gates to the confederates, who immediately proceeded to attack the castle. Courtenay, who commanded the place, determined to maintain it to the last extremity.

The confederates commenced their attack by making a boom across the river, opposite Mockbeggar-mear. This boom—the object of which was to prevent supplies being thrown into the castle by Stradling, who commanded some of the parliament ships in the Shannon—was composed of long aspin trees, fastened by iron links to two mill-stones on the Clare side, and, at the city, to the tower on the quay. The fire from Courtenay's guns delayed the completion of the work for awhile; but the object was finally gained: Stradling was unable to succour Courtenay. Muskerry ordered a gun to be mounted on St. Mary's Church, from which he kept up an incessant fire on the castle; but it still held out. On the 21st of June, three mines were finished, and ready to be sprung. The order was given, and a breach was made in the main wall of the castle. Courtenay was allowed to capitulate, and the city of Limerick was in the hands of the confederates. It was the most important advantage which they had as yet gained, and, when we take into consideration their want of cannon and ammunition, we may be better able to appreciate the great results. Sir William St. Leger, on hearing the defeat of Courtenay, did not long survive the taking of Limerick. The news had a powerful effect on his health. He died broken-hearted, and, if we except his own partisans, no one mourned the death of the man whose public career had been disgraced by the most wanton murders, and rapacious exactions.* Nor were the justices slow in appointing a successor to the late lord president. The man selected for the military administration of Munster was Murrough O'Brien, Earl of Inchiquin. He was the eldest son of Dermid, the fifth of that princely house who had worn an English coronet. About the year 1628, Murrough, son of Dermid, was made ward to P. Fitzmaurice, Esq. The proselytising spirit of the times had two grand objects, which were fully carried out in the person of Murrough O'Brien. The first was to denationalise the heart, and the second to engender such an abhorrence of the Catholic religion, as was calculated to inflict the most unmitigated atrocities on those who adhered to the ancient creed. An apt instrument in the hands of the Justices was this recreant. His sword recking with the blood of the Munster Catholics, and his military experience, the result of his campaigns with the Spanish army in Italy, recommended him to their regards. It is sad to think that a descendant of the illustrious house of O'Brien could have been found ready and willing to rival the barbarities of Coote, and walk in the bloodstained track of St. Leger; but, alas! such was the fact. Although the blood of Brian flowed through the veins of Murrough, it stirred a heart as savage and anti-Irish as that of the Scandinavian, whom his great ancestor vanquished at Clontarf. Tradition still points to many a rifled fane, whose blackened and roofless walls

* See Ferrar's Hist. of Limerick.

arc the mournful mementoes of this Irish **Vandal.**
Round the peasant's hearth, the record of his havoc and
burnings furnishes ample theme for the story-teller.
When the storm sweeps over the ruined shrine of
Cashel, in the dark drear nights of winter, and the
lightning flashes wildly through the desecrated chancel,
the credulous fancy that Murrough revisits earth to renew the work of desolation. When mention is made of
him, his patronymic is forgotten, and an epithet, asso-
ciating his name with conflagration and carnage, is substituted. 'Twas a wise resolve to suppress the name of
O'Brien whenever men spoke of this degenerate son of
that splendid race. "*Murrogh of the burnings*" was
the appropriate designation, significant as it is of the in-
cendiary's torch and assassin's poniard. As long as
the history of his crimes endures, so long shall he be
recognised by this epithet, and no other.

But the capture of Limerick was of the greatest
utility to the confederates. With the cannon* which
they had taken they soon battered almost every castle
and stronghold of their enemies in that county, with the
exception of Loghgur and Askeaton, the latter of which
belonged to the Earl of Cork. But though these trifling
difficulties stood in the way, the entire granary of Munster was in possession of General Barry and Lord Muskerry. Towards the end of July the two generals prepared to march into the county Cork, to chastise
Inchiquin, and rescue from his gripe the seaport towns
which were held for the Parliament by Lord Broghill,
Sir Charles Vavasor, Sir John Pawlet, and Sir William
Ogle. Lord Barrymore, who managed the civil administration of the province, was cooped up in Youghal, and
proceeded to hold quarter-sessions, in which the chiefs of
the confederates were proclaimed traitors.†

While the Catholic arms were thus triumphing in the
south, Owen Roe O'Neill and Preston landed with officers
and arms—the former at Doe Castle, in the north, in the
month of July, and the latter on the coast of Wexford,
towards the end of September. In the west, three

* "One of the guns," says Carte (Orm., p. 43, was of so large a
bore, that it was drawn by twenty-five yoke of oxen.".
† Smith's Cork.

bishops, Malachy of Tuam, Francis Elphin, and John De Burke of Clonfert, addressed a remonstrance to the Earl of Clanricarde, importuning him to join the national cause, "which was," in his opinion, "grounded upon wrong and bad foundations."* In vain did Mountgarret and the bishops endeavour to convince him that he was helping to ruin his country. "No argument," said they, "though you should write it in our very blood, will ever persuade the justices your affections are sincere, while you bear about you those marks by which they distinguish such as they have appointed for perdition Let it not come to you to sprinkle your ancestors' graves with the blood of such as will sacrifice themselves in the justifiable cause."† But they failed to gain him over, and he adhered to the Lord President and young Sir Charles Coote, who were spoiling the country and slaying the people.

But Clanricarde's apathy, and the cruelties inflicted on the people by Coote and Ranelagh, only served to exasperate the minds of the masses. Young Murrough Na Dubh O'Flaherty, at the head of a small band, seized Clanricarde's castle of Aghenure, in jar-Connaught. An English ship, lying in the Bay of Galway, was captured by the discontented populace; she had on board a considerable supply of arms and ammunition. The young men who took the vessel entered a church and bound themselves by an oath of union, in which they swore that they would bear true allegiance to the King, and defend to the utmost of their power the Roman Catholic religion. They then closed the gates of the town, and determined to hold it. They were urged to this step by the example of the Catholics who had been driven out of Cork and Youghal, "whose miserable condition," said the mayor, "did put us in mind of what we were to expect." A large body of men from jar-Connaught were preparing to invest the fortress of Galway, when Willoughby, who held a commission from the Parliament, set fire to all the houses in the east suburb, and wantonly consumed the property in the neighbourhood. Clanricarde, with nearly a thousand men, hastened to succour this ruthless incen-

* Clanricarde's Mem. 117   † Ibid. 171

diary, giving free quarters to his troops from Oranmore
to Clare-Galway. He then proceeded to besiege the
town, and was not long before it when Captain Ashley
entered the bay, in a ship of war, and threw supplies
into the fort. Willoughby thereon determined to bom-
bard the town, but was restrained by Clanricarde.'
Articles were drawn up between the "young men" and
the Earl, and in an evil moment Galway was surrendered to his lordship.

But they soon had reason to repent them of their
haste in submitting to the articles proposed by
Clanricarde. The fiendish malevolence of Willoughby and Ashley was not satisfied with what they
had already done. They were both violent parliamentarians, and cared little for oath or fealty. Willoughby's soldiers openly robbed the people, and without
the shadow of reason executed martial law upon the
harmless and unoffending. In a fit of puritanical
frenzy, he set fire to the suburbs, and burned houses
"which were set for more than a thousand pounds
a-year rent." He killed several of the inhabitants,
scaled the walls by night, and fired his cannon into the
town for an entire day. But the effect was good;
"for," says Mr. Hardiman, "it occasioned and hastened
the general and successful confederacy which afterwards
ensued."[*]

On the 7th of August a squadron of ships, commanded by Lord Forbes, entered the Bay of Galway,
and he immediately put himself in communication with
the fort. He declared against the late pacification,
and landed some men who began to burn and pillage
houses on the coast. Forbes, stimulated by Hugh
Peters, took possession of St. Mary's church, planted
guns against the town, and burned the surrounding
villages. He then dug up the graves in the church-
yard, and burned the bones and coffins; nor did he
quit the bay till the 4th of September. Yet did Clanricarde temporize with the justices in Dublin, and their
fiendish corsairs on the seas. But the hour of retribu-
tion was at hand. The clergy boldly exhorted the

* *Vide* Hardiman's Hist. of Galway, the work of one of the ablest of
our antiquaries, whose friendship I have good reason to cherish and
appreciate.

people to be true to themselves, and imitate the example of their brethren in the south. Coercion failed to check them; the oath of association was cheerfully taken by thousands, and they vowed in their hearts to visit, in the fitting season, their persecutors with vengeance, for all they had endured.

The reduction of the minor castles in the county Limerick engaged the confederate troops during the month of July, and it was not till the 20th of August that General Barry, at the head of 7,000 foot and 500 horse, penetrated into the county Cork. With this force Barry sat down before the castle of Liscarroll, which was garrisoned by Sir Philip Percival. The confederate troops besieged at the same time Annagh and another castle belonging to Percival. Liscarroll was declared by Inchiquin to be the strongest fortress in the kingdom, and such was the marshy nature of the soil around it, that General Barry was obliged to dismount his guns in order to bring them within range. Obstinate was the resistance of the defenders; nor did the place surrender to Barry till he had worn out the garrison after thirteen days' siege.

It was an important victory for the confederates, and struck terror to the heart of Inchiquin and the Earl of Cork. The sept of the Condons were giving the confederate leaders the most effectual assistance in another part of the county. The castles of Cloghleigh and Coote yielded to their bravery, and, when we remember that they were well garrisoned and supplied with the light pieces called sakarets and falcons, we may well afford to admire the valour and efficiency of men who had no other arms than pikes and muskets.

But though it was necessary that the Irish should possess themselves of these strongholds, we may, even now, question the prudence of the act; it had been better if they had fallen on Inchiquin's forces, which were distributed in cantonments, nor given them time to muster in strength. Had this been the case, Murrough could not have brought an army into the field; he was ill supplied with provisions, and the time spent by the confederates before Liscarroll and Annagh, gave him opportunity to collect his forces. He accordingly took the field on the third day of September, with 2,000 foot and

400 horse. The confederates, under Lords Roche, Muskerry, Skerrin, Dunboyne, and General Barry, waited his advance on an eminence in the vicinity of Liscarroll; Inchiquin charged with impetuosity, and was badly wounded in the attack. Kinalmeaky, of whose canine ferocity we have already spoken, was killed by his side; but, after an obstinate resistance, the confederates broke and fled. Sir Charles Vavasour and Inchiquin pursued them to a neighbouring bog, near Kilbolane, where upwards of 700 of them were refused quarter, and slain in cold blood. The loss in arms, colours, and baggage, was considerable. But Inchiquin dared not follow up his victory, and thought it advisable to retire, and secure himself in Mallow. Notwithstanding the boasted success of this action, Inchiquin made very few prisoners; and, as it will be seen, the result of the battle of Liscarroll was nowise important to the arms of the justices. Vavasour succeeded Kinalmeaky as governor of Bandon, whence he sent detachments into the surrounding country, making preys of cattle, and wasting the crops.*

In Ulster, the arrival of Owen Roe O'Neill produced the most signal result; for it would appear that, about the time of this event, Sir Phelim, and the other leaders, meditated following the example of Hugh O'Neill, and escaping to the Continent. The name and reputation of Owen changed their design, and determined them to strike another blow for their native land. The Fabius† of his country, as he is justly called, convened a meeting of the leaders, in the castle of Kinard, and he was immediately declared the chief of the Ulster Catholics. Munroe,‡ at the head of 10,000 men, occupied a strong position in Carrickfergus, and contented himself with seizing and imprisoning those who made any demonstration in favour of the king. The avowed object of the parliament in sending the Scottish forces into Ulster, was to circumvent his majesty, and prevent succours from being sent to him, should he require them from the northern shores. In the month of August, Lord Leven arrived with a detachment for the Scotch general, and addressed a letter to O'Neill, in which he expressed his

---

* Cox, v. 2, p. 113.   † Smith's History of Cork.
‡ Carte's Ormond.

astonishment "that one of his rank and reputation
should have come to Ireland to support so bad a cause."
O'Neill's answer was bold, and worthy of him :—"I have
a better right, my lord," he replied, " to defend my
own country, than your lordship has to march into
England against your king."*

Leven returned to Scotland, after having assured
Munroe that if Owen Roe succeeded in getting an army
together, he would be defeated. O'Neill, undaunted by
the imposing force of Scotch and English, began to
animate his followers, who hailed his advent as the prestige of success. He set about fortifying Charlemont
against any sudden attack, nor did Munroe dare to
molest him ; not a moment did he lose in gathering
together those men who longed to be led by so gallant
a chieftain, and the month of September passed over in
disciplining and organising the forces which hitherto had
little appearance of a military footing.

The justices beheld with alarm these important occurrences. In their addresses to their colleagues in
England, they set forth that their condition was ruinous.
Like superstitious heathens, they trembled at everything
that appeared ominous. "Crows, seagulls, and ravens,
pewling and croaking over the castle towers, portended
disasters which they could not divine."†

But, in fact, the much-dreaded event was the general
assembly of the whole kingdom, the time for which was
near at hand. The retrospective view we have taken of
these events was absolutely necessary, for the better understanding of those which followed in rapid succession.
We now return to the moment at which we set out—the
day before that fixed for the general assembly. It was
about this time that Lord Castlehaven, and others
escaped from prison,‡ and having arrived at the place of
rendezvous, took the oath and were enrolled amongst
the confederates ; nor did the city of Kilkenny at any
time previous witness such excitement and enthusiasm
as on the 23rd of October, 1642.   One who was a
spectator of that scene, which we would fain recal,
has left us a pithy account of it. He tells us that

* Rinun ini.   † Thorpe Papers, R. D. S.
‡ " From Shepes-street, Dublin, thro' Templeoage and over Wick
w mountains."—*Vide* Castlehaven s Memoirs.

on his arrival "he found every one actively engaged preparing for war."* Nor does it require any great power of imagination to conjure up the figure and fashion of those who were then assembling. The Celt had not as yet generally adopted the English tongue and English garb; hence, it was easy to distinguish the chieftains of the north and south from their brethren of the Pale. The *truis barraid*, flowing mantle, and *colun*, were still retained by the Celtic chiefs; while those of the Pale, rigidly conforming to English mannerism, adopted the broad black cloth, and the prevailing fashions of the English court.† In groups through the busy streets might be seen men, whose dusky aspects and foreign costume, pronounced them cavaliers of another clime,—but they were the Irish officers who had accompanied O'Neill and Preston from the Continent.

What a scene for recollection! Prelates and priests were there, who, educated beyond the seas, brought home with them a knowledge of those languages which Dante and Calderon have immortalised, and yet were ignorant of the English tongue;—men who spoke the language of Spenser side by side with the O'Neills from the north and the Macarthys from the south. Happily, however, the language of the western church was understood by them all. But in such angry times it were needless to dwell upon the marks by which the two races might be known, if one were not anxious to bring vividly before the mind of the reader every feature and peculiarity of those who have invested the churches, cloisters, council chambers, and towers of that venerable city with such an intense degree of interest. And surely even the earlier period of its history, when

"Phenecian, and Milesian, and the plundering Norman Peers"

ascended the sacred hill of St. Canice, presents no reminiscence so agreeable as that when the lords and gentry of the Pale came to sit in council with the chieftains and representatives of the Celtic tribes. Memory will ever love to dwell on that extraordinary conjunction, ill-starred though it may have been, or otherwise :—

* Castlehaven's Mem.
† Vide Walker's Letter on the dress of the Irish of the Pale and the Celtic Tribes.

around that old city there is an atmosphere of hallowed antiquity ;—through the vista of ages the forms of Donald O'Brien and Strongbow are still visible, though dimmed and obscured by time. Not so, however, with these of whom we treat: they are visions palpably before us, and it is time that we follow them to the place of assembly.

It is the 24th of October, and within the walls of Kilkenny are assembled eleven spiritual peers, fourteen temporal, and two hundred and twenty-six commoners, to keep watch and ward over the nascent liberties of their native land.

CHAPTER II.

WHEN the Catholic deputies were assembling in Kilkenny, to establish the federative government, and adopt these administrative measures of which we are now to treat, the war had broken out in England between the king and the parliament. Essex had the command of the rebel army, and Charles the First, summoning around him such of the nobles as yet stood firm in their allegiance, raised his standard at Nottingham, and called on his subjects to "give to Cæsar his due."[*]

Those who were up in arms against their monarch, were in close communication with the Lords Justices. They understood each other well, and they mutually vowed to turn all their strength on the Irish Catholics when they had accomplished their designs in England. It is hardly necessary to observe that the confederates were well aware that in the din of arms, and the confusion consequent on the collision between the king and the parliament, they could hope for no amelioration of their condition, or concession of the "graces," which had been so dearly purchased, and so long withheld. To submit to the dictates of Parsons and Borlase, was to sacrifice life and liberty, and nothing now remained for them but to take the government into their own hands, and save themselves and the country

* Lingard, vol. x.

from the machinations of the Puritans. It was a wise
and bold resolve, and promptly was it carried into
execution. War with the justices was inevitable; the
Nore now flowed between them and the Lords of the Pale,
and the latter were fully convinced that if they would
ever cross it to repossess themselves of their estates,
it would be necessary to do so, not as suppliants for
exemptions, but as bold men bent on maintaining their
own inalienable rights, and the lawful prerogatives of
the crown.

The first meeting of the confederates on this important occasion, is said to have been held in the
house* of Sir Robert Shea, in the Market-place of
Kilkenny. The great oaken floors, and massive
solidity of the walls, still attest the opulence of the
family who then possessed the mansion. Belling† informs us that the estates, spiritual and temporal, sat
in the same hall, and that a tier of benches, raised one
above the other, was deemed necessary in order to give
accommodation to the lords and commons. An upper
or private room was appropriated to the lords for consultation; and the clergy who were not qualified by
their sees or abbacies to sit in the house of lords, met
in an adjoining house, which was called the "house of
convocation." Mr. Patrick D'Arcy,‡ "bare-headed,
and seated on a stool, represented all, or some of the
judges and masters of chancery, that used to sit in
parliament upon the woolsack;" and Mr. Nicholas
Plunket represented the speaker of the house of
commons: to him both lords and commons addressed
their speeches. Thomas O'Quirke,§ a Dominican friar of
the convent of Tralee, a man of eloquence and learning,
was appointed preacher and chaplain in ordinary to
both houses. The assembly had all the appearance of
parliament, although the first act of the lay-lords,

* A part of this notable building is now occupied by a coachmaker,
and up to a very recent period the chair, said to have been used by
the speaker, was preserved, till broken up by the owner, who wished
to be rid of the importunities of visitors. Surely the authorities of
Kilkenny ought to look after the venerable residence of the Keth
family, nearly opposite, and if they do not, their city must soon
lose one of its most venerable mansions and greatest attractions.

   † Narrative of the War, Ap. *Desid. Curiosa. Hib.*
‡ Carte's Orm.   Heynus, cited in the *Hib. Dom.*

prelates, and commons was, to declare they did not
intend it as such, fearing to infringe on the prerogative
of the crown, to which belonged the privilege of
calling, proroguing, and dissolving the senate. It was,
however, a provisional government "to consult of an
order for their own affairs, till his Majesty's wisdom
had settled the present troubles."*

The interval between the first day of meeting and the
end of October was occupied in making these pre-
liminary arrangements and administering the oath of
association to such as had not yet taken it. On the
1st of November a committee was appointed, by the
estates spiritual and temporal, to draw up a form of
the confederate government. The committee was
composed, amongst others, of Lords Castlehaven and
Gormanstown, and the lawyers, the chief of whom were
Patrick D'Arcy, Sir Phelim O'Neill, and Richard
Belling. On the fourth of the month the two houses
formally approved the acts of the committee, and on
the same day the prelates issued a mandate to
their clergy throughout Ireland, charging them to
administer the oath of association to their respective
flocks, and pay due obedience to the new government,
the spirit of which may be easily found in the following
extracts:—

"Magna Charta and the common and statute laws of England,
in all points not contrary to the Roman Catholic religion, or inconsistent with the liberty of Ireland, were acknowledged as the basis of
the new government.

"They resolved that each county should have its council, consisting
of one or two deputies out of each barony, and where there was no
barony, of twelve persons elected by the county in general, with
powers to adjudicate on all matters cognizable by justices of the peace,
pleas of the crown, suits for debts, and personal actions, and to restore
possessions usurped since the war; to name all the county officers,
saving the high sheriff, who was to be elected by the supreme
council, out of three whom the council of the county were to recom-
mend. From these there was an appeal to the provincial councils,
which were to consist of two deputies out of each county, and were
to meet four times a year, or oftener, if there was occasion, to examine
the decisions of the county councils, to decide all suits like judges of
assize, to establish recent possessions, but not to interfere with other
suits about lands except in cases of dower.†

"From these there lay a further appeal to the supreme council of
twenty-four persons who were to be elected by the general assembly,
of which twelve were to be constantly resident in Kilkenny, or

* Carte's Orm.   † Carte's Orm.

wherever else they should judge it to be most expedient, with equal
voices, but two-thirds to conclude the rest ; never fewer than nine to
sit in council, and seven to concur in the same opinion : out of these
twenty-four a president was to be named by the assembly, and was
to be always one of the twelve resident, and in case of death or any
other serious impediment, the other residents out of twenty-four
were to select a president."

It was also enacted—"That the council should be vested with
power over all generals, military officers, and civil magistrates, who
were to obey their orders, and send an account duly of their actions
and proceedings ; to determine all matters left undecided by the
general assembly. Their acts to be of force till rescinded by the
next assembly ; to command and punish all commanders of forces,
magistrates, and all others of what rank and condition soever ; to
hear and judge all capital and criminal causes (saving titles to lands),
and to do all kinds of acts for promoting the common cause of the
confederacy and the good of the kingdom, and relating to the support
and management of the war.*

"And as the administrative authority was to be vested in the
supreme council, it was decreed that at the end of every general
assembly, the supreme council should be confirmed or changed, as
the general body thought fit."

Ten days after these enactments had been sanctioned
by the general assembly of the confederate Catholics,
they proceeded to elect the supreme council, when
Lord Mountgarret was chosen president. Six were
selected out of each province, and after the necessary
forms had been gone through, the following were declared duly elected :—

For Leinster—The Archbishop of Dublin, Lord Viscount Gormans-
town, Lord Viscount Mountgarret, Nicholas Plunket, Richard Belling,
James Cusack. Ulster—Archbishop of Armagh, Bishop of Down, Philip
O'Reilly, Col. Mac Mahon, Heber Magennis, Tirlogh O'Neill. For
Munster—Lord Viscount Roche, Sir Daniel O'Brien, Edmund Fitz-
morris, Dr. Fennell, Robert Lambert, George Comyn. For Con-
naught—Archbishop of Tuam, Lord Viscount Mayo, Bishop of
Clonfert, Sir Lucas Dillon, Geoffrey Brown, and Patrick D'Arcy.

On these rested the great national responsibility, nor
were they slow in taking such measures as they deemed
necessary for the welfare of the kingdom. Their first
act was to name the generals who were to command
under their authority. Owen Roe Mac-Art O'Neill was
appointed to command in chief all the Ulster forces.
Thomas Preston, those of Leinster. Barry was named
commander-in-chief in Munster, and John Burke was
to be lieutenant-general in Connaught, reserving the
chief command to Clanricarde, who, it was thought,
would sooner or later declare for the confederation.
But as no act or instrument emanating from the

* Cox, Carte's Orm.

supreme council could be of force, unless sealed with
their own seal, they caused one to be made which may
be thus described:—'Twas circular, and in its centre
was a large cross, the base of which rested on a flaming
heart, while its apex was overlapped by the wings of a
dove: on the left of the cross was the harp, and on the
right the crown. The legend was at once happy, novel,
and classic—" Pro Deo, Rege, et Patria, Hiberni Unani-
mes."*

One of the first acts under the great seal of the
confederacy, was an order to raise thirty thousand
pounds sterling in Leinster, and a levy of thirty-one
thousand seven hundred men in the same province.
This force was to be drilled and disciplined by the
officers who had accompanied Preston, with the least
possible delay. The majority of the new levies was
to garrison such places as the confederates possessed in
Leinster, and the remainder was to be ready to take
the field as soon as circumstances might require. Mr.
Nicholas Plunket was appointed Muster-master-general,
and any locality refusing to contribute its due proportion
of men capable of bearing arms, was to be punished by
a system of "free quarters."

A mint was ordered to be established at Kilkenny,
and those who were wealthy, and heart and soul in the
cause of their country, made large contributions of plate
to the National Treasury; in a very short time four
thousand pounds sterling, in half-crown pieces, "of the
value and goodness of English money" was coined.
The total absence of embellishment or legend on the
silver coin, is evidence of the haste in which it was
struck, for the half-crown piece bears no mark save
that of the cross, and the figures indicating its value.
The copper subsequently produced and circulated, is
far more elaborate, and the legend "Ecce Grex,"
"Floreat Rex," together with the beautiful device,
must be convincing proofs of a more prosperous moment
in the affairs of the confederates.† Along with the
mint the Supreme Council caused a press to be set up
in order to publish their acts, proclamations, and

* Harold in Vit. Lnc. Wadding. This motto is most incorrectly
given in the 4th vol. of Moore's Hist. of Ireland, p. 249.
† *Vide* Simons's Essay on Irish Coins.

manifestoes; nor were they insensible to the great dearth of corn caused by the pillages and burnings which had marred the labours of the husbandman since the rising of 1641.

Anticipating that all the sea-port towns should soon come into their possession, they ordained "that the duty should be taken off wheat and corn imported from foreign countries," till such time as the exigencies which then distressed them should be removed or alleviated. The same exemption was made to extend to such necessaries as "lead, iron, arms, and ammunition." Attracted by such advantages, which were calculated to create a spirit of enterprise, a Dutch captain* had already landed a considerable supply of powder on the coast of Wexford. With the same object in view, they offered "the liberties and privileges of free denizens to all ship-builders and mariners that would settle themselves in the kingdom."

They decreed, moreover, that the bishops and clergy should pay a certain sum out of the ecclesiastical revenues then in their possession, as well as out of the other benefices and church lands which might revert to their rightful inheritors during the progress of the war. But, as the means for prosecuting the struggle for nationality were precarious, notwithstanding the legislative enactments to procure them, they resolved to send agents to the Catholic courts to supplicate aid and succour for a people who had arisen to beat down the strong arm of English despotism, and free their native land.

Father L. Wadding† was named the agent of the Confederates at the Papal court. Who could take such a serious interest in their cause as the annalist? His all-absorbing studies seem to have been forgotten for a time, and the mighty pen which he devoted to record the fame and glories of his order, was now employed in drawing up memorials to the Catholic courts, and supplicating them to look benignly on his suffering and struggling country. Nor were his appeals unheeded. A sum of 26,000 dollars was placed at his disposal, and he sent it

---

* Captain Antonio Vandezepen.—*Vide* Cox.
† Magee's Writers of the Seventeenth Century. See also Harold, in vit. Lucæ Wadding.

by a confidential agent to the National Treasury. Two thousand muskets were landed about this time on the Wexford coast, and although most persons were inclined to ascribe this welcome gift to Pope Urban, it is quite certain that the merit of the work must be given to Father Wadding. The agent sent to the court of Spain was Father James Talbot, an Augustine friar. He soon collected a sum of 20,000 dollars in that land of chivalry; and having visited the French court, he succeeded in procuring an additional sum, together with "two great iron guns, casting balls of twenty-four pounds weight."*

Nor were these acts of the confederate Catholics done in private, as if dreading the light of day; on the contrary, in the face of heaven and earth, they proclaimed by a manifesto, which was published at Kilkenny, "that the Catholics of Ireland, driven by the perfidy and cruelty of the rebel Puritans, had arisen and taken arms for their religion, king, and country." The enemy they had to combat was in each of the four provinces, and they made no secret of their determination to expel him, if God so decreed; but in mentioning the fact, we may be permitted to question the prudence of that arrangement of the supreme council which committed the conduct of the war to four generals quite independent of each other. While the temporal peers were enacting these measures, the prelates were actively engaged sending instructions to their respective dioceses, rousing the torpid and chiding such as thought that there was no hope for their country. The lay lords did not hesitate to pronounce the severest penalties on those who refused to rally round the confederate banners. Nor did the bishops fear to declare such as did not take the oath, traitors to their God, king, and country. Excommunication was decreed against all neutrals and such as assisted the common enemy; but, at the same time, the severest penalties of the church were to be inflicted on all those who made distinctions between the modern and ancient Irish, or wantonly committed murder, pillage, or any act which was incompatible with the holiness of the object for which the Irish of the Pale and the old

* Belling

Celtic tribes were soon to commingle their life-blood on the fair field of battle.

Maligned and misrepresented as they were by the parliamentarian despatches, and the gross calumnies of the justices, the few extracts which have been given must ennoble and exalt that Convention in the eyes of every impartial man. How strangely do they contrast with the bigoted and ensanguined edicts of their enemies? "Reilly, a prime popish priest," wrote some accredited scribe at this period, to the disaffected in England, "like his father the devil, compasses the earth, far and near, to draw into their conspiracy such as had not before been therewith acquainted."* This foul aspersion is an evidence of that lynx-eyed malice with which the assembly was watched, and the ardour and devotion with which the prelates laboured to enlist their people in the confederacy. In the annals of any other country it would be hard to find a convention more pure and patriotic, and certainly the history of the Irish Catholics presents no more agreeable reminiscence than that which is associated with the general assembly of October 1642.

Under the shadow of that old Cathedral, where Clarence's parliament had assembled to sow the seeds of division between the two races, the Norman robbers and the plundered Irish, the representatives of both parties were banded together by a holy league, approved by God, and deplored by those who would keep alive that demon spirit of hate and dissension which had fertilized the soil with torrents of rival blood. Oh! that these jealousies and heart-rending distinctions of caste had never been. But at the period of which we are writing they were forgotten, and merged in oblivion. Two grand objects were to be accomplished: for these life and property, and all that endears both, were to be set at nought, and they had sworn never to lay down their arms till "the Roman Catholic religion was restored to its full splendour, as it was in the reign of Henry VII., and all the penal and restrictive laws were annulled." As a corollary to the foregoing conditions it was to be insisted on—

* Thorpe Papers, R. D. S.

Mountgarret, designing to intercept Ormond on his return to Dublin, took up a position at the bridge of Mageny, four miles from Athy. He had about 8,000 men, badly armed, and far from being disciplined or provided with cannon. These troops had but three or four companies of horse, and were nowise formidable, save in number. They were commanded by Mountgarret, Lords Skerrin and Dunboyne, Roger O'Moore, Hugh Byrne, and Sir Morgan Cavanagh. Orn cial did not move from Athy until the 15th, and, much against his inclination, found that it was necessary to attack the Irish. Three miles further on, was a very narrow defile, through which it was absolutely necessary that Ormond should march. Mountgarret's men, being unencumbered with baggage, rapidly advanced to seize the pass; but a rising ground concealed from his view a corresponding movement of the English forces; he was mortified at finding himself outmarched, and was obliged to halt; he then took up a position on a neighbouring height. Some ditches in his front gave him a considerable advantage over Ormond, who ordered Coote to advance and dislodge his enemy. A well-aimed volley from the Irish, staggered the advancing column. For awhile they seemed sure of success, till they saw Lucas and Grenville on their left, with Ormond's cavalry. An opening in a hedge, which had not been noticed by Lord Mountgarret, gave access to Ormond's horse. The Irish, thus taken by surprise, did not long resist the cavalry; but broke and fled to the bog at the foot of the hill. Mountgarret, who commanded on the right, still maintained his ground. Against him, Ormond and Sir John Sherlock now led the main body, which was not yet engaged. As they ascended they were met with spirit, volley after volley swept their ranks; but, as the two lines in front of each other were about to "cross their pikes," Mountgarret's men fled, nor stopped till they joined their companions who had taken refuge in the bog.

In this fatal action, since known as the battle of Kilrush, the Irish are said to have lost 700 men, and some of their most distinguished leaders. Mountgarret and Lord Skerrin fled that night to Tullogh; Roger O'Moore and his brother Lisagh, to his own house "near the

Boyne;" and the O'Byrne of Wicklow to the fastnesses
of Glangaran. Ormond, even after this signal victory,
was in no mood to follow it up; it was quite enough for
him that he forced his way to Dublin, where he was
soon after congratulated by a message from the parliament extolling his bravery, and lauding his untiring
zeal in pillaging, murdering, and burning the crops.

Yet the heart of Ireland was only humbled by this
disaster—it was not crushed; new energy and a bolder
spirit were soon to be infused. Those who listened to
the recital of that failure, did not despair. The tree of
hope, which they beheld prospectively blossoming and
laden with fruit, was but a sapling; the storm had
only bowed it as it swept by; and those who, to escape
the hurricane, had retired for awhile, were soon to rally
round it and guard it more faithfully. But after the
battle of Kilrush, one bright name* disappears: the last
time the inspiriting war-shout of his followers fell on his
ear was on that hill side. What reasons there may
have been for the retirement of the gallant chief, whose
name was linked with that of "God and our Lady," are
not apparent; but it is said upon authority that he proceeded to the Fews, "and devoted the rest of his days to
peaceful pursuits in the bosom of his family."†

During these transactions in Ireland, King Charles I.
was actively engaged with his English subjects. It was
quite impossible that he could pay much attention to Irish
affairs, busied as he was with the factions who were
already meditating the ruin of his crown. The two houses
had voted a levy of 10,000 men, in opposition to the
king, who intended to levy war against the parliament.
The royal arsenal at Hull had been forcibly seized by
the parliamentarian party, and the arms removed to the
Tower. A forced loan, at eight per cent., paid in
money and plate, replenished the treasury. The Earl
of Warwick took the command of the fleet; and the
Earl of Essex was appointed lord general, with a
solemn promise from both Lords and Commons that
they would live and die with him in the national
quarrel.

* Roger O'Moore. Carte says he died at Kilkenny.
† V. the map of Ulster in the admirable History of the Confiscation, by Mac Nevin.

"That all primates, archbishops, bishops, ordinaries, deans, and chapters, archdeacons, chancellors, vicars, and other pastors of the Roman Catholic secular clergy and their respective successors, shall have, hold, and enjoy all the churches and church-livings, in as large and ample manner as the late Protestant clergy respectively enjoyed the same on the 1st day of October, together with all the profits, emoluments, perquisites, liberties, and their rights to their respective sees and churches belonging, as well in all places then in possession of the confederated Catholics, as also in all other places that shall be recovered by them from the adverse party, saving to the Roman Catholic laity, their respective rights according to the laws of the land." *

It is needless to dwell at any length on the altered circumstances of the Irish Catholics at this moment. We have seen that judicatories for the administration of justice were established throughout the land, and that officers were appointed to the various departments. A mint and a press were the creation of a moment. Envoys or ambassadors were sent to the foreign courts, and their credentials were recognised by Philip IV. of Spain, Urban VIII., and Anne of Austria, during the minority of Louis XIV. Richelieu,† who was then prime minister, seems to have taken a lively interest in their proceedings, but he did not live to witness the ulterior movements of the confederates. Incredible do their exertions seem. They gave letters of marque, and chartered some light vessels, which were to protect the shores, and sail under the confederate colours; in a word, they took the government on themselves, and issued orders for the levying of armies, and gave commissions under their own seal to the generals who were to take the command. Cusack was named Attorney-General, and Plunket held the office of Chancellor of the Exchequer, other officers having been appointed to the various departments, civil and military. The declaration of their independence, saving their allegiance to the crown of Charles I., may be easily found in the following extract from the manifesto which they published at the termination of the first General Assembly :—

"It is hereby declared that no temporal government or jurisdiction shall be assumed, kept, or exercised in this kingdom, or within any

* Unkind Deserter, p. 55
† He died December 4, 1642, and was succeeded by Cardinal Mazarin.

county or province thereof, during these troubles, other than is before expressed, except such jurisdiction or government as is, or shall be, approved by the General Assembly, or Supreme Council of the Confederate Catholics of Ireland." *

The last act of the general assembly was to draw up a remonstrance to the King, declarative of their loyalty, and reprobating the vexatious tyranny of the justices, and the Irish parliament, which, composed for the most part of men who were of the lowest and basest class, thought of nothing but spoliating and persecuting the Irish Catholics. The remonstrance detailed the wholesale plunder of the O'Byrnes in the county Wicklow, and the bigotry of the justices who made it penal to tolerate a Catholic school-master. It implored his Majesty to confirm the graces withheld by the artifices of Parsons and Borlase, who, by bribing jurors, and promising them a portion of the lands which they contemplated confiscating, on the plea of defective titles, left little chance for fair and impartial trial. The many murders committed on the natives under the semblance of law, were detailed at length, and means were taken to transmit the remonstrance to his Majesty and Queen Henrietta Maria. † The confederate assembly did not break up till the 9th of January, and the next general meeting was fixed for the 20th of May following. ‡

This manifesto is signed by Lord Mountgarret, President, and Sir Nicholas Shea, Clerk of the Supreme Council.

+ Carte's Orm. L. 270.   ‡ Walsh, Second Part, First Treatise.

CHAPTER III.

BEFORE the general assembly rose the parliament was sitting in Dublin, and strange and unconstitutional were its proceedings. The Catholics were unrepresented, nor was there a friendly voice to speak in their favour. The justices, intent on forging new fetters, and extirpating the Papists, were for suspending Poyning's act, and thus leaving themselves free to pass new penal laws without transmitting the bills to England. In this, however, they were opposed by Ormond, now made still more important by the title of Marquess, the patent having been issued on the 18th of the preceding August. Nor was there wanting a representative of the fanatical party in England to infuriate the enemies of the confederates, and canonise those who would march against them. This man was Stephen Jerome: patronised by the hypocritical justices, he preached in St. Patrick's cathedral each morning at seven o'clock to the soldiers, and on the 13th November, in Christchurch, the "state" and other persons of rank being present. "Empty, illiterate, and turbulent,"* he was an apostle in the eyes of his pay-masters; nor did he spare the king, upon whom he heaped slander and obloquy. To such a length did he carry his invectives that it was thought desirable to interpose the authority of Launcelot Bulkely, the Protestant archbishop, who inhibited the spiritual champion of Parsons and his colleagues. The justices, it would appear, had little respect for the authority of their diocesan; nor did the preacher resign his office till he found it inexpedient to continue. He was the prototype of those enthusiasts, who, subsequently, in the name of the God of charity, evangelized not peace, but strife—not mercy, but extermination; nor would his name be mentioned here were it not necessary to show that the pulpit was employed by the

* Carte's Orm.

authorities to propound these rabid dogmas, of which a
more enlightened age is happily growing weary.

But the proceedings of the confederates were calculated to alarm the justices. They wanted money to
pay their troops, who were daily becoming mutinous;
their appeals to England were unheeded, and they
determined to take such measures as were likely to
still the clamour of their hirelings. Imitating the confederates "they called in all the plate," which their
partizans gladly gave them, and caused it to be coined
into half-crown pieces by John Neale, Peter Vander-
troven, and Gilbert Tongues, goldsmiths.*

These precautions were necessary; for the levy of the
troops in Leinster, ordered by the supreme council, as
well as the alacrity with which the Catholic gentry and
their dependents furnished the national treasury, made
them tremble for their security. The poorest gave his
mite, and all were ready to gird on the sword. The exertions of Preston's officers were beyond praise, and they
hoped soon to be at the head of a large and well-disci-
plined force. True it is that they could not all be furnished with arms, if we except the pike, which was
readily procured; but the artillery which Preston brought
with him supplied many defects. One thousand five
hundred muskets of the two thousand landed at Wexford
were bestowed on him; the remainder was apportioned
to Owen O'Neill.

Burke, who was to command in Connaught, was actively engaged in enlisting the sympathies of his province; nor, indeed, had he much difficulty in drawing
multitudes into the confederacy. With a small band of
followers, he entered the church of Athenry, and caused
Clanricarde's chaplain to bless his banners. The fact
came to the knowledge of the Earl, and the chaplain was
dismissed. But the petty tyranny and officious zeal of
this nobleman could not stem the popular enthusiasm.
The bishops and clergy were to a man opposed to him,
and the recent barbarities of Willoughby made them
long for an opportunity in which they might expel the
English garrison.

In the south, Inchiquin had remained inactive since

* Carte's Orm. Simons's Essay.

the battle of Liscarroll. Forbes, however, landed at Kinsale, and marched into the country, as far as Rathbarry. A section of his forces consisted of a Scotch regiment; and the peasantry, who were far from being well armed or disciplined, rose and slew them in an ambush. Groves, who was a captain under Forbes, immediately afterwards fell on this rude array, and forced 600 of them into the island of Inchidony, where, the tide being in, they were all drowned.[*] Inchiquin, however, remained shut up in Cork, in need of provisions; nor did he dare to take the field.

Nor did Owen Roe confine himself to Ulster. The Scotch general had endeavoured in vain to bring him to an action, but as yet he had not sufficient strength to meet him. Munroe, however, had been compelled to retire into Down and Antrim. Sir Robert Stewart, a descendant of one of the most distinguished of the Scotch undertakers, had a strong force on the Donegal side; and O'Neill retired for a while into Longford and Leitrim, with the intention " of nursing up an army in these rugged districts" which would make him a match for his enemies.[†]

Indeed, the chieftain of Ulster could not have selected a fairer field for his enterprise than that which lay open to him in these two counties. The tyranny of such men as Sir Frederick Hamilton, of Manor Hamilton, and Coote, (under whose orders he appears to have acted,) had driven the unfortunate peasantry to madness. The cruelties inflicted on the Christians of Spain by Aben Humeya[‡] and his Morisco captains, pale before the atrocities perpetrated by Hamilton on the inhabitants of Leitrim and Longford. His bawn, or castle, was the rendezvous of a ferocious banditti, who spread death and desolation around them. By day and night he sent from within its walls a savage soldiery, who robbed and murdered with impunity. When they returned to their leader, the most acceptable gifts they could offer were the heads of the wretched people, which they brutally severed from the bodies. Women and tender girls were

[*] Smith's Cork.
[†] Appendix to the Poems of T. Davis.
[‡] *Vide* History of Spain and Portugal, vol. v., p. 65, in Lardner's Cab. Cyclop.

not exempt from the horrors which this fanatic inflicted in the holy name of God. Upon a hill near his castle he erected a gallows, from which every day a fresh victim was suspended. The brother of the O'Rourke shared this ignominious death, with his wife and dependents. Nor was the gallant Sir Frederick ashamed to bequeath to posterity a journal which he kept of these barbarities.* The result may be easily imagined. The O'Rourkes, O'Connors, MacGaurans, and other septs, were only anxious for a leader. Their people were ready—nay, constrained—to follow them ; and O'Neill's exertions were employed to bring them to a state of discipline and organization.

Such was the state of the country about the close of November, 1642. The two hostile parties—the Confederates and Parliamentarians—were actively engaged making preparation for the coming struggle. The enthusiasm of the Irish was at its height, and their enemies, who calculated on a rich harvest of plunder, only waited an opportunity of meeting them in the field.

While the respective generals were mustering their troops and disciplining the new levies, the supreme council remained at Kilkenny, anxiously watching the progress of events. About the middle of December they proceeded to Wexford, escorted by their guard of 500 foot and 200 horse.† Their object was to compose ani-

---

* This journal, or diary, written by Sir F. Hamilton, was printed in London, 1643. It is to be found in the Thorpe Papers, under this title, "Another Extract of more Letters sent out of Ireland." A portion of it has been since reprinted by my talented friend, Mr. Battersby, in the Catholic Directory for 1846; 'tis a pity he did not give it whole and entire in one number. We.must, however, content ourselves with one extract from it, which cannot fail to exhibit the animus of Hamilton and his godly mercenaries:—" March 17—Being their patron St. Patrick's day, our colonel, sending for one of his prisoners, the rogues being drawn up in a body right before us, we called to them since they durst not come to perform their promise, and take the castle, they would rescue their countryman who was there to be hanged in honour of St. Patrick, which prisoner being hanged, and proving but an old sack of straw, long stockings being sowed to it, as it was throwne over the gallowes, our hangman sitting on the gallowes, calling to them if they had charity in them to send the poore prisoner a priest, they imagining that sack to be a man, fell all on their knees in our view praying for the prisoner's soule."

† This force was to accompany them wherever they went, and garrison whatever town they visited.

tuosities, and release from prison those who had been
committed for offences against the government of the
justices. It does not appear what these dissensions
were, but the fact is recorded by one of themselves.
They feared any disagreement which tended to diminish
their strength, and certainly set great value on the heart
and nerve of the capital of that county, so signally remarkable for its bravery and patriotism. " The towns-
men of Wexford," says Belling, " were naturally as violent and stubborn at land as they were famous among
the nation for being daring at sea." *

It is at this period we have evidence of the growing
importance which the confederacy was attaining in the
estimation of foreign powers. When the supreme
council had arrived at Ross they were waited on by M.
de Overmere, a man of quality from Flanders, and a
relative of General Preston. This gentleman made the
supreme council an offer of frigates, on a proviso that he
was to command. They deliberated on the expediency
of the proposal and finally declined it. Overmere was
a subject of Spain, and they feared to offend the French
and the United Provinces then actually at war with the
Spanish king. A number of light vessels soon after
came from Flanders, to which they gave letters of
marque, and thus, in great measure, succeeded in inter-
rupting the passage between Chester and the Irish
coast.† From Ross they proceeded to Clonmel, for the
purpose of drawing Limerick into the confederacy;
for although the city and county had declared for the
national cause, such was the influence of the Earl of
Thomond with the citizens, that they wished to maintain
themselves as " a free state." When the mayor was
advertised of their approach, he politely represented the
great dearth of corn which rendered it unsafe to introduce any body of troops; but the chief anxiety of the
confederates was for the castle of Bunratty and the
other strongholds on the Shannon, then held by

* Belling's Narrative of the War, p. 163.
† Borlase, p. 97, has a copy of a commission given by the
supreme council to Francis Oliver, a native of Flanders, to command
the "St. Michael the Archangel," a ship of 120 tons or lasts, empowering him to " prejudice all such as he shall meet of his Majesty's
enemies, and the enemies of the general Catholic cause."

Thomond, who they feared was in league with the parliament, and might be induced to admit their garrisons. The mayor, however, gave a solemn assurance of his friendship, and that of the citizens, who were determined to resist all overtures on the part of the parliamentarians. This communication quieted their apprehensions and they retired, after having given a commission to Sir Daniel O'Brien to seize on the castle of Bunratty, and on the person of the Earl of Thomond; for, it was resolved—

"That if he could be forced to join the confederates without touching on his religion (as he was a Protestant), he should be in the condition of their confederates ; or if he continued neuter, without adhering to the enemy, a competent part of his estate should be set apart for him, and no declaration made, by which he would be subject to the penalties of neuters."*

Meantime the confederates were actively engaged in Leinster. Preston was now at the head of about 6,000 foot and 600 horse, and Lord Castlehaven, who acted as his lieutenant-general, burned for an opportunity to distinguish himself. The first encounter between the new levies and the Puritan forces was at Ballinakil, in the Queen's county, which was a colony of English, planted there by James I. The celebrated Moncke, afterwards Duke of Albemarle, relieved the place, and coming up with some detachments of the confederates, defeated them at Tymahoe. It was, however, nothing more than a skirmish, for Preston immediately afterwards proceeded to besiege the castle of Burros, in the King's county, which surrendered on the 30th of December. This partial triumph was regarded as an auspicious termination of a year in which Ireland had raised herself to such an extraordinary eminence, and many a heart "beat high with hope" for ultimate success, ere the year which was now dawning had drawn to a close.

From Burros the Leinster forces marched to Birr, of which place the infamous Parsons was governor. They sat down before it on the 13th of January, and after a brave, but ineffectual resistance, it surrendered to Preston. •Nothing could equal the humanity of the confederate generals on this occasion, for they

* Belling's Narrative of the War.

caused all the prisoners who had fallen into their hands, amounting to 800, men, women, and children, to be escorted by detachments till they reached Athy.*

Bannagher was soon after besieged by Preston, and yielded without firing a shot. From this place he marched to Fort Falkland, on the 26th of January. The garrison was strong, and such was the zeal of Clanricarde for the justices, that he supplied it with provisions. When the confederates were about to open a fire, the governor, Lord Castlestewart, thought it better to surrender, and Preston immediately took possession of the fortress. "Thus," says Carte, "the confederate general having strengthened himself with new forces, reduced all the forts in the King's County. †

While these successes were attending them in Leinster, the province of Connaught was up and stirring. Alarmed by the growing power of the Irish, Ranelagh, the lord president, accompanied by young Coote and the other English commanders, fled out of the province. This was in the beginning of February. On the 5th of that month, as they approached Dublin, they halted at Rathconnel, where they were met by Preston, whose mercurial character could not forego the opportunity of risking a battle, when he might have hung on their march, and cut them up in detail. Ranelagh had but a small force, and he fought with desperation. He succeeded in repulsing Preston, and making his way to Dublin, where he charged the justices with a dereliction of duty in not sending him supplies. The withdrawal of the lord president had a salutary influence on the men, who were every day rallying round Colonel Burke. He proposed amicable terms to Willoughby, who still held the fort of Galway; but they were all rejected, and circumstances made it apparent that the garrison was in the interest of the parliament. This fact served to rouse the people to more strenuous exertions, and about the middle of February Clanricarde's castle of Clare-Galway was seized for the confederates by Captain Thomas Burke, of Anbally, who was ably seconded by a Franciscan friar. When the lieutenant-general of the province had information of this event, he called upon

* Castlehaven's Mem.   † Carte, i. 382.

several gentlemen of the ccuntry to levy forces and besiege the fort of Galway. *

The supreme council returned to Kilkenny when the
news of Preston's defeat at Rathconnel reached them.
There was an old prophecy that whoever should win the
battle of Rathconnel should win Ireland. Fearing that
these absurd superstitions should damp the ardour of the
people, measures were taken with promptitude to repair
the recent disaster. Some of the new levies, who had
not yet seen service, were given to Preston, and in less
than a week he was in condition to take the field.

General Barry had mustered his forces in the south,
and had reduced Inchiquin to such straits that he was
obliged to drive all the cattle left in the baronies of
Imokilly and Barrymore into the garrisons of Cork,
Kinsale, and Youghal. Such was his distress that it became necessary to seize on part of the tobacco belonging
to patentees, of which there was a great quantity in the
above-mentioned towns, and sell it for the subsistence of
his troops. Purcell, who was lieutenant-general to
Barry, had orders to besiege Cappoquin, which was garrisoned by Lord Broghill for the parliament. Purcell
proceeded to execute his commission, when an event occurred which ultimately delayed the reduction of the
place.

The justices found that they could not maintain their
troops in Dublin without producing famine; and as they
had now some money in their hands, they made arrangements with Ormond to take the command and bring in
provisions. Accordingly, on the 2nd of March, the lieutenant-general left Dublin with an army of 3,000 foot,
700 horse, two demi-culverins, and four field-pieces.

His instructions were to capture Wexford and Ross, as
the confederates were masters of the sea, and were daily
seizing barques laden with provisions as they were passing through St. George's Channel.† The justices agreed

* Hardiman's Galway, 120. .Mr. Moore, in his account of the two
actions at Tymahoe and Rathconnel, gives them the most undue importance. "The ominous victory" of Rathconnel did not "strike dis-
may into the hearts" of those whom he calls "rebels;" on the contrary,
they grew daily bolder and more determined.—*Vide* Hist. of Ireland,
vol. iv. p. 254.

† Carte's Orm.

to send a ship laden with victuals for Ormond's troops;
and according to agreement this vessel was to anchor at
Duncannon. Having taken Castle-Martin, in the county
Kildare, Ormond continued his march towards Carlow,
and on the 4th of the month he sat down before the small
castle of Timolin, which was garrisoned for the confederates by four-score men. He called on them to yield,
and they stoutly refused. He then opened a fire on that
devoted band of heroes; nor did they ask for quarter till
the blazing rafters were crackling about them. They
were then permitted to march out, and when they expected the same forbearance which they had shewn at
Fort Falkland and Birr, they were massacred on the
spot. Elated with this victory, Ormond advanced on
Carlow, and having held a council of war, it was determined to lay siege to Ross. Orders were then issued by
the supreme council to abandon the siege of Cappoquin,
and Purcell was directed to throw 300 men into Ross,
which was greatly exposed. Belling tells us that it
had little or no fortification—a rampart of earth was
its only protection; but within that feeble barrier there
were stern hearts. On the 11th of March Ormond approached the town, and sent a herald to Nicholas Fitz-
harris, the mayor, commanding him to surrender. Fitz-
harris replied that he held it for his Majesty, and would
not yield. A second summons was as boldly rejected,
and the townspeople immediately hoisted the confederate colours. Ormond then opened his fire, and having
effected a breach in the earthen rampart, ordered his
men to advance. They did so, and were encountered
by the heroic people. Men and women guarded every
avenue, and repulsed the justices' soldiers; again and
again did they push forward to gain an entrance, but a
shower of balls and stones drove them back. While the
people were thus engaged a vessel of war had dropped
down the river from Duncannon, and commenced battering the town; but the bravery of the inhabitants was
not to be daunted. They brought some light pieces to
bear on the ship, and sunk her. Ormond, who witnessed the devoted courage of the men of Ross, was con-
sulting what step he should take, when word was brought
him that Purcell was advancing with a large force from

Cappoquin, and he felt himself constrained to raise the siege, after having remained five days before the place.

Fearing to be cut off from his reserve, which he had left in Carlow, he sounded the march, and resolved to get back to Dublin as he might. Preston advanced with an army of 5,000 horse and foot to intercept him, but in his haste he brought no cannon. He halted at Temple Wodigan, about two miles from Ross, and waited Ormond in a pass through which he should necessarily march. "The pass," says Castlehaven, " "was at least half-a-mile through a bog, where no more than four horses could march in a breast, with water up to the belly; but Preston had not the patience to expect the enemy's coming to him, which they must do, or starve, but went over the pass to them, and put himself under as great disadvantage as his enemy could wish. Ormond took hold of this unexpected advantage, and gave Preston no time to form his army, but charged still as they went over, besides what he did all along with his cannon, till at length, after a considerable loss of men, killed and taken prisoners, he was wholly defeated and routed."† Ormond, however, rapidly retired to Dublin, quite satisfied that he was not 'totally destroyed. A better system of military supervision would have removed Preston from the command; as it was, however, he was censured by the supreme council, and his conduct pronounced uncircumspect. He stood high in the estimation of Mountgarret, whom he materially served, notwithstanding his recent failure. Soon after the battle of Ross, he marched with all his force on Ballinakil, (the property of Mountgarret) which had been in the possession of an English colony. Father Talbot, who had just then arrived from his mission to the Spanish and French courts, had brought with him supplies of money, and "two great iron guns." These were forwarded to Preston, and he commenced battering the castle, which soon yielded. The undertakers were permitted to depart whither they would, and Mountgarret got possession of his estate. Could this circumstance have blinded

* Castlehaven's Mem. 35.

him to Preston's rashness and unfitness for such a responsible post?

The eulogists and apologists of Ormond would have us believe that he undertook the expedition to Ross much against his will, and that the justices had a secret design in sending him, which was, to prevent his negotiating with the confederates. Be this as it may, we cannot find any claim, on his part, to such humanity as ever characterised the confederate armies.— On every occasion where blood might be shed, he knew no mercy, and where the interposition of a generous man might have saved many, Ormond was an impassive spectator. All the apologies made for him by Walsh, and O'Connor* who falls into the strange blunder of calling him an Irishman, would not wipe away his guilt, in permitting the wanton massacre at Timolin. But a more congenial occupation than that of war, now presented itself. England was in a flame, and the king had got a check which induced him, on retiring to Oxford, to consider the remonstrance which the confederates had forwarded after the first general assembly. He looked to the future, and began to calculate on the succours he might derive from Ireland, in case he succeeded in making terms with the leaders.

Influenced by these considerations, and affecting to believe that their demands were moderate, and the representations which they had put before him well grounded, he issued a commission, under the great seal, on the 11th of January, 1643, directed to the Marquis of Ormond, the Earls of Clanricarde and Roscommon, the Lord Viscount Moore, and others, any three or more of them being authorised to meet and act for the purpose aforesaid, namely, to receive in writing what the petitioners had to say or propound. This document was in the hands of Ormond on the 30th of the month, but the justices, taking this commission for a step towards the peace of the kingdom, and their own ruin, "were displeased that a wish should be manifested by any one that the war from which they promised themselves revenge and fortunes, should in any

* Columbanus, who was ably handled by Plowden, *passim.*

other way be ended, than with the blood and confiscation of all those whom they could propose to be guilty
of the defection." They, therefore, hit on an expedient
which was well calculated to promote their ends. The
supreme council was at Ross when a trumpeter was sent
to inform them of this communication from the king,
with a safe-conduct from Ormond and Parsons to such
as the council chose to employ to represent their
grievances to the above-named commissioners. When
the safe-conduct was submitted to the supreme council,
they were astonished on reading the following words,
which had been artfully introduced by the justices, with
the cognizance of their lieutenant-general :—" That,
albeit, his majesty hath not thought fit to admit any
of them to his presence who were actors or abettors of
so odious a rebellion," they might regard themselves as
peculiarly favoured in being allowed to treat with his
justices. The answer returned to this lying fabrication
was worthy of these chivalrous men :—" We take God
to witness," said they, " that there are no limits set to
the scorn and infamy that are cast upon us ; and we
will be in the esteem of loyal subjects, or die to a man."
In the heat of the moment they had resolved not to
treat with the commissioners, and stated " that there
was a necessity laid upon them to absent themselves
from the meeting." Their answer was published, and
the people applauded their firmness.*

However, on more mature deliberation, they suspected that the insulting words had been written, not
by the king, but by his enemies, and they appointed the
18th of March for a conference, to be held at Trim.
The justices, seeing that the confederates were well-
disposed towards his majesty, resolved to try what
cruel and perfidious actions might do.† They, therefore, got the consent of the council in Dublin, to
an act which was calculated to put a stop to anything like a treaty. At the battle of Rathconnel,
Lisagh O'Connor and the son of Garret Aylmer had
been made prisoners by Sir Richard Grenville; in
order to exasperate the Catholics, Parsons and his
colleagues wrote to Sir H. Tichbourne to have them

---

* Belling's History of the War.   † Carte's Orm. i. 407.

executed by martial law. Nor did they confine themselves to this unwarrantable proceeding. At the very
time they had the king's orders to quiet troubles, and
bring about a peace, they sent their lieutenant-general
to attack Ross; and when he should have been engaged
in pacific negotiations, he was actually in conflict with
General Preston, though he well knew that he was
doing the bidding, not of the king, but of Parsons
and his council.

In fact, he undertook the expedition with the consent
of the justices, and at the desire of an English committee then sent over by the parliament "to direct and
superintend the affairs of Ireland, against the king's
command."[*] Though expressly named in the commission, he was burning and spoiling the country without
opposition, on the very day when Lord Gormanstown,
Sir Lucas Dillon, Sir R. Talbot, John Walsh, Esq.,
and others were assembling at Trim.. What wonder,
therefore, if the Irish Catholics distrusted this man of
craft and faithlessness?

The commissioners from the confederates were met
at the above-named place by the Earls of Clanricarde and
Roscommon, Sir Maurice Eustace and others, on the
part of the king. A remonstrance[†] of grievances
was produced, which entered at great length into a
history of the cruelties practised on the Catholics by
the justices and their adherents. "This remonstrance,"
says Borlase, "was solemnly received by his majesty's
commissioners, and by them transmitted to his majesty."[‡]

But before it was sent to the king it came to be considered in the commons' house of parliament in Dublin,
seemingly disliked by all, whereby the business growing
hot, the house was prorogued till the 6th of May.[§]

When the justices heard that Preston was besieging
Ballinakil, they sent Colonel Lawrence Crawford, with
1,300 foot and 150 horse, to endeavour to beat up the
Leinster general's quarters. He set out on the 13th of
April; but as he approached, he halted before the castle

* Borlase's Irish Reb. p. 142.
† This lengthy document is to be found in the Appendix to Curry's Review.
‡ Ibid, p. 154.   § Borlase, 155.

of Ballybrittas. He called on the confederate garrison
to surrender, but he was soon beaten off. Castlehaven
was ordered to fall on Crawford as he was retiring.
Having got together 1,500 horse, he came up with the
English at Monastereven, charged and dispersed them.
As they were retreating over the Barrow, their commander had his thigh broken by a musket-shot in his flight.

From Ballinakil, Preston proceeded with his army
into Westmeath; and the English garrisons of Carlow
and the Queen's County, taking advantage of his absence,
alarmed the county Kilkenny to the very gates of the
city. Castlehaven took the field again and scattered these
marauding parties, which were commanded by Sir Michael Emle and Major Verney. He subsequently took
the castles of Ballynunry and Cloghgrenan, and relieved
the supreme council from any further apprehension.
Flushed with success, he passed rapidly into the Queen's
County, and besieged the castle of Ballylennan. Here
he was joined by Sir Walter Butler, who informed him
that a strong reinforcement, drawn from the English
garrisons, was on march to raise the siege. Castlehaven, having reconnoitred the advancing troops, determined to give them battle in sight of the besieged; and
finding that they did not amount to more than 800 foot
and 300 horse, he ordered Butler's cavalry to follow,
when they immediately betook themselves to flight, pursued by the confederate light troops till they got shelter
in Athy. The castle, seeing those who had come to
their succour defeated, yielded on honorable conditions.
Thus, in the course of a few months, did the confederates prosecute the war in Leinster with the most signal
success, taking almost every place of strength which had
been held for the justices, who were terribly apprehensive of being ultimately shut up and starved in Dublin.

But their hopes of plunder, and undisguised desire of
shedding the blood of the Irish Papists, were doomed to
be disappointed. Whether Charles I. was made sensible
by the remonstrance recently forwarded of the evils inflicted on the Irish people by Parsons and Borlase, or
apprehensive that, by continuing them at the head of affairs, he was only injuring himself, it is not our province
to examine. He certainly saw that the justices would
ever stand in the way of any peace between him and his

Irish subjects, and he determined to remove them. On the 23d of April, 1643, Sir Francis Butler arrived from England with a supersedeas for Parsons' government, and a commission to Lord Borlase and Sir Henry Tichbourne to be lords justices. Yet there may be question whether this act of tardy justice on the part of the king was ultimately beneficial to Ireland. There are many who think that it was quite the reverse. Had Parsons been allowed to retain the government, there never could have been room for the craft and intrigue which followed. His love of pillage and hypocritical cant had roused such feelings of abhorrence and detestation in the breasts of the Irish Catholics, as must have ever stood in the way of any accommodation between them and their tyrants. From what we have seen of their success since the sitting of the first general assembly, it is evident that they were becoming daily more skilled in the use of arms, and firmly bent on establishing their independence. The open and flagrant villanies of this man could not have subdued their spirit, or checked them in their onward march; but it was reserved for the policy of one who was well skilled in the principles of Macchiavelli to break that bond of union which must have rendered them irresistible and triumphant; but let us not anticipate.

In the beginning of May, whilst Preston and Castlehaven were reducing the strongholds of Leinster, Munroe was obliged, by the most pressing want, to advance into the neighbourhood of Armagh. Owen Roe occupied Charlemont, which he had fortified and garrisoned.— 'Twas Munroe's object to seize the Ulster general, and thus dash the hopes of his followers, who sanguinely reckoned on his great military character for ultimate success. So secretly did the Scotch general conduct his march, that Owen Roe was out hunting with but few of his staff when he was surprised. His first thought was to escape by spurring rapidly back to Charlemont; but he was intercepted by a detachment of the Scotch. His superior knowledge of the locality was his only advantage; but even this did not prevent collision. Beset by Munroe's men, in a lane thickly enclosed with copses, he fought, hand to hand, for an hour; and such was the steady bravery and coolness of his retinue, that Munroe

shouted to his men, "Cam awa frae awheen rebels,"*
*and suffered the great prize to elude his grasp.   On the
following day he had reason to repent him of his teme-
rity, for he was encountered by O'Neill and Colonel
Sandford, and routed with loss.   A small army, under
Montgomery and Chichester, menaced him soon after;
but the phlegmatic general was not to be provoked.
He knew that these officers were chiefly intent on making
preys, and he determined to husband his resources for a
better opportunity.   He contented himself with having
secured the cattle from their foragers, and then retired
into Leitrim.

In the west, the confederate arms were signally prosperous.   The son and grandson of Lord Athenry, the
three Teige Kellys of Aughrim and Mullaghmore, together with Sir Roebuck Lynch, Sir V. Blake, and other
gentlemen marched, under Lieutenant-Colonel Burke, to
Galway.   Willoughby was shut up in the fort, and in
want of provisions.   He was obliged to send boats' crews
to pillage on the coast.   They were intercepted, after one
of these predatory excursions, by the confederates, and
cut off to a man.   The town undertook to defray the
expense of the siege, and two batteries were erected—
one on the west, and the other on the opposite point of
Rinmore.   A chain was drawn across the harbour, and
access by sea was thus hindered.   Clanricarde, who had
hitherto rejoiced at any reverse sustained by the confederates, "was," says Mr. Hardiman, "unable to afford
any relief."†   The condition of Inchiquin in the south
may readily be imagined from a letter which he sent in
the early part of May to the Earl of Cork :—

"Our present state falls out now to be more desperately miserable
than ever : in regard we have no manner of help or relief amongst
ourselves, and the provisions we depended on out of England do h-fail
us, which will put us to a terrible extremity, here being nothing to deliver forth on the next pay day.   I request your lordship to lend or
borrow £300, for victualling those in Youghal.   To-morrow, ith a
heavy heart, I shall march forth, to linger out a few days in the field
where I am not likely to continue so long as to enterprise anyt ing of
advantage, for want of provisions for the men and money for the of
ficers."‡

  * O'Neill's Journal, in the *Desid. Curiosa Hib.*
  † Hist. of Galway, p. 120.
  ‡ From an original letter.   See Smith's Cork.

Nor, in fact, did he effect anything of advantage, save seizing some small supplies. His troops amounted to 4,000 foot and 400 horse. Some of them were sent into Kerry in order to forage, whilst he himself invested Kilmallock with 700 men. Purcell and Barry held it against him, and he was obliged to raise the siege and go to the aid of his colleague, Vavasour, who, after committing the most revolting murders on those who surrendered themselves, was preparing to meet Castlehaven on the borders of the county Limerick.

It was now the 20th of May, and pursuant to their resolution, the general assembly had met in Kilkenny. The six months which intervened between this and their first sitting, had witnessed the most extraordinary changes. By an act of the general assembly, the supreme council was confirmed, nor were there any material changes made in the administration. But, as it will appear, it was a moment of the greatest importance to the Catholics of Ireland. Their armies in the four provinces were preparing for a conflict, on the result of which everything depended. The hopes and enthusiasm of the Irish people never were higher, and they hastened from the mountain fastnesses and sequestred glens to swell the number of those who marched under the confederate banners. On the land and on the sea triumph and success had followed their movements. The eyes of Catholic Europe watched their progress, for their fame had travelled over the Alps and Pyrenees. The French court sent M. La Monaric as its envoy, with all the powers of an ambassador; he was soon followed by M. Fuysot, a Burgundian, from the court of Spain, and letters from Father Wadding announced that Urban VIII had determined to send an agent from the Vatican. with supplies of arms and money. Charles I. no longer published his intolerant threats against "Popish recusants." Hampden was proposing to besiege him in Oxford, whilst Essex was thundering at the walls of Reading. His treacherous eyes were at last opened to the perils that beset him, and the injustice which he had contrived to inflict on the confederate Catholics. He, therefore, resolved to pursue a different course

Lord Taaffe, according to the parliamentary pasquinades[*]
of the times, had been plotting with the king since his
return to Oxford, and he was made the bearer of an
important communication to Ormond; it was a com
mission from the king to the marquess, to treat with
his subjects, "and to agree on a cessation of arms for
one year."

In an evil moment the supreme council consented to
entertain the proposal, and ordained that the Lords
Gormanstown, Muskerry, and others, should be appointed their commissioners, with power and authority to treat with Ormond of a cessation for one whole
year, or shorter, upon such terms, conditions, or
articles, as to the commissioners aforesaid should be
thought fit and expedient. The promptness with which
the assembly caught at any overture of peace on the part
of the king, was ample evidence of their loyalty and
affection to the throne. But the message which elicited
their reply, is at once evidence of their strength and
weakness. Had they determined to stand aloof from
all factions, parliamentary and royal, and struggle manfully for their country's independence, they must have
succeeded, and made themselves more than a match for
any army that could have been sent against them.
But, alas! the attachment of the Irish to the worthless
house of Stuart, was destined to be their bane and ruin.

But Ormond was in no hurry to carry out the intentions of the king. There was one objection in the way
which he knew would prove insuperable to the confederates. They had determined to insist on a dissolution
of the parliament, which was made up of "Clerks,
soldiers, serving men, and others not legally, or not at
all, chosen or returned," who had passed an act that
no person should sit, either in that or in any future
parliament, till hey had taken the oath of supremacy."[†]

Another condition on which the confederate commissioners were ordered to insist was, that they should have
liberty to use arms against all such persons as should
make war against the contracting parties; but Ormond,

* Mercurius Melancholicus.
† Remonstrance from Trim. Warn. Irish Reb. p. 217.

who knew well that this was meant to engage him against
the Scotch in Ulster, demurred, and caused the treaty
to be adjourned to the following month.

During these negotiations, the conflict between the
confederate generals and their enemies was raging in the
four provinces. Owen Roe, at the head of 3,200 men,
of which force 1,000 were immediately with him—the
rest being in attendance on a large collection of cattle—
was on his way into the county Leitrim, when he was
overtaken by Sir R. Stewart at Clonish, on the borders
of Fermanagh. Stewart had a large body of well-dis-
ciplined troops, commanded by Sir W. Balfour and Colonel Mervyn. O'Neill posted his main strength in a
narrow pass, which he lined with musketeers. Stewart
determined to force it; but O'Neill's cavalry repulsed
him for the moment, and then rapidly retired. Stewart
immediately advanced at a gallop; but had scarcely entered the causeway when a terrible fusilade from within
scattered his men, and drove them back. A forlorn-
hope was now ordered to seize the pass, and the battle
raged fiercely on both sides. A nephew of the English
commander engaged in single combat with Owen Roe;
but the clansmen of the latter attached too much importance to his life to suffer it to be risked in this species
of wild tournament. Stewart was struck by a shot, and
a dozen pikes pinned his horse to the ground. At this
moment Shane O'Neill advanced with some troops of
cavalry; both parties then engaged, and the encounter
lasted fully half an hour, when the Irish retired, after
leaving many of their companions dead in the gap.—
Stewart did not venture to pursue his partial victory,
and, before O'Neill arrived at Mohill, he received an accession of men and arms, which more than compensated
for his loss.*

Twelve days after this much exaggerated skirmish,
Owen Roe, at the head of a considerable force, marched
into the county Westmeath, within fifteen miles of Mul-
lingar; whilst Preston, with 7,000 foot and 700 horse, was
carrying everything before him in the King's County.
'Moncke was sent to oppose him, but dared not meet him;

* In this action Con Oge O'Neill was murdered by a Presbyterian
minister, after quarter given.—*O'Neill's Journal.*

and thus left the Leinster general master of every strong place in that county, with the exception of Castlejordan. The state of the English garrisons in at about Dublin is described by Carte and others to have been desperate. There was the greatest dearth of provisions, and nothing but the saddest necessity could induce Ormond to attack the confederates, who spread terror even to the very walls of the city. Moncke was sent into Wicklow to seize whatever corn and cattle he could; but was soon recalled to reinforce Lord Moore, who was sent to dislodge Owen Roe,—who, with Sir James Dillon, held a strong position five miles from Trim, at a place called Portlester-mill. O'Neill threw up a breastwork, placed sixty men in the mill, and waited patiently for the enemy. Moore[*] was about to advance, when he was killed by a cannon-ball, and his whole force fled, being routed with slaughter. O'Neill was amply avenged for his loss at Clonish; and the way to Dublin was open to him, had he been directed to advance. The victory at Portlester was the prestige of success, as well as a subject for mirth. Some "camping chaplain" commemorated Moore's death in a distich, which Borlase gravely remarks had more sallies of wit than skill. It is, however, too good to be lost:—

"Contra Romanos mores res mira Dynasta,
Morus ab Eugenio canonizatus erat."[†]

Ormond, who had left Dublin at the head of 6,000 men, accompanied by Lord Lambert, failed to bring Preston to an action; nor did the conduct of this general fail to engender suspicion, for he had an army which was well supplied, whilst that of the marquess was, according to the testimony of Carte, "ready to starve for

* He was of English descent, and his ancestors came in for a large share of the confiscated church property in the time of Elizabeth.

† See Borlase, p. 129. The following is an attempt at the translation:—
"Rome's ancient rights are now but lightly prized,
Since Moore by Owen Roe was *canonized!*"

Lord Moore, the subject of this distich, was a Protestant. I mention the fact most respectfully, and simply because the verses in Latin or English would have no point if the religion of his lordship was not known.

want of provisions." Far different, however, was the spirit of the leaders in the west and south. The siege of Galway was pressed with vigour; and so straitened was Willoughby, that he offered to surrender the fort to the Marquess of Clanricarde after Rear-Admiral Brook had failed to throw in supplies. Burke would not hear of such an overture, unless the Marquess consented to take the confederate oath, which he sternly refused, and the parliamentary general surrendered the fortresses of Galway and Oranmore to the heroic Burke on the 20th of June. Three days afterwards a squadron entered the bay; but the colours of the confederates were streaming from the flag-staff. The Archbishop of Tuam was one of the parties who drew up the articles with Willoughby; and this infamous murderer was permitted to depart in peace. "Thus," says Mr. Hardiman, "the second fort of importance in the kingdom was in the hands of the confederates."*

And now, to crown these signal triumphs, couriers were spurting across the plains of Munster to announce to the supreme council the intelligence of a defeat sustained by Inchiquin and Vavasour. We have already said that Castlehaven had marched to the borders of the county Limerick, and it is necessary that we should see what he accomplished. Barry, the Munster general, was old and infirm,† and perhaps had no greater value in the eyes of the supreme council than that which resulted from his local influence.

Castlehaven, who was beginning to grow tired of adventure, seemed at first reluctant to take the command; nor did he move till urged by Lord Muskerry and the assembly. Accompanied by Fitzgerald, commonly called Garret-Garrough, he marched hastily to Cashel, where he was met by General Barry and Lieutenant-General Purcell, with 700 foot and some troops of horse. His whole force now consisted of about 3,000 men, together with a troop of boys, mounted on fleet horses. Vavasour was at Castle-Lyons, after allowing a number of women and children to fall into the hands of one of his officers, by whom they were stripped and murdered. Inchiquin having notice of the approach of the confede.

* Hist. of Galway, p 123.　　　　† Castlehaven's Mem.

rates, sent orders from his camp to Moyalloe * for detachments to strengthen his lieutenant-general, but before they could arrive, Vavasour was set upon by squadrons of cavalry from the neighbouring hills. Fearing that
he would be surrounded, he sounded a retreat, and his
cannon and carriages were ordered to Fermoy, while he
himself rapidly crossed the Funcheon. His van was led
by Lieutenant King, the main body by Major Howell,
and the rear by Vavasour in person. Pierce Lacy, Captain Hutton, and Lieutenant Stadbury commanded the
forlorn hope. Their last man had not forded the Funcheon, when the confederate cavalry was at their heels.
—The vanguard had ascended the hill which over-
hangs the river, and was dashing in haste through a
narrow defile which leads to Fermoy, when Vavasour
ordered a halt, and prepared to contest the pass; but
that troop of boys, mounted on fleet horses, was pressing on the forlorn hope, not after the fashion of drilled
and disciplined men, but rather like "the Moorish and
Getulian horsemen," says Borlase, "mentioned by Salust
in Jugarth's war." In vain did the forlorn-hope strive †
to resist the impetuosity of their assailants. They were
driven in on the main body, which disordered those who
still held the pass. In a moment the rout was univer-
sal. The confederates pursued the flying columns, and
cut them up in detail. All the cannon and colours were
, taken. Vavasour and his officers were made prisoners.
and 600 of his best soldiers were sabred between the Man-
/ ning-water and Fermoy. It was a sad blow to Inchiquin, for by this action he was reduced to about 2,000
men, and obliged to shut himself up in garrison. The
confederates soon after prepared to besiege Cappoquin
and Lismore, but abandoned the design when it was announced that the supreme council was negotiating a
truce with the Marquess of Ormond.

Alas! that craft and intrigue should have stayed them
in their glorious career, for there never was a moment
so prosperous and bright with hope. Owen Roe was
master of the north, as far as the borders of Westmeath
He had slain Lord Moore, and driven Moncke within th:

---

* Mallow, the birth-place of my lamented friend, T. Davis.
† Irish Reb

walls of Dublin. Preston hung on the outskirts of the city, and threatened Ormond. The Munster army had covered itself with glory. Drogheda, Dundalk, and the garrisons in the north, were reduced to the direst want. Was this a moment for diplomacy? Certainly not. But had the command of all the confederate troops been committed to Owen Roe, instead of dividing it between four generals, Ireland would have achieved a glorious independence, and must have been spared that long and bloody catalogue of pains and sufferings, the recollection of which must ever pain the heart, while it teaches us that all our miseries have been the result of treachery on the part of pretended friends, and disunion amongst ourselves.

CHAPTER IV.

ABOUT the middle of July, 1643, while the confederates were gaining those important advantages which we have described, there arrived on our coast a commissioner from the Holy See, who was sent by Urban VIII. to report on the state of Irish affairs. This was Father Peter Francis Scarampi, a native of Piedmont, and a priest of the oratory; nor did he come empty-handed. The Pontiff made him the bearer of a bull, in which he lauded the zeal and earnestness with which the Irish fought for the independence of their religion, and Father Luke Wadding committed to his charge a sum of 30,000 dollars, which he had collected from the Barbarini,* Spada, and other noble families who took an interest in the cause of the confederates. Nor did the holy father confine his liberality to transmitting such spiritual weapons as a jubilee, with a plenary indulgence,

* In the library of this noble family there is a vast store of material for Irish history. When the author of "Rome, under Paganism and the Popes" visits the holy city again, it is to be hoped that he will turn his attention to the archives of the Barbarini palace. Who more equal to the task than the eloquent and erudite Dr. Miley?

to all who had taken up arms in defence of religion.[*]
He also sent a large quantity of arms and ammunition,
of which he knew there was then much need. When
the supplies had been safely landed, Scarampi at once
proceeded to Kilkenny, where he found the confederates
engaged discussing the question of a cessation of arms.
Division and dissensions had manifested themselves in
the council, and the spirit displayed by the contending
parties, clearly evinced that the oath of association
was their only "essential tie." The Irish of the Pale
were tired of the war, whilst the "old Irish" were bent on
following up their success; in fact, the former had been
drawn into the confederacy contrary to their inclination,
and were now anxious to make terms with Ormond.
The "old Irish," on the other hand, influenced by the
bishops and clergy, and fondly hoping to establish their
independence, were inexorably opposed to all overtures
which did not tend to secure to them freedom of conscience,
and the public exercise of their religion. Naturally
enough, Scarampi advocated the views of the bishops,
and, in his capacity of envoy from the Holy See, exhorted the assembly, in the name of the Sovereign Pontiff, not to recede an inch from their 'vantage, but to
prosecute the war and insist on such terms as a weak
and beleaguered government could not dare to refuse.
And, although it has been the lot of this man to fall
under the censure of such writers as Carte and Leland,
he was perfectly right in principle; nor let us, who daily
echo the sentiment that "England's infirmity must be
Ireland's opportunity," dare to impeach the policy of a
friendly stranger, who, two hundred and three years
ago entertained the same view and gave utterance to a corresponding conviction. It has been the work of more
than two centuries to shake off these penal fetters which
must ever be a disgrace to English legislation. The
man who has done the mighty work stands proudly pre-
eminent as the greatest of his day. Had he done nothing
more than unrivet those chains, he should go down to
his grave canonized in the remembrance of his country-

---

[*] Borlase says that the Pope sent the Irish a pardon for all manner
of sins. The charge was repeated by Lord Orrery, but is nobly re-
futed by Dr. French in the "Bleeding Iphigenia."

men; and shall we join our own misrepresenters when they endeavour to cast blame on the head of him who strove to do, in a moment of our greatest triumph, that which O'Connell has effected after centuries of division, weakness, and misrule? Forbid it, justice; for, come honest counsel whence it may, or a helping hand from the most distant region—be it Greek, Hindoo, or Roman—we should not be ungrateful for kindness. And what was required in Scarampi's time?—unanimity, stern resolve, and a march on Dublin. With an army in each of the three provinces, and the most unparalleled enthusiasm on the part of the people, and some great leader whose command to "follow" all would have hearkened to—what bitter ages of hate, and strife, and degradation, might we not have escaped! But it was otherwise ordained—there was yet wanting a spirit of union; and even now, after so many painful lessons, what but the same prolific source of evil stands in the way of our nationality? But, thank heaven, "we preach a land awoken."[*]

We have already seen that the question of the truce with Ormond had been adjourned for a month; but, although he had the king's peremptory order to carry it into execution, he was in no hurry to comply with the royal mandate. However, the reverses which he had sustained began to make a deep impression on him, and determined him to adopt another course. Want of money and provisions had reduced him to the direst straits; and the condition of his troops and chief garrison is thus described by an eye-witness:—"The state and the army," says Sir P. Percival, "were in the greatest distress. The streets of Dublin had no manner of victuals many times for one day, so that the soldiers would not move without money, shoes, and stockings; for want of which, many had marched barefooted, and had bled much on the road; and others, through unwholesome food, had become diseased, and died." Yet, notwithstanding this state of misery, Ormond was more anxious to cater to the parliamentary faction than serve the king; but he hated the federative government, and set his heart upon destroying it; in fact, nothing, save

---

[*] Duffy, in the Spirit of the Nation.

the ruin which stared him in the face, could have induced him to resume the negotiation which had been broken off. Towards the end of June he called the richest of the citizens of Dublin before him, when he delivered a motion in writing, "that if £10,000 could be raised, the one-half in money, and the other in victuals, to be brought in within a fortnight, he would break off the treaty, and proceed in the war;" but the citizens were unable to supply his demand. Sir H. Tichbourne, a gloomy fanatic, then tried to raise £300 a-piece from the members of the council board; but he, too, failed; and yet, at this very moment, the confederates were well supplied with men, arms, and money, and might have overwhelmed the designing Ormond and his faithless colleagues, had the councils of the "old Irish" happily prevailed. "'Twas the crisis of their affairs"*—the most active moment of two conflicting principles, and the conduct of the time-serving Pale lords, ruined and disgraced the country. They well knew that at this moment the country might have been their own, and that they could have driven Ormond, Tichbourne, and their famished mercenaries into the sea, and then flung themselves heart and soul into the royal cause, and saved the monarchy; but such was not their policy, for they lacked the proper spirit.

But a rumour was industriously circulated by the Pale lords, that the king was inclined to dissolve the present parliament, and call a new one by the 10th of November following, and Ormond was authorised to assure them of his majesty's good intentions. The latter was aware of the dissensions which were at work, and by his agents artfully contrived to foment them. Many, nay, nearly all the lords and gentry of the Pale were his relatives or dependants, and he cajoled them with soft words, and flattering compliments. Astutely hiding his own distressed condition, he pretended that he was acting with friendly feelings, and his artifice prevailed to his satisfaction.

One event, however, had well night marred his plans. Though the supersedeas for Parsons had long since come, it had not been acted on. Thus was this infamous

---

* Dublin Review, June, 1844. Percival's Statement in curte.

man allowed to take share at the council board in Dublin. A short time before that appointed for the meeting between Ormond and the confederate commissioners, Parsons wrote a letter to the supreme council, touching an exchange of prisoners, couched in the following terms :—

"We, the lords justices, do declare, that if Captain Farrer be released by the rebels, we will give orders for the releasing Synnott lately employed as captain among the rebels, the jailor's dues being first paid."

To this insolent document the supreme council returned the following reply :—

"We do not know to whom this certificate is directed, neither shall it be safe hereafter for any messenger to bring any paper to us containing other language than suits our duty, and the affections we bear to his majesty's service, wherein some may pretend, but none shall have more real desires to further his majesty's interests, than his majesty's loyal and obedient subjects,

"MOUNTGARRET. MUSKERRY."

Startled by this manly reply, which nothing but insult could have drawn from them, Ormond became alarmed. He did not know how soon Preston might be on the north bank of the Liffey, there was no time to be lost, and he determined to strike a blow which he knew would give pleasure to his friends and partisans in the supreme council. Parsons, Loftus, Meredith, and the veracious Sir John Temple, of ghost-seeing notoriety, were arrested. Parsons pleaded impaired health, and the rest were committed prisoners to the castle on charge of contravening the royal will. Sir Henry Tichbourne and Sir John Borlase were appointed lords justices, and Mountgarret, Gormanstown, and Muskerry openly boasted that they had got rid of their most inveterate enemies. Ormond's policy triumphed, and the question of the cessation was immediately resumed. In vain did the few members of the "old Irish" who were in the supreme council inveigh against it; they were in a minority from the beginning, and those who were opposed to them placed all their hopes in the genius of the marquess.

Perhaps there is no more humiliating scene in the entire of these transactions than that which followed. On the 16th September 1643, Muskerry, Dillon, Plunket,

Talbot, Barnwell, Neale, Brown, Walsh, and Maginnis stood bare-headed before Ormond's tent, at Sigginstown, in the county Kildare, while "he alone wore hat and plume," prepared to sign a truce which was intended to last an entire year. It will be necessary to extract some of the articles of this treaty for the satisfaction of the reader, but before we do so, it is necessary to premise, that before the ink in which it was written dried, the confederate commissioners discovered that Ormond had no notion of calling a new parliament, although he knew that the present one was irregular and illegal.*

ABBREVIATE OF THE TREATY.

"It was agreed that the Roman Catholics now in arms at any time during the cessation, may send to his majesty such agents as they shall think fit, and that the said agents shall have a free conduct from the chief governors of this kingdom.

" It is agreed that the quarters in the province of Connaught be the following, viz. :—that the county Galway, the county town of Galway, the counties of Mayo, Roscommon, Sligo, and Leitrim, now in possession of the Roman Catholics, shall, during the said cessation, remain in their possession.

" It is agreed that the quarters of the province of Leinster be the following, viz. :—that the county Dublin, the county of the city of Dublin, the county of the city of Drogheda, and the county Louth, shall remain in possession of his majesty's Protestant subjects.

" It is agreed that the county Tipperary, the county Limerick, the county Kerry, the county Waterford, and the county Clare, shall be in possession of the Roman Catholics, except Knockmorne, Ardmore, Pilltown, Cappoquin, Ballinetra, Stroncally, Lismore, and Lisfinny.

"The quarters in Ulster are to be as followeth, viz. :—That such counties, baronies, tenements, hereditaments as are now possessed by any of his majesty's Protestant subjects, or any that adhere to them, and all places protected by any commanders deriving authority from the king, shall be in their possession, excepting such lands, castles, &c. &c. as are now in possession of the Roman Catholics."

The rest of the articles regard traffic and free intercourse between England and Ireland, and the rules to be observed by both parties regarding the exchange of prisoners.

Sorely annoyed as were the "old Irish," by the conclusion of the truce, the parliamentary party did not feel it less. The Earl of Cork, according to Borlase, "took it so much to heart that he died soon

+ Carte, iii. 430.

after, as he did not wish to survive what he suspected might not be conducible to the English interest." Broghill and Inchiquin were altogether opposed to it; and the latter, seeing it carried against his unavailing remonstrance, betook himself to England, and made an offer of his services to the king. It is probable that Charles set no value on his assurances; and as soon as he learned that the presidency of Munster was about to be bestowed on the Earl of Portland, he returned to Ireland, confirmed in his hatred of the faithless monarch. But as for Ormond, he had gained all he could have wished. Jealousies and rancorous feelings grew up amongst the confederates, and the men who hitherto dared not to cross the Liffey without hazard to their lives, became fawning courtiers and expectants of office; but to none did the cessation give less satisfaction than to the Catholic inhabitants of Ulster. The provisions which were made for that province gave Munroe and his adventurers both claim and title to all the lands and tenements which they then held, as they did to those intruders who had long since hunted out the rightful owners. Yet, as the orders emanated from the supreme council, they were rigidly observed, though the population smarted under a sense of the injustice which was done them.

The advantages derived by Ormond from his able diplomacy may be collected from the fact, that hitherto the confederate ships intercepted all supplies, and left Dublin in such a state, that upon search being made in the city and suburbs, there could not be found fourteen days' provisions for the inhabitants and soldiers.*

But now the ports and the approaches to them were left open, and he began to gather in supplies of corn and other stores, which restored to him the confidence of the soldiers and citizens, and made him a match for any section of the confederate army which might be induced to violate the cessation. One article of that fatal instrument obliged Ormond to join his forces with those of the confederates in punishing those who would be guilty of the slightest infraction of the treaty; but

* Sir Phil. Percival's Statement.

we shall soon see how faithlessly he regarded it. The
Scotch forces, " recent and veterate," in Ulster at this moment, amounted to 20,000 men; and " memorable Munroe"* was in direct communication with the parliament.
About the beginning of November the infamous Owen
Connolly (who betrayed the plot of Lord Maguire† and his
brave associates to seize the Castle of Dublin in 1641) came
over with a commission from the parliament, and an order to the Scotch to take the covenant as the parliament
had done on the 25th of September.   On bended
knees, in the kirk of Carrickfergus, Munroe complied with the wishes of the rebels, who sent him
supplies of money, arms, and provisions, with an in-
junction to denounce with fire and sword all who
should observe the cessation.

It was at this period that the Marquess of Antrim (who
having escaped from Carrickfergus and proceeded to
England) returned to Kilkenny.   A zealot in the royal
cause, he gladly took the oath of association.   He meditated being appointed to some high post of honour
amongst them.   This nobleman found the supreme
council in every way favourable to his views, and apparently intent on squandering their resources. Antrim,
now created marquess by the king's privy seal, proposed
to raise 3,000 men to assist Montrose in Scotland, and
they agreed to furnish him with 2,000 muskets, 2,400
pounds of powder, and 200 barrels of oatmeal, which
were to be ready by the 1st of May following, and
shipped to Scotland by Mr. Archer, a merchant of Kilkenny—an instance of fatuity which was quite in keeping with the voluntary offering of £30,000, which was
not, in the strict sense, what its advocates pretended, inasmuch as it was to be levied on a people who had been
basely plundered by the ministers of the crown.

Another disadvantage which this cessation brought on
the Irish, was the departure from their coasts of most of
the ships which had been chartered by the supreme

* Legend of Montrose.
† Corn. Maguire (Lord Enniskillen) was executed at Tyburn on the
20th of February, 1644. No martyr at the stake ever died more true
to God and his faith. His trial is to be found at the end of Temple's
Hist., and also in the State Trials. See Dub. Review, March, 1845, where
there is a letter concerning him

councils in the earlier time of the war. Every creek and harbour suddenly became infested with the parliamentary cruisers, so much so, that it was difficult to send men or money out of Ireland. The orders issued by the parliament to their partisans, on the land, were only equalled by the Algerine ferocity of their cruisers on the seas. Out of 150 men, who about this time sailed for Bristol, and who were taken by one Swanly at sea, seventy, besides two women, were thrown over board because they were supposed to be Irish.* Nor did the Irish retaliate; for, soon afterwards falling in with a ship which had on board fifty kirk ministers deputed to preach up and administer the covenant in Ulster, they contented themselves with making them prisoners. This fatal truce was the source of all these miseries, and the coast which hitherto had been so watchfully guarded, was now swarming with rebel ships, "whose commanders showed no mercy to such as had the misfortune to fall into their hands."†

When the news of the cessation had reached Oxford, the king determined to appoint the Marquess of Ormond lord lieutenant of Ireland ; but, on account of the tempestuous state of the weather, and the difficulty in adjusting the form of procuring the Earl of Leicester's resignation, the commission was not issued till the middle of January, 1644. On the 21st of that month he was sworn in with all proper forms and ceremonies.‡ We have now arrived at the beginning of a year which witnessed many sorrows and reverses in Ireland, and it is necessary that we pass them rapidly in review before us.

Ormond's elevation to the viceroyalty was calculated to raise the hopes of that portion of the confederates who placed all confidence in him, and naturally gave him a fairer opportunity of deluding and deceiving them. The "old Irish," on the other hand, did not reckon on any advantage to be derived from his administration. He had no real sympathy with them, and they deeply deplored the conclusion of the treaty, which was likely to give another direction to the popular mind. Some were of opinion that the truce tended to abate that martial ar-

---

* Ormond's Let. Collect. of his papers, vol. i. p. 48.
† Carte's Orm. vol. iii. p. 246. ‡ Carte, t. 476.

dour which characterised the people since the rising of
1641 ; and others, like Father O'Ferrall,* bitterly regretted that the lords and gentry of the Pale had ever
been "trusted in so holy a league." That such should have
been the sentiments of the "old Irish" is only natural,
when we find it admitted, on the authority of Carte, that
they had nothing to get by a cessation, and "were only
fit to be sent to Scotland to deliver his majesty out of
his troubles."† In fact, such was the dislike entertained
by them for the entire proceeding, that De la Monarie,
the envoy from the French court, and Francisco de Fos-
set, the envoy from Spain, had no difficulty in getting
men to embark in the service of their respective crowns,
while the greatest reluctance prevailed against going into
England ; in truth, the continental courts had strong
claims on the affections of the Irish, for even a short time
before Ormond's inauguration his Catholic majesty had
forwarded 20,000 dollars to the confederates. This sum
was expended on arms and ammunition. Their agents,
too, were kindly received in the foreign capitals, and
were willingly aided by the nobility and gentry, who regarded them as engaged in a holy crusade. But the
lord lieutenant well knew that the treaty itself would
furnish ample material for dispute and bloodshed, and
he calculated wisely. The question of boundaries, which
was not well defined, was of itself fashioned to engender
broils between the parties; but what cared he if the Catholics became broken up and disorganised? Division
was his object, and he had copiously sowed its seeds. He
only looked to the dissolution of that union which was
once so formidable, and diplomacy like his was capable
of effecting it.

It was at this period that the supreme council commissioned Edmund O'Dwyer‡ to proceed to Rome, and
present to Pope Urban a memorial, signed and sealed by

---

* He was a Capuchin friar, and wrote a book with the following
title—"Modus Eversionis Cath. Religionis in Hibernia." Lynch, the
author of "Cambrensis Eversus," published a reply under the name of
"Eudoxus Alithinologus." It is quoted by Walsh in the Hist. of the
Rem., p. 740.

† Carte's Orm., i. 477.

‡ He was afterwards Bishop of Limerick, and signalised himself when
Ireton besieged the city.

them, praying his holiness to promote Wadding to the college of cardinals. *

But that portion of it which must interest us most is their report on the state of Catholicity in Ireland at this period of the confederacy. It was thus described :—

" It is now manifest to the whole Christian world with what fidelity the Catholics of Ireland have clung to their ancient faith, and how they braved death, and exile, and the confiscation of their substance, rather than renounce the religion of their ancestors. To you, most holy father, it is particularly known how heroically the Irish people, without arms or munitions of war, have struggled against the phalanxes of those who, sworn enemies of the holy see, had vowed and sworn to pluck up our religion by the very roots. Our holy war has had a glorious result. The Lord God is now publicly worshipped in our temples, after the manner of our fathers; most of the cathedrals have been restored to our bishops; the religious orders possess the monasteries, and seminaries have been opened for the education of our youth. This great work has been accomplished through the goodness of God and the many favors bestowed on us by you; verily, in future times the brightest page in the history of your pontificate shall be, that you found the Catholic religion despised and prostrate in our island, and ere that pontificate closed beheld it raised up in splendour, and magnificently attired, even as a bride for her spouse." †

During these transactions the supreme council held its sittings at Waterford, and a question was raised as to the prudence of pawning that portion of the kingdom then in their possession to some foreign court, in order to raise money. Owen Roe was summoned to give his opinion, when he repudiated the idea of giving any foreign power " an interest in Ireland." He then proceeded to Charlemont, where he remained some time with Theobald Magauly, the governor of the fort, and finally fixed his head-quarters at Belturbet. Lulled into false security by the cessation, the supreme council proceeded to Galway, and some of the other towns, to hear cases touching usurpations of property, and adjudicate on civil concerns which, in the din of arms, could not have been properly attended to.

Having returned to Kilkenny, a very considerable period seems to have been wasted in collecting those supplies which it was their intention to have transmitted to England. It was agreed that the sum of £30,800 should be paid by instalments of money and "beeves;" but it

* In the Writers of the Seventeenth Century Mr. M'Gee has beautifully treated this subject.

† *Vide* Hib. Dom., in Append. p. 876

would appear that there was great difficulty in procuring advances of kind and coin. Charges were made almost daily of a violation of the articles of cessation by both parties: and Ormond did not conceal his displeasure at the slowness with which the confederates sent the beeves to Dublin. One of the strangest of the charges advanced against the supreme council at this moment was, that they forwarded cattle of a very inferior description, and took away 369 head of the choicest English cows and bullocks from the suburbs of Dublin, thus exposing the inhabitants to the very danger from which it was the object of the cessation to protect them. This charge is made upon dubious authority, for it is certain that the confederates had the best intentions, however short-sighted their policy may have been. Perhaps no fact is more calculated to vindicate them from such aspersions than the conduct which Ormond was forced to adopt regarding the forces which he sent to the king's aid in England. When the cessation was concluded, several regiments, drawn from the garrisons in and about Dublin, got orders to proceed to Chester; "but such was the reluctancy of the common soldiers, that the sharpest proclamations hardly restrained them from flying their colours, both before and after their arrival in England." [*] Indeed, to such a state of insubordination and disaffection had they been brought, that Ormond was forced to administer an oath obliging his mercenaries to remain firm in their allegiance to the king. Not so, however, with such of the Catholics as could cross the sea, and stand by his majesty in his struggle against the parliament. Their fidelity was only equalled by their valour and chivalrous conduct against the overwhelming forces under the command of Fairfax.

But, as to the cessation, the only towns which can be said to have observed it were Newry, Dundalk, and Drogheda. Munroe was encouraged by the parliament, as we have already seen, to disregard it; and, if he required any further stimulant, he had already got it in a commission, under the parliament's broad seal, to command in chief all the English as well as Scotch forces in Ulster. On receipt of the commission he commenced a

[*] Borlase's Hist. of the Irish Insur., p. 135.

campaign against the Catholics, who religiously obeyed the orders of the supreme council, which, on the intelligence of his perfidy, wrote to Ormond that these Covenanters "were diverting them from assisting his majesty, and eating further into the bowels of the country."* This was obviously meant to induce Ormond to declare Munroe and his followers rebels to the crown. But the wily lord lieutenant did not find it his interest to take such a step.

A subject of the most momentous importance was now mooted by the supreme council, regarding propositions to be submitted to the king; and in order to take their attention from mere matters of war, Ormond encouraged them to proceed to Oxford, and lay their case before his majesty. At the very same time a cabal in Dublin was maturing a scheme to counteract any advantage which the Catholics were likely to derive from an interview with the king. Muskerry, MacDonnell, Plunket, Sir Robert Talbot, Dermid O'Brien, Richard Martin, and Severinus Browne, formed the deputation, which reached England about the beginning of April, and, having arrived at Oxford, presented a statement of grievances, and earnestly prayed for the repeal of all the penal restrictions, which not only disqualified them from holding civil offices in the state, but weighed most heavily on their religion and the practices it inculcated.

To all their demands the king gave willing ear, and flattering assurances; but one grand subject, which had been warmly debated by the council at Waterford, previous to the departure of the delegates, was regarded by his majesty as little less than scandalous. This was the secure possession of the churches then in their hands; and the king declared that he would reserve it for his future consideration. An earldom was offered to Muskerry, which he declined, and the commissioners retired from the royal presence with an abundance of soft words, but without a single practical result.

It is hard to imagine any state of greater difficulty than that of the king at this moment; for the confederate commissioners had not left England, when Sir Charles Coote and others, deputed by the Protestants of

* Borlase.

Ireland, presented propositions asking, amongst other
concessions, that " the king would abate his quit-rents,
and encourage and enable Protestants to replant the
kingdom, and cause a good walled town to be built in
every county for their security, no Papist being allowed
to dwell therein." The second demand was not less
extravagant. They prayed his majesty " to continue the
penal laws, and to dissolve forthwith the assumed
power of the confederates, and banish all Popish priests
out of Ireland, and that no Popish recusant should be
allowed to sit or vote in parliament." The king was
amazed at the peremptory manner in which these
propositions were enforced ; but it was conjectured that
they were concocted in London, with a view to obstruct
any accommodation with the Irish, and, in all pro-
bability, to induce them to a violation of the truce.
But commissioners soon after came from the council
in Dublin, at the head of whom was Archbishop
Usher, who condemned Coote's extravagance, and
requested him to withdraw these revolting demands.

But, though Archbishop Usher inveighed against
the proposals of these fanatics, the propositions which
he submitted to Charles I. were not far removed from
the intolerant spirit of Coote. On the part of the
Irish Protestants, he desired :—" That all the penal
laws should be enforced, and all Papists disarmed."
The king clearly pointed out the impracticability of such
measures, at a moment when the confederate Catholics
possessed more than three parts of the kingdom. The
queen, too, influenced the royal will on this occasion,
and sought to impress on the mind of her consort,
that the Catholics were well worthy of his confidence.
Indeed, it is more than likely that whatever kindness
he had shown the confederate commissioners, was the
result of her majesty's interference. And, before we
close this brief glance at this portion of our subject,
we may sum up in a few words the amount of his
good intentions towards the Irish Catholics. He was
willing to pass an act for removing from them any
incapacity to purchase lands or offices, and had no
objection to allowing " recusants their seminaries of
education." He was content to call a new parliament
in Ireland, but, without the suspension of Poyning's

law. In all matters regarding penal enactments, he stated that these statutes were too odious to be enforced, and that his recusant subjects, on returning to their duty, should have no reason to complain. He then dismissed them with a pathetic admonition to consider his circumstances as their own.

Whilst the king was cajoling the commissioners with these kind promises, on which they placed but too much reliance, Munroe was carrying the orders of the parliament into execution. The general assembly, alarmed by the imposing force of the Covenanters, sent orders to Owen Roe to appear in Kilkenny on the 1st of May. It was about this time that the Scotch general had seized Belfast. O'Neill complained bitterly of the distress of the men under his command, stating that he would be obliged to quarter them on the other provinces. He then made an offer to prosecute the war against Munroe, if he was seconded by the supreme council, for whom he promised to raise 4,000 foot and 400 horse out of his own province. The council accepted his offer, and agreed to give him 6,000 foot and 600 horse. When the question of command was raised, it was put to the vote, and Castlehaven was declared by a majority commander-in-chief. O'Neill took it seriously to heart, but subsequently went to congratulate Castlehaven. But, even at this time, the effects produced by the cessation were deplorably visible, for the man who now was vested with the chief command, declared that the troops who were to take part in the approaching campaign, came to the rendezvous "like new men half changed."[*]

Men and horses were unfit for service; and the accoutrements were not in a better condition. With 2,000 men, Castlehaven marched rapidly into Connaught to enforce the orders of the supreme council, and soon after detached some parties to reduce the Ormsbys, who would not submit to the cessation. Owen Roe was encamped at Portlester about July, when Castlehaven marched on Granard, in the county Longford, where he was met by his main force, consisting of 3,000 horse and foot, with three field-pieces. He was soon informe'

* Castlehaven's Mem. 447.

that Munroe, with an army 17,000 strong, was marching
to meet him. Fearing to encounter such superior num-
bers, he retired on Portlester. Munroe, having accomplished his object, which was to get preys of cattle,
marched back to the north, after having wasted the
country in his rear, and dealt death about him.—
Throughout these marchings and counter-marchings
there was a misunderstanding between the two commanders. In some skirmish with outposts, one Fennell,
who commanded under Castlehaven, stood passively by
while some of O'Neill's kinsmen were hacked to pieces
before his face. O'Neill, who had been sick during the
action, styled Castlehaven's officers cowards, and the
commander bitterly resented it, when O'Neill repeated
the charge, saying: " This Fennell, the cowardly cock
with the feather, had the craven-heartedness to look on
whilst my relatives were being slain, and moved not an
inch to their succour—to the supreme council, who employed us both, he shall answer for this."

Castlehaven, soon after this occurrence, called on
O'Neill for the supplies he had promised ; but the latter
excused himself, saying: " That as soon as they had
entered Ulster he would make good his word." They
then united their forces, and proceeded to Tanderagee,
and erected a fort to protect their magazine. Nothing
of consequence transpired during their progress; they
were, however, engaged in perpetual skirmishes with
outposts; nor did Munroe dare to face them. He had
advanced as far as Armagh; but soon broke up his
camp. Castlehaven finally grew tired of a war, which
he had not patience or military talent to appreciate, and
hastened back to Kilkenny, where he boasted that the
confederacy owed its preservation to his skill and perseverance. The army under his command now amounted
to 8,000 men ; and commissioners were appointed to see
them quartered in different parts of Leinster, within the
confederate boundaries. O'Neill, disgusted with the
vapourings of the man wh had been preferred to him,
retired to the county Cav n, anxiously watching the
progress of events.

Scrupulously as the Irish Catholics observed the cessation, it was treated with contempt by Inchiquin and
Lord Broghill in the south. Early n July they for-

warded letters to the king, beseeching him to proclaim
the Irish, "rebels," and stating that they were resolved
to "die a thousand deaths" sooner than condescend to
any peace with them.* They then set forth that their
quarters, which extended from Youghal to Mogeely, and
thence to Cork, had been pillaged by the Catholics, who
were intent on prejudicing the royal cause. The parliament seconded Inchiquin's designs, as it did those of
Munroe in the north. One Mathews, a friar, was accused of a design to seize the city of Cork, and Inchiquin caused him to be tried, and soon after executed;
nor did this miscreant content himself with these atrocities—aping the pharasaical cant of the parliament, he
justified all his barbarous proceedings by an appeal to
his religious sentiments, which taught him that "he
was acting for the gospel, and that if he died for it, he
should be held as a perfect martyr."† Early in August
he collected a large body of troops, and expelled all the
Catholic inhabitants out of Cork, Youghal, and Kinsale.‡ The parliament applauded the act, gave him
promise of supplies, and hinted that he might be appointed to the presidency of Munster. It was idle to
think that the plundered and persecuted inhabitants
would not resent these cruelties; and yet such was the
anxiety of the supreme council for the inviolate observance of the cessation, that they ordered Lieutenant-
General Purcell to punish those who had been guilty of
the slightest infraction. Ormond was importuned by the
confederates to enforce the obedience of Munroe and
Inchiquin; but he was secretly encouraging the conduct
of those rebels, and rejoiced at every misery which befel
the Catholics.

And yet, in the midst of these multiplied troubles, the
confederates were not unmindful of the promises which
they had given to aid the king. It is true that the im-
poverished state of the kingdom would not allow them
to raise such an enormous sum as they had promised to
advance; but they sedulously endeavoured to forward

* Borlase, p. 146.
† Inchiquin's letter to the parliament, in Borlase, p. 149.
‡ "Allowing them to take no more of their goods with them than
what they could carry on their backs."—*Carte's Orm.*

all they could through the agency of Ormond. The troops which they had guaranteed to raise for Montrose were three months waiting for an opportunity of crossing the sea, while the parliament ships were watching to intercept them. Lord Antrim, however, contrived to embark 2,500 men at Waterford and other ports, and, though it be a digression, we may not overlook their services.[*]

These men were commanded by a Catholic—Alexander M'Donnell, alias Colkitto. When they arrived in Scotland, within Argyle's bounds, they marched to Castleblair, in Athol, where they were joined by Montrose, "who went on foot, with his target and pike." On the 1st of September they were reinforced by the bowmen under Lord Kilpunt, and encountered the Covenanters, who had an army of 8,000 foot and 800 horse, at St. Johnstown. The Covenanters[†] were three or four to one, but the Irish routed them with such fearful effect "that men might have walked upon dead bodies to the town, being two miles long from the place where the battle was pitched." On the 13th of the same month they defeated 3,000 foot and 500 horse, with three pieces of cannon, at Aberdeen. They then marched to Glengarry and Inverloughy Castle, which they stormed, routing Argyle and Aghenbracke, and taking their standards, arms, and ammunition. [‡]

Such signal valour made due impression on the king, who did not fail to commend it in his despatches to Ormond. Indeed, he could have had no more convincing reason for impressing on the mind of his lieutenant-general the necessity of a speedy accommodation with his

* It is worth remarking that Clarendon, who disparages Lord Antrim, has drawn an over-coloured picture of Clanricarde. No one doubts the loyalty of the latter; but viewing him as an Irishman, he seems to have had little or no feeling of nationality. On the strength of Clarendon's statement, Mr. Moore, in the fourth volume of his History of Ireland, calls Antrim " an absurd lord." Clarendon hated Antrim personally, as appears from Carte's Orm., vol. ii., p. 282.

† One's hand must tremble in transcribing the battle-cry of these fanatics; but it is an evident proof of the frenzy to which that horrid enthusiasm, so often mistaken for religion, can raise men's minds. " Jesus and no quarter" were the words uttered by the Covenanters in this engagement with Montrose.—*Graing. Biograph.*, vol. ii., p. 245.

‡ Collection of Original Papers, found among the Duke of Ormond's papers, vol. i., p. 75.

Irish Catholic subjects; and it is likely that his desire for concluding a peace with them originated in the consideration of the effectual services of the men who humbled these stern Covenanters on their own mountains. Ere we close this rapid view of the events of this year, it is necessary to observe that Urban VIII., who had so cordially befriended the confederates, died early in July, 1644, and was succeeded by Innocent X., on the 15th of September of the same year.

The time for the expiration of the truce was now approaching, and the general assembly, which met in August, appointed commissioners to treat with Ormond for a renewal. Amongst those named to manage it was Thomas Fleming, Catholic Archbishop of Dublin; but as Ormond objected to him, Muskerry, Sir R. Talbot, Browne, D'Arcy, Dillon, and Plunket, set out on the 31st of August for Dublin. Upon their arrival the cessation was renewed to December 1, and afterwards continued to a longer time. *

CHAPTER V.

WHEN the confederate commissioners returned to Kilkenny, Charles I. was congratulating himself on the brilliant victories achieved by Colkitto and Montrose in Scotland. The hapless monarch naturally began to think that nothing could prove so conducive to his interests as a peace with the Irish Catholics; but, well aware as he was of their oath of association, he must have inwardly grieved at the idea of being obliged to purchase it at such a price as the free and public exercise of the Catholic religion. Yet, in truth, the confederates, as it will appear, were the only loyal subjects in Ireland on whose willing hearts he could place true reliance. Disaffection was contagious, and Inchiquin was already tampering with Lord Esmond, the governor of Duncannon, and persuading him to declare for the parliament, or sur-

* Carte, L, 516.

render that strong place to their forces. As to himself,
he had entered into a truce with General Purcell, which
was not to expire till the 10th of April following. This
act, as precipitate as it was unwise, had been done to
propitiate Ormond, who had an overweening notion of
Murrogh O'Brien. The consequence was, that he had
time to collect forces, and strengthen himself in the
towns out of which he had expelled the Catholics. The
truce which had been renewed with Ormond, left the
supreme council free to look closely into their circumstances; and they resolved to send their agents beyond
the seas to the courts of the Catholic princes. "Their
design was, that they might know themselves what they
had to trust to, and what succours they might really depend on from abroad; and that, in case they should
be forced to serve God again in holes and corners, the
world might know they had laboured all they could to
prevent that misfortune."* For this purpose Father
Hugh Bourke was sent to the court of Madrid, to solicit
the King of Spain; Belling, the secretary of the council,
had orders to proceed to the vatican, to congratulate Innocent X., and to visit the Italian princes, and the Marquess of Castle-Rodrigo, governor of the low countries.
Hartegan, a priest, remained as their envoy at the French
court. The articles of the treaty with Ormond were religiously observed; and towards the end of December,
the king wrote to the lord lieutenant in the following
terms:—"I have thought to give you this order, to seek
to renew the cessation for a year; for which you shall
promise the Irish, if you can have it no cheaper, to join
with them against the Scots and Inchiquin."† Ormond,
however, did not attach much importance to these orders,
and was in no mood to oppose either Munroe or Inchiquin; on the contrary, he had already hinted to his partisans in the council that he meditated a peace which
was calculated to prove advantageous to them. But the
flagitious acts passed in the parliament towards the end
of September caused the supreme council to take such
steps as were necessary for their immediate security.
Unprotected as the coast was at this moment, they knew
not how soon a descent might be made by their enemies;

* Carte's Orm., I, 529.   † Reliq. Sacræ. Carol.

and the orders to execute all Irish-born and papists who might be found upon the seas, struck salutary terror into their hearts. The most important seaports then in their possession were Waterford, Wexford, and Galway. The loss of any of them must have done incalculable mischief; and a rumour reached them that Esmond was about to surrender Duncannon. About the beginning of January, Preston was ordered to blockade the fortress; but this proving too slow a process, he resolved to convert the blockade into a siege. The weather being extremely bad, and a whirlwind prevailing, " which blew the priming off the guns, filling the pans with dust," seriously retarded the operations of the besiegers.* A flotilla was ordered by the parliament to succour the place, but such was the perseverance of the confederates that they finally drove out the garrison, after ten weeks' siege. During this time they expended 19,000 lbs. of powder, † and were ably helped by the inhabitants of Ross and Wexford. Esmond, who was old and blind, died soon after, and thus escaped a punishment which his disloyalty amply deserved. Whilst the confederates were engaged at this siege, the king sent an order to Ormond to conclude a peace with the confederates. The general assembly, which was then sitting, immediately despatched Sir Nicholas Plunket and Lord Muskerry to confer with him, on the 6th of March, 1645. Ormond, who was fully empowered by the king to abrogate the penal statutes, artfully concealed the royal orders, and referred the commissioners to the decision of his majesty, who had determined that these obnoxious statutes should not be put in execution after the conclusion of a peace. He then laboured sedulously to convince them that a suspension of Poyning's law could not be conducive to their interests. Amongst some new *graces* to which he yielded, the Catholics were to be released from all the king's rents and revenues which they had received since the beginning of the war, with an abolition of all outlawries, attainders, and indictments against any of them. The king, he assured them, was willing to confer all places of trust and honour indiscriminately on Catholic and

* Belling. 276.   † Carte, I. 528.

Protestant subjects; but he indignantly denied that ne had any notion of employing an equal number of bo th parties. With this unsatisfactory arrangement, the delegates hastened back to Kilkenny, to report the result of their conference to the assembly.— But as the lord lieutenant made no guarantee for religious immunities, save such as the king might be subsequently induced to cede, the great body of the assembly would not subscribe a peace which did not secure the public exercise of religion. Scarampi and the bishops would not make any compromise, and as the peace on which Ormond reckoned made no real provisions for the hereditary possession of the Catholics of Ulster, a great majority of the confederates would not hearken to the wily artifices of the viceroy. And no wonder that such terms should be rejected with scorn. The clergy, who exercised the most unbounded influence over their flocks, were secretly informed of the king's intention to grant their most sanguine demands, and, notwithstanding the unseemly haste of Plunket and Muskerry to negotiate a peace with Ormond, contrived to obstruct it. But, although the commissioners, who favoured Ormond's views, desisted from pressing it in the assembly, they managed to carry on an under-hand negotiation with the lord lieutenant in Dublin. Throughout the entire summer this unhappy question furnished matter for acrimonious discussion, and strengthened the animosities which had grown up between the lords of the Pale and the "old Irish," at the conclusion of the armistice in 1643.

But it is necessary to relinquish this important matter for awhile, in order to witness events of another character. The truce with Inchiquin expired on the 10th of April, and the confederates were unanimous in their resolve to destroy him and his adherents. For this purpose they ordered Castlehaven to proceed into Munster with an army of 5,000 foot and 1,000 horse. In a very short time he reduced all the castles in the baronies of Imokilly and Barrymore. Cappoquin, Dromane, Mitchelstown, Castlelyons, Mallow, Doneraile, Liscarroll, and Lismore surrendered on articles. He next reduced Rostellan, and in it took

Colonel H. O'Brien* and Colonel Courtenay. Inchiquin could not resist, and was obliged to shut himself up in Cork, pursued by Castlehaven, who wasted the country to the very walls of the city. He then besieged Youghal, but owing to some misunderstandings between himself and Preston, he did not act with vigour, and thus left the place in possession of Lord Broghill, who had got a supply of arms and ammunition from the parliament. Towards the beginning of September Castlehaven returned to Kilkenny after disbanding his forces.

The parliament in England, hearing of these movements in the south, lost no time in strengthening Munroe's forces in Ulster. Having nominated young Coote to the presidency of Connaught, they sent over £10,000 to the covenanters, with a considerable supply of clothing. On the 8th of June Sir Charles Coote presented letters from a committee of both houses, desiring Munroe to send 500 men into Connaught, who were to be joined by Sir F. Hamilton's regiment, in order to reduce Sligo. They complied, after some hesitation, and determined to march a body of 4,000 foot and 500 horse into the counties of Mayo and Galway. Their progress was marked by carnage and burnings. Sir Robert Stewart took possession of Sligo, and Coote set about raising 1,400 horse, in order to overrun the entire country. Clanricarde, who had been appointed president by Ormond, could offer but little resistance. His apathy in the earlier period of the war had so diminished his influence, that the people had little regard for him, and Ormond beheld the critical position of his friend with a stoic's indifference. Clanricarde, however, got about 2,500 men to oppose the overwhelming force which was now devastating the country, and appointed Lord Taaffe to the command; but he effected nothing of importance, his efforts being confined to the reduction of such minor places as Castlecoote and Jamestown. The supreme council,

* This man caused a Roman Catholic dean to be hanged a short time before, and betrayed his trust at Warcham in England, which he yielded to the parliament forces. He was brother to Inchiquin, and partook of his savage character.

alarmed for the safety of Galway, ordered Sir James
Dillon and Malachy O'Kelly, archbishop of Tuam, to
drive the Scotch and English out of Sligo; and they
attacked the place on Sunday, October 26th, with a force
far inferior to their enemies. They succeeded in getting
into the town, but word was brought that a large
force was now coming to succour the garrison. The
confederates took alarm and fled, pursued by the
Scotch. Malachy, archbishop of Tuam fell into their
hands, and was brutally murdered,* after quarter
given. The noblest Catholics of the province were
either slain or made prisoners, and Sligo was in the
hands of the parliament.

Now, long before these events occurred, the king,
feeling his difficulties daily increasing, and well
knowing that Ormond was so zealous a Protestant as
to be absolutely averse to granting the Irish confederates such terms as they insisted upon, determined to
send them a Catholic envoy, in the person of Lord
Herbert, afterwards Earl of Glamorgan. He arrived
in Dublin about the end of July or beginning of
August.† Having conferred with the lord lieutenant,
Glamorgan soon after proceeded to Kilkenny, where the
supreme council was sitting, and discussing the terms
proposed by the lord lieutenant. Glamorgan had been
empowered by the king to treat with the confederates,
"and also to levy any number of men in Ireland and
other parts beyond sea, commanding of them, putting
officers over them, governors in forts and towns, and giving
him power to receive the king's rents." He, therefore,
in virtue of a commission given him by his majesty,

---

* Bruodin, in the *Hib. Dom.*, p. 652, states, that the archbishop was
cut into bits by the Scots.—" In minutas sectus est partes, absciso
brachio dextero, etiam post datam fidem." Mr. Hardiman, in the
History of Galway, p. 123, has this curious note on the subject :—
" Here is a true tragidie of the unhappie expedition of Sligoe,
viz. :—Last Sunday our forces, after taking the abbie of Sligoe,
and hearing of the approach of Coote with a strong relief, began to
march back, and though they beat the enemie that day and the day
before, yet, then, a few horse of the said enemie put them most
shamefully to flight, in which flight (proh dolor) my Lord Archbishop,
Father Teige Conel, Father Augustine Higgin, with other clergymen,
were killed and pittifullie mangled, and so left in the way near
Sligoe."

† Transactions of Glamorgan, pp. 60, 61, 67.

entered into a treaty with the confederate body, by
which it was agreed, and accorded by the said Earl, on
the part of his majesty, and Richard Lord Viscount
Mountgarret, Donogh Lord Muskerry, as commissioners
appointed by the said confederate Catholics :—

"I.—That all the professors of the Roman Catholic
religion in Ireland, shall enjoy the free and public use
and exercise of their religion.

"II.—That they shall hold and enjoy all the churches
by them enjoyed, or by them possessed, at any time
since the 23rd of October 1641, and all other churches
in the said kingdom, other than such as are now
actually enjoyed by his majesty's Protestant subjects.

"III.—That all the Roman Catholics shall be ex-
empted from the jurisdiction of the Protestant clergy,
and that the Catholic clergy shall not be punished or
molested for the exercise of their jurisdiction over
their respective flocks. And, also, that an act shall be
passed in the next parliament for securing to them all
the king's concessions.

"IV.—That the Marquess of Ormond, or any others,
shall not disturb the professors of the Roman Catholic
religion in possession of the articles above specified.

"VI.—The Earl of Glamorgan engages his majesty's
word for the performance of these articles.

"VII.—That the public faith of the kingdom shall be
engaged unto the said Earl by the commissioners of
the confederate Catholics, for sending 10,000 men by
order and declaration of the general assembly at
Kilkenny, armed, the one-half with muskets, and the
other half with pikes, to serve his majesty in England,
Wales, or Scotland, under the command of the said
Glamorgan, as lord general of the said army; which
army is to be kept together in one entire body, and all
other the officers and commanders of the said army are
to be named by the supreme council of the said confederate Catholics, or by such others as the general
assembly of the said confederate Catholics of Ireland
shall entrust therewith."

When these articles were signed by the supreme council
and Glamorgan, the general assembly, on the 28th of
August "ordered and declared that their union and
oath of association shall remain firm and inviolable.

and in full strength, in all points, and to all purposes until the articles of the intended peace shall be ratified in parliament, notwithstanding any proclamation of the peace." But, in order to avoid the inconvenience which the publication of these concessions might produce to the king, it was thought proper to be deferred till the forces designed for his majesty should arrive in England, when he might more confidently avow and confirm the concessions made, by his authority, by the Earl Glamorgan."*

Such were the terms offered on the king's behalf by Glamorgan, copies of which had been already submitted to the archbishops and other leading members of the confederates. Ten weeks were spent in Dublin debating with Ormond on the articles which had nothing to do with this, which may be regarded as of a spiritual nature. But the delegates from the supreme council had likewise endeavoured to gain from the lord lieutenant some concessions in favour of their religion, as he had the public authority of his majesty, but, not so ample a one, in that respect, as the Earl.

The commissioners were charged to hear of nothing which was contrary to, or inconsistent with, the private concessions made by the Earl. But the terms which the lord lieutenant would grant, especially with regard to religion, were by no means such as were satisfactory to them. While these matters were being negotiated at Dublin and Kilkenny, another event took place which aggravated the loss of Sligo. Towards the end of the year a parliament flotilla sailed up the Shannon, and the Earl of Thomond, who remained neutral, and was not molested by the confederates, (as it would appear that their orders had been rescinded,) gave possession of his castle of Bunratty† to the parliament's troops. The result was, however, in one respect propitious, for Limerick abandoned its neutrality, and declared for the confederates.

But it is necessary that we follow the secretary, Belling, to Rome, and introduce one who was destined

---

* Glamorgan's Transactions, p. 74.
† Belling describes Bunratty as "a noble antient structure, reputed strong when engines of battery were not so frequent." —*Narrative of the War*, p. 332.

to act a conspicuous part in these important and varying scenes. Belling reached Rome about the end of February 1645, and was presented to his Holiness Innocent X., by Father Luke Wadding, and received as the accredited envoy of the confederate Catholics.

The Pontiff—who is described by Muratori* as of rough and repellent aspect, yet, still of majestic manner, was suspected to be hostile to the policy of the French court, and of a strong leaning to the interests of Spain—succeeded in removing the apprehensions of both parties; and now seeing the war which had so long desolated the Continent drawing to a close, scarcely needed the memorial of the Irish Catholics to turn his attention to their then far off region. But in applying to the court of Rome, it is quite evident that they calculated on finding unity and power in obedience to the supreme chief of that religion which was their only common bond, disunited as they were in every other respect. His Holiness having heard from Belling the actual state of affairs, determined to forward to Ireland considerable supplies of arms and money, and while the secretary was at the court of Florence he resolved to send to the confederates a minister with the high and influential dignity of nuncio extraordinary.

He first selected Luigi Omodei, whom he afterwards made a cardinal, but in consequence of the objections of Mazarin against the appointment of a prelate who, as a Milanese, was a subject of Spain, he substituted John Baptist Rinuccini, who, being of Tuscan origin, should be regarded as belonging to a neutral power. This distinguished prelate was born at Rome, on the 15th of September, 1592. From his earliest years he manifested a decided predilection for the ecclesiastical profession, and commenced his studies under the tutelage of the Jesuits. In his eighteenth year he went to Bologna, and thence to *Perugia*, to study canon law; and in the latter city, when but twenty-two years of age, he received his doctor's degree, and was at the same time elected a member of the learned academy, "Della Crusca." He soon

* Annali D'Italia, ann. 1644.

afterwards returned to Rome, at the desire of his uncle, the Cardinal Octavian Bandini; and it appears that during his sojourn in the Eternal City, immoderate application to studies of a varied nature made such fearful havoc of his health, that he never afterwards recovered that strength and corporeal energy which render life so dear, and sustain it in great and arduous trials. *

To repair a constitution which had thus early suffered, he retired for a while to the patrimony of his fathers, on the banks of the Arno; but quiet and seclusion ill according with an active mind, he retraced his steps to Rome, where he practised law under Monsignor Buratti, a celebrated canonist in the court of Gregory XV.

In Rome, as elsewhere, he earned considerable celebrity, and was appointed by his holiness clerk of the chamber, and was soon afterwards nominated one of his domestic prelates, and secretary to the congregation of rites. On the demise of Gregory XV., Urban VIII. was called to the vacant throne, and the successor of Rinuccini's first friend and patron, to evince the high esteem he entertained for his piety and talents, conferred on him the archiepiscopal see of Fermo, in the marches of Ancona, then vacant by the death of Monsignor Dini, which took place in the year 1625.

His biographer informs us that his conduct in the archiepiscopal see was distinguished by the most exemplary piety and consummate wisdom; and, as a proof of his devoted attachment to the flock over which he presided, we learn from the same authority that he declined the more exalted dignity of the metropolitan see of Florence, which he was invited to accept by the pontiff himself and the Grand Duke Ferdinand II. in the year 1631.

This is not the place to enter into a critical analysis of the character of the nuncio, which should be learned from the history of the events in which he took such a prominent part. Were we to place implicit reliance on the representations of his biographer, we might not hesitate to pronounce him a man of genuine piety and great political acumen. Without pausing, however, to

* Alazzi, p. 10.

examine the portraiture which is given of him by such interested parties as Walsh and Callaghan,[*] we may be allowed to borrow an eulogium from one who cannot be accused of partiality to Rinuccini, which would reflect honour on the character of any man, and is, perhaps rarely deserved by those placed in similar circumstances:—" He was," says Carte,[†] " regular and even austere in his life and conversation, and far from any taint of avarice or corruption."

Having received his instructions from Pope Innocent X., he set out from Rome early in the year 1645, and proceeded to Florence, where he was joined by the secretary, Belling, who was so much astonished on learning that a nuncio had been appointed for Ireland that for three days he was unable to speak. Passing rapidly through Genoa and Marseilles, he arrived in Paris on the 22nd of May. According to the instructions which he had received, he was led to believe that he should have an opportunity of negotiating personally with the Queen of England;[‡] but on his arrival at Paris circumstances transpired which totally removed the possibility of a personal interview. Sir Dudley Wyat had been sent to Paris to communicate to the queen and the French court the news of the overthrow of the royal army; and Rinuccini, seizing the opportunity of impressing on her majesty's mind the necessity of making terms with the confederate Catholics, offered to visit her in person, and in his ministerial capacity. She, however, refused to receive him, alleging that if she did so she would violate the English law, which forbade her to recognise him and the confederate government of which he was the accredited agent. Indeed, it is evident that some interested parties, who had no sympathy with the Irish, sedulously laboured to prejudice the queen's mind against the nuncio and the Irish themselves. She had been taught to believe that the object of Rinuccini's mission was to usurp the prerogatives of the crown; and the impression does not appear to have been wholly effaced, notwithstanding his solemn declaration that the pope

* The author of the Vindiciæ Hibernorum.
† Orm. i. 558.
‡ She had been forced to fly out of England some time before.

was actuated by no other motives than his ardent desire
of protecting the Catholic religion, and furnishing his
majesty with those aids which he required to sustain him
against the faction which had vowed the destruction of
Ireland.

A prey to grief and despair, the queen retired from
Paris to St. Germains, where the disastrous intelligence
of the king's defeat at Naseby was brought her; and
changing her opinion of the confederate Catholics, whom
she hitherto designated with the false epithet of "rebels,"
she determined, if possible, to conclude a peace, which
would leave them free to send troops into England.
She sent to inform the nuncio that she regretted that she
could not receive him without the king's consent, and
earnestly desired that he would exert himself to conclude
a peace which would serve to release her royal consort
from the dangers which were impending. Sir Dudley
Wyat was the person selected to carry on this indirect
negotiation. He insisted, on the part of the queen, that
the peace should be concluded at Paris, and asserted that
she was ready to procure its confirmation on the part of
her husband, provided the nuncio sent to Ireland to have
it ratified by the supreme council.

Wyat insisted on the necessity of speedily coming to
an arrangement. He argued that the king's condition
was desperate, and that if he were obliged to make
terms with the parliamentary faction, the ruin of Ireland would be inevitable, as it was utterly hopeless to
think of resisting the combined powers of England and
Scotland.

To these entreaties on the part of the queen the nuncio
replied that he had nothing so much at heart as the conclusion of a peace which would secure to the Catholics of
Ireland the free and uncontrolled exercise of their religion, and the immediate removal of all the penal laws
by which they had been so long and so grievously afflicted; and that nothing could give more heartfelt satisfaction to the pope than to learn he had witnessed the
conclusion of a peace which would allow him to proceed
to Ireland to employ himself with the ecclesiastical concerns of the kingdom, exclusive of all political interference; but he clearly saw that nothing really beneficial
could result from such indirect negotiation, and he be-

gan to think that the promises of the queen were delusive, and only meant to retard his departure.

It had been hinted that it was the object of the queen's
adherents to obtain from him the supplies of arms and
money which were destined for Ireland, and have them
transported for the king's service into England; and
Mazarin suggested to him the possibility of such an event,
at the same time that he deprecated the fruitless expen-
diture of those large sums which had been sent from
France for the support of the royal cause.

He was, moreover, strictly forbidden by Cardinal
Paufilio to consent to a private interview with Henrietta
Maria, on the ground that he could not uncover his head
to a queen;[*] and on being informed that she could not
receive him without this mark of respect to royalty, he
was driven to the alternative of employing Sir Dudley
Wyat and her majesty's chaplain to open this indirect
communication with her. There can be no doubt that
the queen was determinedly opposed to Rinuccini's landing in Ireland, for he informs us that when he sent one
of his retinue, Dominick Spinola, a Genoese of noble
birth, to present her with the pope's brief, she asserted
with considerable vehemence that the Irish in general,
and the secretary, Belling, in particular, were anxious
to renounce their allegiance to the king, on plea of their
devotion to the Catholic religion; nay, more, that Hartegan, the agent of the confederates at Paris, had been
heard to boast that the Irish were determined to prosecute the war to the last extremity, if the terms on which
they insisted were not fully confirmed. In a spirit of
bitterness, which may readily be excused, when we reflect on the difficulties which then beset the king, she
deprecated the conduct of the Irish, "who," she said,
"seemed to rejoice at the reverses of her consort, when
they placed him in such a position as would make him
yield to their demands, on threat of their assistance being withheld." This, however, was but the passion of
the moment, for, from the correspondence which describes this ebullition of the queen's feelings, we learn
that, in a subsequent interview with Spinola, she ex

* Card. Paufilio's letter in Rinuccini's Corresp., 450.

pressed her entire confidence in the firmness and prudence of the nuncio, and his devotion to the royal cause.

Anticipating the application which would be made on him for the monies which he had brought from Rome, the nuncio stated, that seeing the straits to which the king had been reduced, the sums he had in his possession could be of little use, and as to any agreement between the king and the parliament, Ireland had little to fear from their combined efforts, as she had carried on a war against Elizabeth, in the time of Hugh O'Neill,* for sixteen years, independent of the sympathy with which she was now regarded by the pope and the Catholic powers. It would appear, moreover, that he was in concert with the English Catholics, who, declaring their inability to be of any use to his majesty, pointed to the effective aid of the Irish Catholics, who, if seconded in their demand, would be ready at the shortest notice to turn all their energies against the parliament. Meantime letters from Rome chided him for his delay in the French capital, and Scarampi had written from Ireland to urge his departure. The nuncio, for the last time, sent Spinola to wait on the queen to renew his avowals of attachment to her cause, and that of her consort, and with this mutual interchange of compliments terminated their negotiations.

The instructions which he had received on leaving Rome urged him to proceed to Ireland with all possible expedition, and strictly forbade him to hold any unnecessary intercourse with the English Catholics at the queen's court, who, far from sympathising with the Irish were more inclined to lament any triumph to their arms, as they were afraid that they would, in consequence, be deprived of those places of dignity and emolument in that kingdom, which were the natural accompaniment of superiority and command.

Cardinal Mazarin† was most anxious to detain him,

---

* See his life by Mitchel, one of the most beautiful pieces of biography which we possess.

† Mazarin commenced his career as a soldier, and commanded in the Valteline for the Pope. His character is variously estimated. The Spaniards hated him, and Corneille immortalized him. He was a liberal patron of the arts, and introduced the opera in France. He was made Cardinal in 1642.

and it was not till after repeated commands that the nuncio resolved to leave Paris, after having been there fully three months. He had not been long in France when he received a promise from the Duke de Ventadour of 100,000 dollars for the purposes of the war in Ireland, but the news of the king's reverses changed his intention. Having got from Mazarin the sum of 25,000 livres, that is to say, 5,000 for the purchase of some vessels, and 20,000 as a present, he left Paris for Rochelle, where he arrived about the beginning of October. On his arrival at Rochelle he was met by Galfrid Baron, who brought him letters from the Earl of Glamorgan informing him that the confederates anxiously awaited his arrival, as they stood in need of the military stores which he was to bring them. This determined him to make all the necessary arrangements for the voyage. There seems to have been some misunderstanding as to the means of transport into Ireland, for, Hartegan informed the nuncio that Cardinal Mazarin had promised to place four ships at his disposal to serve as a convoy for himself and the supplies; whereas, when application was made, he learned to his mortification, that there was but one ship in the harbour, which would require at least 1,000 dollars and six weeks to make her ready for sea.

To suppose that Cardinal Mazarin was not influenced by some sinister motive on this occasion, would be to differ presumptuously from those who have written concerning the character of this remarkable man. He must evidently have looked with a jealous eye on any enterprise which tended to involve the affairs of Charles I., whose queen had all the sympathy of the French court. It is likely, too, that he had formed a hasty notion of the confederates, and apprehended that they meant to throw off their allegiance to the crown of England. The man "who could listen to the murmurs of the people, as one listens on the shore to the noise of the waves of the sea,"* was not much affected by the progress of events in Ireland; it afforded too small a field for the finesse of the great minister, who, whether riding in the trenches of

---

* President Henault.

Casal* with bullets whistling about him, or returning
to power, after having had a price set on his head,
proved himself to be the greatest politician of the day.
One thing, however, is certain, that Richlieu would
have taken a livelier interest in the affairs of Ireland.

The French admiral, the Duke de Brezé, then in the
harbour was applied to for a ship, but as he had no
orders to furnish one, it was not till considerable time
had elapsed that Rinuccini succeeded in purchasing the
San Pietro, a frigate of twenty-six guns. His retinue
consisted of twenty-six Italians together with a number
of Irish officers, and the secretary Belling. On board
the frigate he embarked the following supplies :—2,000
muskets, 2,000 cartouch belts, 4,000 swords, 2,000
pike-heads, 400 brace of pistols, 20,000 lbs of powder,
with match, shot, &c. &c.†

The money, which was considerable, he took with him
in Spanish gold. Wadding's generosity had not
abated, and he furnished 36,000 dollars, in addition to
the sum contributed by Pope Innocent X. He weighed
anchor about the middle of October, and sailed from
St. Martin, in the Isle de Rhé. The two first days of
the voyage were prosperous, for they met no interruption,
but on the third they were alarmed by the appearance
of a flotilla, which was evidently in pursuit. The experienced eyes of the sailors pronounced them to be
the parliament's ships, under the command of one
Plunket, whom Belling calls "a noted scourge."‡ Two
of the squadron soon made sail in the wake of the *San
Pietro,* whereon the Irishmen cast loose the guns and
cleared the deck for action ; having sent the non-com-
batants out of the way into the forepart of the ship. The
nuncio meanwhile was sick in his berth when word was
brought him that one of the pursuing vessels had dropped

* Bussy Memoirs.
† During his sojourn at Paris the nuncio was allowed by the Pope
3,000 dollars for the maintenance of himself and suite. On his arrival
in Ireland, 200 dollars a month were assigned him, but he expended
during his stay 15,800 dollars, of his own private income. His biographer (Aiazzi) remarks that this was a great outlay considering the
low rate at which all the necessaries of life were then to be had in
Ireland; a fact which is made still more clear by the letter of the
nuncio's confessor, Arcamont, in the Appendix to this vol.
‡ Narrative of the War.

astern; but to his horror, they informed him that the larger vessel of the two was still making all sail on his frigate. The chase continued for more than a hundred miles, and an hour before sunset the *San Pietro* lost sight of her pursuer. In a transport of jubilee, the Italians sang a hymn of thanksgiving, and the nuncio expressed his joy that none had suffered, as he sickened at the thought of seeing the blood of his Irish sailors staining his decks. He attributed his delivery from Plunket to a manifest interposition of Divine Providence, and pronounced it miraculous; but he must have subsequently learned that the escape of his pursuer was still far more wonderful, for Plunket's cooking-room had caught fire, and being alarmed for his magazine, he was obliged to shorten sail, and thus suffer the *San Pietro* to distance him. On that night, owing to the darkness of the weather they did not know their bearings, though they had passed Cape Clear, but on the following day they were visited by birds which gave them notice of their approach to the coast; and when the haze which concealed the land from their view had disappeared, they found themselves in the Bay of Kenmare, where they dropped anchor on the 21st of October. Next day the nuncio came on shore, and his first abode on the Irish soil was in the hut of a shepherd, where he celebrated mass on the feast of St. Mabilia, surrounded by the peasantry, whom the unusual sight of a dignitary from the Vatican, and his Italian retinue, had brought down from the fastnesses of the mountains.[*]

Having rested for some time, and taken ashore all the arms and equipments at Ardtully, he proceeded on a rude litter towards Macroom, the frigate having been sent round to Duncannon. The supreme council on intelligence of his arrival, despatched some troops of cavalry to escort him through Inchiquin's quarters; and at Dromsecane,[†] on the Blackwater, he was joined by Richard Butler, a Catholic, though brother to the Marquess of Ormond, Lord Netterville, and others. From Dromsecane they continued their route through

[*] Aiazzi. Nunziatara in Irlanda. *Vide* Appendix.
[†] A strong castle of the O'Keeffe's, about fourteen miles from Macroom.

Kilmallock to Limerick. Here, in the cathedral, he celebrated the obsequies of Malachy, archbishop of Tuam, and was received with generous hospitality by the municipal authorities. At the door of the cathedral the bishop of Limerick presented him with the mitre, saying:—"Ab Ecclesia apostolica hæc recepi, nunc eidem ecclesiæ prompte restituo." His instructions charged him to proceed to Kilkenny without delay, and having congratulated the people of Limerick on their recent acknowledgment of the confederate government, he journeyed slowly to his destination, and on the 12th of November rested at a village, distant three miles from Kilkenny.

The confederates had resolved to receive him with every demonstration of respect, and deputed four gentlemen, accompanied by the secretary Belling, to bid him welcome. Next morning, having ascended his litter, surrounded by thousands of the gentry and peasantry, together with a vast concourse from the neighbouring counties, he set out for the city. Conspicuous amongst this vast assemblage was a troop of fifty students on horseback, armed with pistols, the leader of whom, in a distinguished costume, and wearing a crown of laurel, recited some Latin verses, and conveyed to him the compliments and congratulations of his companions.

At a short distance from the gate he descended from the litter, and having put on the cape and pontifical hat, the insignia of his office, he mounted a horse caparisoned for the occasion. The secular and regular clergy had assembled in the church of St. Patrick,* close by the gate, and when it was announced that the nuncio was in readiness, they advanced into the city in processional array, preceded by the standard-bearers of their respective orders.†

* The site of this church may still be traced in the graveyard adjoining the modern parochial church of St. Patrick, outside the city wall.
† That Ireland was rich in ecclesiastical furniture is quite evident from the splendid collection in the Royal Irish Academy. Pugin, in his grand work on Ecclesiastical Ornament and Costume, p. 77, speaks of a cope of cloth of gold of the fifteenth century, with excellent orphreys, and hood of needle-work," which was discovered not long ago in the cathedral of Waterford. It is now in England. One of the banners probably carried in the procession, has been preserved by a venerable gentleman in Kilkenny, who is as learned in the antiquities of his native city, as he is affable and kind.—I mean Mr. B. Scott.

Under the old arch, called St. Patrick's gate, he was met by the vicar-general of the diocese of Ossory and the magistrates of the city and county, who joined in the procession. A canopy was held over him by some citizens, who remained bare-headed, although the rain descended in torrents. The streets were lined by regiments of infantry, and the bells of the Black Abbey and the church of St. Francis pealed a gladsome chime.

In the heart of the city, and nearly opposite to the ancient residence of the Roth family, there stood a cross* of beautiful workmanship and great antiquity. Here the nuncio halted, while a young student pronounced an appropriate oration in the Latin tongue. The procession then moved on till it ascended the gentle eminence on which the splendid old fane, sacred to St. Canice, is erected. At the grand entrance he was received by the venerable Bishop of Ossory, whose feebleness prevented him walking in the procession. After mutual salutations, the bishop handed him the aspersorium and incense, and then both entered the cathedral, which, even in the palmiest days of Catholicity, had never held within its precincts a more solemn or gorgeous assemblage. The nuncio ascended the steps of the grand altar, intonated the "Te Deum," which was caught up by a thousand voices, till crypt and chancel resounded with the psalmody, and when it ceased he pronounced a blessing on the immense multitude which crowded the aisles and nave. Three years before the occurrences here narrated, David, Bishop of Ossory, had erected a monument to commemorate the restoration of St. Canice's cathedral to the ancient worship, and it needs no flight of fancy to suppose that on this memorable occasion he may have echoed the words of the canticle, " Now dismiss thy servant, because my eyes have seen thy salvation, and the glory of thy people, Israel." These ceremonies concluded, he retired for awhile to the residence prepared for him in the city, and shortly afterwards was waited on by General Preston and Lord Muskerry. He then proceeded on foot to visit Lord Mountgarret, the presi-

* This cross was barbarously thrown down in the year 1771. It bore date MCCC. Its site is now occupied by a pump !

dent of the assembly. The reception took place in the
castle. At the foot of the grand staircase he was met by
Thomas Fleming, Archbishop of Dublin, and Walsh,
Archbishop of Cashel. At the end of the great gallery*
Lord Mountgarret was seated, waiting his arrival, and
when the nuncio approached, he got up from his chair,
without moving a single inch in advance. The seat
designed for Rinuccini was of damask and gold, with a
little more ornament than that occupied by the president. He tells us that it was placed on the right of
Mountgarret's, but yet so situated that it looked rather
to the left, and thus made it a matter of doubt as to the
personage who held the most central position. The
nuncio immediately addressed the president in Latin,
and declared that the object of his mission was to sustain
the king, then so perilously circumstanced; but, above
all, to rescue from pains and penalties the people of Ireland, and to assist them in securing the free and public
exercise of the Catholic religion, and the restoration of
the churches and church property, of which fraud and
violence had so long deprived their rightful inheritors.
He implored those who heard him to banish from their
minds the insinuations of some who were artfully endeavouring to misrepresent the motives of the pope in sending him, and concluded his remarks by solemnly asseve-
rating † that, far from wishing to do injury to King
Charles, it was his earnest anxiety to prop up his tot-
tering throne. Heber MacMahon, Bishop of Clogher,
to whom Rinuccini had been specially confided by the
holy see, followed the nuncio in a spirited appeal, and
echoed the sentiments to which the papal minister had
given utterance. After mutual compliments, the assembly broke up, and the nuncio retired to his residence,
accompanied by Preston, Muskerry, and the troops.
The cold formality of Mountgarret did not escape his
observation, for, in writing to his court, he mentions
that, as he retired from the gallery, the president never

* Little now remains of the castle as it was in Rinuccini's time, save
the towers at the grand entrance. The gallery must have been splendid
that elicited the praise of a man who had seen the Vatican and Medi-
cean palaces.

† " In verbo principis," says Callaghan, in Vindic. Hib., was his fa-
vorite expression.

moved an inch from his place. But the supreme council
soon after did not fail to impress on the pope's mind the
advantages the people of Ireland might derive from his
prudence and counsels. The following is their letter:—
" Most Holy Father—One of the first acts of your pontificate has been to send to us a nuncio from your court,
in the person of John Baptist, Archbishop of Fermo, and
we hasten to return our acknowledgments of the paternal solicitude thus shown us. If we have been unable to
receive so exalted a personage with that pomp and splendour which the occasion called for, we humbly pray that
the joy and overflow of heart with which we have hailed
his advent, may make amends. Grateful for the supplies
which the nuncio has brought us from you, we earnestly
implore that your paternal bounty may not be withdrawn
till the most Holy Innocent shall have beheld the Catholic religion flourishing in our island, and the enemies of
our faith vanquished by the potent arm of the God of
hosts."*

Now, it so happened that Muskerry, Plunket, and the
other commissioners did not return from Dublin till the
12th of November, the day before Rinuccini's entry into
Kilkenny. That their chagrin must have been great, cannot be questioned, for they learned from the events
which had transpired that the " old Irish" in the
assembly would be animated by more hostile feelings to
their projects by the interference and influence of the
nuncio. Muskerry, and those of his party, had toiled
with unwearied exertions all the summer to conclude the
peace, and were willing to sign it, without obliging Ormond to any concession of a religious nature, save such
as the king might be pleased to grant as a " grace" when
triumphant over his enemies. But, without pausing to
examine the prudence of this resolve, the " old Irish"
had begun to tire of begging favours and immunities,
when they felt themselves in a position to insist on them
as rights. Elated by the magnificent promises of the nuncio, they looked beyond the seas for sympathy and sup
port. The Head of the Church, it was expected, would
use all his influence to sustain them. The impassioned
oratory of the Italian conjured up prospects as bright as

* *Vide* Borlase's Dismal Effects of the Irish Insurrect.. p. 144.

ever passed before the mental vision of Celtic bard.
In the recesses of his domicile bishops listened to his
plans; and the enthusiastic Heber of Clogher already
fancied that he saw the " thieving Scot" driven out of
Ulidia, and the temples and possessions of the Catholics
restored to their rightful owners. It was no wonder that
estrangement should soon have grown up between the
parties who, long before now, were mutually opposed.—
Those who adopted the nuncio's views bitterly regretted
that all that Rinuccini dreamed of had not been accomplished before his coming. Surely, thought they, if
craft and intrigue had not marred our progress, all might
have been realised. Fond enthusiasts! brave hearts!
grand and simple souls! little did ye then think of the
storm which was soon to burst on the land and destroy
your brightest hopes! As in every other feud, the parties who were now to work the ruin of the country began to be recognised by the names of their leaders.—
Those who were ready to swear by Rinuccini, were denominated Nuncionists; and those who placed reliance
on the lord lieutenant, were designated Ormondists. The
solemn vow recorded at Knockcrofty, to merge all divisions in the struggle for fatherland, was forgotten or unheeded; and the demon strife had come from the abyss
to exercise his power. Alas! for those who dream of
nationality with hate and dissension rankling in their
hearts!

To add to the embarrassment of the Ormondist party,
they were now informed that the nuncio, during his sojourn in Paris, had received a memorial from Rome,
which had been transmitted thither from the English
Catholics, representing their grievances, and desiring
that the Irish would insert among the articles of the
peace, about which they were treating with the king,
some conditions in favour of the Catholics of England;
and that the peace be concluded upon such terms as
might secure the Irish in their own country, and at the
same time enable them to come to his majesty's assistance in England with an army, which should be joined
by the English Catholics. The conditions laid down in
this memorial were the following; and they were regarded as the most effectual:—

I. That the Irish do not come to England with less

than 10,000 or 12,000 men; that they may subsist of themselves without any fear of being cut off even by those English Protestants who serve under his majesty.

II. That two seaport garrisons be delivered up to them.

III. That the general and all the officers be named by the Irish.

IV. That the general be subject only to the immediate orders of the king.

V. That this army be kept together in a body, and not obliged to go upon any particular service, except by order from the general and council of war.

VI. That the English Catholics, by the king's command and authority, have a power of meeting in a body, and with a corps of horse, answerable to the Irish foot, forming one army.

VII. That the Catholic general of this body of English horse be such a man as shall not be distrusted by the Irish, but approved of by the Irish general.

As the necessary consequence of those conditions, the English Catholics had pledged themselves that nothing should be omitted which was essential and necessary to the complete establishment of the Catholic religion in Ireland."

This subject afforded ample room for discussion in the assembly, and a considerable time was spent by the Ormandists and the party opposed to them in debating on the practicability of such proceedings.

But, for the elucidation of this matter, it is necessary that we know in what relation Glamorgan stood to the king and the Irish people. He was a Catholic, and son of the Marquess of Worcester; for the king he entertained the most chivalrous devotion, and had already advanced, in conjunction with his father, £200,000 towards the maintenance of the royal cause. He was married to Margaret O'Brien, daughter of Henry Earl of Thomond; and his religion and connexions gave the king good reason to believe that his influence in Ireland should be considerable. As it has been already stated, his majesty was well convinced that Ormond would make no terms with the confederates which they would

* Glamorgan's Transactions, pp. 41, 42, 43.

regard as satisfactory. He, therefore, entrusted Gla.
morgan with a commission to levy men, coin money,
and to use the revenues of the crown for their support.
He gave a warrant to him to concede to the Catholics
such terms as it was not prudent for the king or Ormond openly to make, and a solemn pledge to ratify
whatever engagements he (Glamorgan) might conclude.
He also furnished him with letters to the pope, the nuncio, and the Catholic princes from whom he expected
aid. When the nuncio arrived in Kilkenny, the earl
produced the commission, empowering him to treat with
the confederates. This letter, dated April 30, 1645,
expressed the king's hope "That the work commenced
by the late pope, in behalf of the Irish Catholics, would
have a happy accomplishment in the hands of his present
minister, aided by the assistance of his dear cousin
(Glamorgan), with whom he was at liberty to make
whatever terms he thought best, all of which he (the
king) would ratify on Glamorgan's return." He informed the nuncio "that an acquaintance of twenty
years had confirmed his love and respect for Glamorgan,
and that whatsoever he promised in his name, he would
feel himself obliged to ratify as the price of the favours
he received." "Depend, therefore, on him," concludes
this authentic document, "but on the understanding
that the whole matter is to be kept strictly secret, since
you see that necessity demands silence, this being the
first document which we have ever addressed to any
Papal minister, but hoping that it is not to be the last.
Signed, Charles R., from our court of Oxford, 30th of
April, 1645."—Nor less curious is the warrant which
Glamorgan produced to the nuncio and the council, concerning the authenticity of which document there cannot
be any doubt:—

" CHARLES R.
"Charles, by the grace of God, King of England,
Scotland, France, and Ireland, Defender of the faith,
to our right trusty and right well-beloved cousin, Edward
Earl of Glamorgan, greeting. We, reposing great and
especial trust and confidence in your approved wisdom
and fidelity, do by these (as firmly as under our great
seal to all intents and purposes) authorise and give you

power to treat and conclude with the confederate Roman Catholics in our kingdom of Ireland, if upon necessity anything be to be condescended unto, wherein our lieutenant cannot so well be seen in, as not fit for us at the present publicly to own; and, therefore, we charge you to proceed according to this our warrant with all possible secrecy; and for whatsoever you shall engage yourself upon such valuable considerations as you in your judgment shall deem fit, we promise in the word of a king and a Christian to ratify and perform the same, that shall be granted by you, and under your hand and seal, the said confederate Catholics having, by their supplies, testified their zeal to our service: and this shall be in each particular to you a sufficient warrant."

But all these concessions depended on the landing of the troops in England; nor was there a single favour to be conceded unless this agreement was fully carried out.

Along with the foregoing documents, which Glamorgan produced, he exhibited to the nuncio another in the king's hand, addressed to " Our most Holy Father, Innocent X." With such assurances, as to political advantages on the one side, and the concessions made in behalf of the Catholic religion on the other, Rinuccini found it impolitic to resist the inclination of the confederates for the conclusion of peace, yet he seems all through to have had some misgivings as to the sincerity of the king, and, in a private interview with Glamorgan, he got a solemn assurance that, when the term of Ormond's vice-royalty had expired, his successor should be a Catholic; and that the Catholic bishops should be entitled, as soon as a free parliament could be assembled, to sit as spiritual peers, and take part in all matters concerning the well-being of the kingdom. Glamorgan had no difficulty in satisfying the nuncio on all these particulars, provided the negotiation was kept strictly secret till the king, relieved from his present embarrassments, might be at liberty to confirm all the articles in the light of day. The nuncio, not fully satisfied with the solemn promises of Glamorgan, urged that some contingency, such as shipwreck, or the death of Glamorgan himself, might prevent the transmission of the troops, in which case the king would not be bound by a promise which

was purely conditional. He insisted, moreover, that in
case the English Catholics did not assist the Irish levies,
a failure of the enterprise might result; but Glamorgan,
overruling all these considerations, bound himself by
oath, in the presence of the nuncio, that the 10,000 Irish
infantry, for which he stipulated, should not strike a
blow before the treaty had received the royal signature;
and in case the king might withhold his consent, the
troops should be put to sea, and landed again in Ireland.
But it was useless to continue in opposition to the under-
hand negotiation carried on by the abettors of the peace.
Mountgarret and Muskerry urged the necessity of
speedily sending the succours; and Doctor Leyburn, on
the part of the queen, charged the Irish people with
cruelty in insisting on too much, and sought to convince
them that a bare toleration of their religion was as much
as they might reasonably demand from a king so straitened as was his Majesty Charles the First. Apprehensive of some failure of Glamorgan's treaty, the nuncio
had gained over nine bishops, who signed a protest
against any arrangement with Ormond or the king,
which did not fully guarantee the maintenance of the
Catholic religion; and this was to be kept in reserve,
and afterwards produced as occasion might require.
This precaution was necessary, inasmuch as he saw that
no power of persuasion could moderate the desire of Ormond's adherents for a peace, and more particularly as
they were now enabled to point to the letters exhibited
by Glamorgan, in which Charles promised, on the word
of a king and a Christian, to make good, to all intents
and purposes, whatever he should perform. " And although you exceed," said his majesty, " what law can
warrant, or any powers of ours extend to, as not knowing what you have need of, yet it being for our service,
we oblige ourself not only to give you our pardon, but
to maintain the same with all our might and power."*

A considerable time had been spent in the negotiations
with Glamorgan, and it was not till near the close of
December that he set out for Dublin, accompanied by
two commissioners from the supreme council, to treat
with Ormond on the levying of troops, and their tran-.

* *Vide* Lingard, in Appendix to vol. x.

mission to England. The king's condition was every day becoming worse, and Chester, the only city by which he could maintain a communication with Ireland, was besieged by the parliament army. Glamorgan was aware of the urgent necessity of immediately relieving that place, and confidently calculated on being furnished with three thousand infantry, as an instalment of the ten for which he had stipulated in the secret treaty.

Meanwhile the nuncio turned his thoughts to the state of Ireland. He did not hesitate to tell the supreme council that the time which had been consumed in armistices and cessations with Ormond, had been productive of the most disastrous results. The popular ardour was beginning to cool, and gave their enemies leisure to recruit their forces and strengthen the fortresses which had fallen into their hands. Peace or no peace, he had determined to make a vigorous attack on the Scotch, in Ulster. Cork, Youghal, and Kinsale were garrisoned by the troops of Murrogh O'Brien, Lord Inchiquin. Sligo had been recently reduced by the Scotch, which was of the greatest advantage to them, inasmuch as it was favourably situated for communicating with Ulster and Scotland. In Ulster, the Scots, under Munroe, held nearly all the principal places, and extended their incursions to the very borders of Leinster, which were but feebly protected by the troops under Preston. The success of Munroe in Ulster was attributable in a great measure to a want of unanimity in its generals, as there was a dispute between Owen O'Neill and his kinsman Sir Phelim, on the question of precedency. Thus were the keys of three provinces in the hands of the avowed enemies of the Catholics, who, by temporising policy and subserviency to Ormond, were made to forget the value of the adage, " Aid yourselves, and God will aid you."

Rinuccini's views were those of an uncompromising prelate. He had learned to appreciate the impulsiveness of the true Irish character, and determined to convince the confederates that they had within their own body all the materials which were required to insure success. He set his mind on one grand object, the freedom of the church, in possession of all her rights and dignities,

and the emancipation of the Catholic people from the
degradation to which English imperialism had condemned them.   The churches, which the piety of
Catholic lords and chieftains had erected, he determined
to secure to the rightful inheritors.   His mind and
feelings recoiled from the idea of a people worshipping
in crypts and catacombs.   He abhorred the notion of a
priest or bishop performing a sacred rite as though it
were a felony; and, spite the wily artifices of Ormond
and his faction, he resolved to teach the people of
Ireland that they were not to remain mere dependants
on English bounty, when a stern resolve might win for
them the privileges of freemen.   His estimate of the
Irish character was correct and exalted.   He formed
it in the proper quarter.   On the Janiculum at Rome
stands the Franciscan convent of St. Peter; many an
hour did he spend there listening to Wadding, as he
narrated the history of his own dear land—the persecutions of her children, and their constancy to the
Catholic faith.   What place more fitted for the recital?
On that same hill, Tasso, who sung of her rugged war-
riors marching to Palestine, oft reposed; and within
the church that crowns its summit was the tomb of
Hugh O'Neill, whereon the history of Erin's chivalry
may be said to have been epitomized.*

It was, therefore, with evident and cogent reason that
he regarded the flattering attention of the modern Irish
as the homage that is paid to the treasurer of a prince,
whilst he received the spontaneous and heartfelt devotedness of the ancient race as a manifest declaration of
their love for the religion of which he was a minister,
and one in whom they expected to find a deliverer from
penalties and persecutions.   And why should he not
cherish an ardent admiration for the representatives of
the old Celtic tribes, and a cordial abhorrence for the
sickly policy of the Catholics of the Pale?   Ormond had
charmed, as never did any magician, "with spell and
philters,"† these ductile men and silken lords, who were

---

* All these inscriptions are to be found in "Rome Ancient and
Modern," by Dr. Donovan.
† Unkind Deserter.

willing to make terms with him which a noble and persecuted race scorned to accept. Their religion was a
dearer consideration than their plundered homes and
confiscated estates. The war which they had waged was
in the cause of that religion, for those whom they had
met foot to foot in many a bloody field had vowed its
destruction ; and, now that a treacherous king and his
faithful lieutenant were driven to the alternative of
throwing themselves on the protection of that people,
had they not an incontrovertible right to seek—nay, to
demand—terms which would secure and guarantee the
exercise of their religion, unfettered by those penal enactments which were worthy the ministers of a Nero or
Domitian ?

Having maturely considered the state of the country
and its immediate exigencies, the nuncio concluded that
a bold and unanimous effort would, in one campaign,
drive the enemy out of the three provinces before the
parliamentary faction could send troops to Ireland. He,
therefore, caused all the arms and ammunition which
he brought with him to be transported to Kilkenny.
Meanwhile the party in the interest of Ormond busied
themselves in nominating bishops to some of the vacant
sees, and coadjutors to those prelates who, by reason of
age or infirmity, were unequal to the episcopal duties.
Six of those named by them were men who were
the creatures of their masters, and in the same relation to them that Walsh was to Ormond, "what the
shadow is to the substance."* But the nuncio firmly
denied that any power was vested in them to nomi-
nate the bishops or their coadjutors; and in vindicating this grand principle, he taught the Irish Catholics that their hierarchy could never be more pure and
independent than when it was free from the patronage
and control of secular dominion. But expectation was
on tiptoe, and, now that the year 1645 had drawn to a
close, the confederates anxiously awaited intelligence
from Ormond and Glamorgan.

* Lives of Irish Writers.

CHAPTER VI.

It was about the 1st of January, 1646, that the two commissioners who had accompanied Glamorgan returned in hot haste from Dublin to Kilkenny. Few were prepared for the intelligence which they brought. On St. Stephen's day, about dinner hour, Glamorgan had been arrested by the order of Ormond, and committed a close prisoner to the castle on a charge of high treason. Had the fleet of the parliament anchored in the bay, it could not have caused greater alarm than that which was feigned by Ormond and Digby on this occasion. The gates of the city were closed, and none were permitted to depart, save the confederate commissioners. They, too, had been brought to the castle; and Digby, in the presence of Ormond, informed them that they had reason to congratulate themselves on their escape from the severities which were in store for the unfortunate earl. "You must know," said he, "that a document* has lately come into my hands, which was found on the person of Malachy, Archbishop of Tuam, who was slain at Sligo by the Scots. This paper, which is signed by the Archbishop of Cashel, certifying that it is a true copy, is the following :—

"Whereas much time hath been spent in meetings and debates betwixt his Excellencie Ja. Lord Marquesse of Ormond, lord lieutenant and general governor of his majesties kingdome of Ireland, commissioner to his most excellent majesty, Charles, by the grace of God, king of Great Britaine, France and Ireland, &c , for the

---

* A copy of all the papers had been found on the person of the Archbishop of Tuam, when killed at Sligo by the Scots. It was forwarded to England, and published by order of the parliament, under the title of "The Earl of Glamorgan's Negotiations and Colourable Commitment in Ireland." Sir Thomas Fairfax was the man who seized the captain of the ship in which the papers had been sent. The captain was a native of Waterford, and was arrested at Padstow, in Cornwall.—V. Appendix.

treating and concluding of a peace in the said kingdome :
of his majesties humble and loyall subjects, the confederate Roman Catholiques of the said kingdome of
Ireland, of the one part, and the Right Honourable
Donnog. Lord Viscount Muskery, and other commissioners deputed and authorized by the said confederate
Roman Catholique subjects, of the other part; and thereupon many difficulties did arise, by occasion whereof,
sundry matters of great weight and consequence necessarily requisite to be condescended unto by his majesties
said commissioner, for the safety of the said confederate
Roman Catholiques were not hitherto agreed upon,
which retarded, and doth as yet retard the conclusion
of a firm peace and settlement in the said kingdome.
And whereas the Right Honourable Edward Earl of
Glamorgan, is intrusted and authorized by his most
excellent majesty to grant and insure to the said confederate Roman Catholique subjects farther graces and favours which the said lord lieutenant did not, as yet, in
that latitude as they expected, grant unto them. And
the said earl having seriously considered of all matters,
and due circumstances of the great affairs now in agita-
tion, which is the peace and quiet of the said kingdome,
and the importance thereof in order to his majesties
service, and in relation to a peace and settlement in his
other kingdomes, and hereupon the place having seene
the ardent desire of the said Catholiques to assist his
majestie against all that doe, or shall oppose his royall
right or monarchique government, and having discerned
the alacrity and cheerefulnesse of the said Roman Catholiques to embrace honourable conditions of peace,
which may preserve their religion, and other just interests ; in pursuance thereof in the twentieth of his reign,
granted unto the said Earle of Glamorgan, the tenour
whereof is as followeth, viz. CHARLES R.—Charles,
by the grace of God, king of England, Scotland, France,
and Ireland, defender of the faith, &c. To our right
trusty and well-beloved cousin, Edward Earle of Glamorgan, greeting. Wee, reposing great and especiall
trust and confidence in your approved wisdome and fidelity, doe by these (as firmly as under our great seal,
to all intents and purpose) authorize and give you power
to treat and conclude with the confederate Roman Ca-

tholiques in our kingdome of Ireland, if upon necessitie
anything be to be condescended unto, wherein our lord
lieutenant cannot so well be seen in, as not fit for us
at this present publicly to owne, and therefore we charge
you to proceed according to this our warrant, with all
possible secrecies; and for whatsoever you shall engage
yourself, upon such valuable considerations, as you in
your judgment shall deeme fit, we promise in the word
of a king and a Christian, to ratifie and performe the
same that shall be granted by you, and under your hand
and seal, the said confederate Catholiques having by
their supplyes testified their zeal to our service : and
this shall bee in each particular to you a sufficient warrant.   Given at our court at Oxon, under our signet,
and royall signature, the twelfth day of March, in the
twentieth year of our reigne, 1644.   To our right truly
and well-beloved cousin, Edward Earle of Glamorgan.
It is therefore granted, accorded, and agreed, by and
between the said Earle of Glamorgan, for and on the
behalf of his most excellent majesty, his heirs and successors on the one part, and the Right Honourable
Richard Lord Viscount Mountgarret, lord president of
the supreme council of the said confederate Catholiques,
and the said Donnogh, Lord Viscount Muskery, Alex.
Mac Donnell, and Nicholas Plunket, Esquires ; Sir
Robert Talbot, Baronet ; Dermid O'Brian, Jo. Dillon ;
Patr. Darcy, and Jeffrey Browne, Esquires ; commissioners in that behalf appointed, by the said confederate
Roman Catholique subjects of Ireland, for and in the
behalf of the said confederate Roman Catholiques of the
other part, in manner following, that is to say :
"That an act shall be passed in the next parliament
to be held in this kingdome; the tenour and purport
whereof shall be as followeth, viz. An act for the relief of his majesties Catholique subjects of his highnesse
kingdome of Ireland. Whereas by an act made in parliament held in Dublin, in the second year of the reigne
of the late Queene Elizabeth, intituled, an act for restoring to the crown the antient jurisdiction over the
state ecclesiasticall and spirituall, and abolish all for-
raigne power repugnant to the same, and by another
statute made in the said last mentioned parliament, intituled, an act for the uniformity of common prayer and

service in the church, and the administration of the sacraments, sundry mulcts, penalties, restraints, and incapacities, are and have been laid upon the professors of the Roman Catholique religion in this kingdome, in and for, and concerning the use, profession, and exercise of their religion, and their functions therein, to the great prejudice, trouble, and disquiet of the Roman Catholiques in their liberties and estates, to the general disturbance of the whole kingdome; for remedy whereof, and for the better feeling, increase, and continuance of the peace, unity, and tranquillity of this kingdome of Ireland, his majesty at the humble suit and request of the lords and commons in this present parliament assembled, is graciously pleased, that it may be enacted, and bee it enacted by the kings most excellent majesty, the lords spirituall and temporall, and commons in this present parliament assembled, and by authority of the same, that from, of, and after the first day of this session of parliament, it shall and may be lawfull to, and for all the professors of the Roman Catholique religion, of what degree, condition or quality soever, to have and enjoy the free and publike exercise and profession of the said Roman Catholique religion, and of their severall and respective functions therein, without incurring any mulct and penalty whatsoever, or being subject to any restraint or incapacity concerning the same, any article, clause, sentence, or provision in the said last mentioned act of parliament, or in any other act or acts of parliament, ordinances, law or usage to the contrary in anywise notwithstanding. And be it also further enacted, that neither the said statutes, or any other statute, act, or ordinance heretofore made in your majestics raigne, or in any the raigne of any of your highnesse most noble progenitors or ancestors, and now of force in this kingdome, nor all, nor any branch, article, clause, and sentence in them, or any of them contained and expressed shall be of force and validity in this realme, to extend to be construed or adjudged to extend in anywise to enquiet, prejudice, vexe or molest the professors of the said Roman Catholique religion, in their persons, lands, hereditaments, or goods, for anything, matter, or cause whatsoever touching, and concerning the free and publique use, exercise and enjoying of their sayd religion,

function, and profession. And be it also further enacted
and declared by the authority aforesaid that your majesties Roman Catholique subjects in the said realme
of Ireland from the first day of this session of parliament
shall be and be taken, deemed, and adjudged capable of
all offices of trust, and advancement, places, degrees, and
dignities, and preferments whatsoever within your said
realme of Ireland, any act, statute, usage or law, to
the contrary notwithstanding. And that other acts shall
be passed in the said parliament, according to the tenour
of such agreement or concessions as herein are expressed,
and that in the meantime the said Roman Catholique
subjects, and every of them shall enjoy the full freedom,
benefit, and advantage of the said agreement or concessions and of every of them.

"It is accorded, granted, and agreed by the said earle,
for and on the behalfe of his majesty, his heirs and successors: that his Ex. the Lord Marques of Ormond, lord
lieutenant of Ireland, or any other or others authorized
by his majesty, shall not disturbe the professors of the
Roman Catholique religion in their present possession,
and continuance of the possession of their said churches,
jurisdiction or any other the matters aforesaid in these
articles agreed and consented unto by the said E. untill
his majesties pleasure be signified for confirming and
publishing the grounds and agreements hereby articled
for, and condiscended unto by the said earle. And the
said earle of Glamorgam doth hereby ingage his majesties royall and publique faith unto all and singular the
professors of the said Roman Catholique religion within
the said kingdome of Ireland, for the due observance
and performance of all and every the articles, grounds
and clauses, herein contained, and the concessions
herein mentioned to be performed to them.

"It is accorded and agreed that the publique faith of
the kingdome shall be engaged unto the said earle by
the said confederate Catholiques for sending 10,000 men
to serve his majesty by order and publique declaration
of the generall assembly now sitting: and the supreme
councell of the said confederate Catholiques shall engage themselves to bring the said number of men armed,
the one-half with musketts, and the other half with
pikes, unto any port within this realme within the elec-

tion of the said earle, and at such time as he shall appoint to be by him shipped and transported to serve his majesty in England, Wales, or Scotland, under the command of the said Earle of Glamorgan, as lord generall of the said army : which army is to be kept together in one entire body, and all other the said officers and commanders of the said army are to be named by the supreme councell of the said confederate Catholiques, or by such others as the severall assembly of the said confederate Catholiques of this kingdome shall entrust therewith. In witness whereof the parties of these presents have hereunto enterchangeably put their hands and seals the 25th day of August, 1645.

" GLAMORGAN.

" *Copia vera collata fideliter originali,*
   Thomas Cashell, P. Partricius,
   Waterford and Lismore."

Digby denied the authenticity of the document—and asserted that it was either forged or surreptitiously obtained. In a tone of indignation which subsequent events must prove to have been affected, and without a particle of sincerity, he told the commissioners that their offer of the subsidies, on the terms which they proposed, should be scornfully rejected. "And for my part," continued he, "sooner than counsel his majesty to accept your assistance on the terms which you have made with Glamorgan, I would sacrifice the lives of my wife and children. Go back to Kilkenny, and inform the president of the federative assembly that the Protestants of England would fling the king's person out at his window, if they believed it possible that he lent himself to such an undertaking." *

When the commissioners returned with this strange intelligence, consternation and amaze seized every one who heard it. At the time there were but few of the confederates in the city; the rest were spending the Christmas holidays in their homes, and anxiously awaiting the result which, they fancied, would restore peace to Ireland, and leave them free to succour the unfortu-

nate king. The nuncio immediately summoned as
many of them as he could collect, for the purpose of
ascertaining what was to be done in such a critical
emergency. All of them protested vehemently against
the injury which was inflicted on Glamorgan; and some
were of opinion that they ought to march on Dublin,
and demand his liberation from an unjust imprisonment,
which they regarded as an insult put upon themselves.
Far from regarding Glamorgan's powers as fictitious,
they avowed their belief that he had been commissioned
by the king to treat with them, and that the conditions
on which they had agreed could not but be pleasing to
his majesty, as they stipulated nothing which they had
not a right to demand. Five of the confederates waited
on the nuncio in his own house, to learn from him what
supplies he could give in case they came to a resolution
to besiege Dublin (an enterprise which he anxiously desired); but on hearing from him that he could not give
an exact account of the money till his agent, Invernizi,
had returned from Flanders, where he was sent to purchase some frigates, their ardour began to cool. Mountgarret and Muskerry gave a different version of the arrest, and, in their overweening estimate of Ormond's
probity, sought to screen him from any suspicion which
might reflect on his honour and loyalty. But, notwithstanding the palliation which they offered for the conduct
of the lord lieutenant, a great number of the confederates were for active measures, and were fully satisfied
with the answer they subsequently received from the
nuncio, who asserted that at the time he could take
upon himself the expenses that might be incurred by a
campaign in any one of the provinces, if they could
assure him that it would tend to bring about a peace on
the conditions which they had already made.

Nothing could be more acceptable to the prelates and
people than this proposal. They had long since lost all
respect for the promises of Ormond; but that section of
the confederacy which called itself the Ormondist party,
fearing that they might be involved in a war, laboured
against the popular feeling, and pressed their resolution
to have the whole matter submitted to the general
assembly.

This resolution had not the concurrence of the

prelates or the people, for although the truce with
Ormond could not expire till the 17th of January, they
regarded the recent transactions as justificatory of an
infraction. But there were, of the confederates, some
who did not hesitate to avow that, in case of hostility,
the marquess would make terms with the parliamentarians, and turn all his powers against the assembly.
Whether this might have been the case or not, certain
it is that if they had resolved to advance on Dublin,
it could not have stood a siege of eight days, open as it
was to attack, and the castle without means of holding out
against a vigorous effort.* Meanwhile, the nuncio wrote
to the English queen and Cardinal Mazarin, informing
them of Glamorgan's arrest, and deploring the state of
insecurity into which the artifices of Ormond had drawn
the Irish people. In his letter to Henrietta Maria, he
assured her of the devotedness of the Irish Catholics to
the interests of the king, and lamented the interruption
which the expedition under the command of Glamorgan had met, by reason of his incarceration.

According to their resolutions, the assembly of the
confederate Catholics met at Kilkenny early in January.
The prelates and clergy approached the meeting with a
feeling against Ormond, which was only embittered by
his recent proceedings; and, now that Glamorgan's
peace had been set aside, they calculated on terms to be.
proposed by the lord lieutenant, to which their oath
of association, and the sweat and toil of five years in
the cause of Catholicity, forbade their assent.

Their first act was to write to Ormond threatening to
suspend all further negotiation, if the Earl of Glamorgan was not immediately freed from arrest. The
release of the prisoner, they said, was absolutely necessary for the relief of Chester. Three thousand men
were ready to embark,† and only waited the transports;
all was at a stand by his imprisonment, and further
delay compromised the king. Sir Robert Talbot was

* At this moment Ormond was in concert with Munroe in the north,
and in great want of provisions. The castle, which at that time was
the principal magazine of Ireland, had not arms or food to resist a
siege.—*Rinuccini's Corresp.*

† These troops had been drawn out of the armies in the three
provinces.

sent by the confederates to second this letter, and on
the 22nd of January an order was given for his being
bailed upon £40,000 sterling, security, given by the
Earl of Kildare and the Marquess of Clanricarde. He
was also bound to appear before the board within thirty
days after notice. Nor need it be wondered at that
Ormond could thus dismiss the man whom he impeached of high treason, for he was a party to the
collusion, and professed himself quite satisfied with
Glamorgan's commission, which had subjoined to it
*a defeasance** or *starting hole*, stipulating that the king
should be no further bound than he himself might
think fit, after he had witnessed the efforts of the Irish
Catholics in his favour. Nothing can be more clear
than that the whole transaction was meant as a blind
for the English Protestants, and a delusive hope for the
Irish Catholics.

On his release, Glamorgan proceeded to Kilkenny,
where he was received by the assembly. Far from
resenting the treatment he had received from Ormond,
he praised and extolled his conduct, declaring that,
under the circumstances, he could not have acted
otherwise.

But these professions were far from satisfying the
nuncio and the prelates. They immediately concluded
that there was something fraudulent in the transaction,
and determined to receive any proposition, which Glamorgan might advance, with greater caution for the
future.

The assembly was now unhappily divided into two
parties. The clergy were obstinately opposed to any
peace which did not secure the free and open exercise of
the Catholic religion. Their oath of association, they
asserted, bound them to identify the interests of religion
with the support of the king : nor would they accede to
any terms which did not stipulate the restoration of all
the cathedral and parochial churches with the revenues
which had been wrested from them by "the reforma-
tion."

On the other hand, the lords and gentlemen of the
Pale insisted on a peace, which, committing this import-

---

* The nuncio seems to have been ignorant of this defeasance.

ant question to the ulterior decision of the king, would
leave them free to succour him immediately. This expedient, they contended, was a sufficient security for the
church, and the only means of effectually uniting the
Protestant loyalists with the Catholics. They contended,
moreover, that the articles of Glamorgan's private
treaty (provided it was a *bona fide* transaction) were
ample, and in every respect satisfactory. But the recent
imprisonment of the earl had shaken the confidence of
the clergy, and they regarded the devotion of Muskerry and Mountgarret to the interests of Ormond as the
necessary consequences of their connexion with him.
So generally did this feeling of distrust pervade the
popular class, that Emerus, bishop of Clogher, was
obliged to write to the Ulster chieftains, rebuking their
adherents for having come to a determination not to join
the troops intended to be sent to Chester. *

The division which now reigned in the assembly was
nothing less than the reflex of the popular feeling. The
old nobility, slighted by Ormond, and excluded from any
participation in the management of the treaty, had identified themselves with the clergy, and preferred all the
horrors of civil war to what they termed an ignominious
peace. The nobility and gentry of the Pale were chiefly
concerned for the security of their temporalities and the
toleration of their religion, beside which they had nothing in common with the indigenous population. So
deeply rooted was the aversion of the latter to the king's
representative, that they hailed the nuncio's arrival as
that of a general who was to raise the pontifical standard, and lead them against Ormond and the puritans,
whom they identified in hostility to their creed and
country.† It required no trifling labour, on the part of
the nuncio, to remove the erroneous impression under
which they laboured. It was industriously circulated
that he came to make the pope protector of Ireland; and
deep as was their sense of loyalty, they required no sti-
mulus to shake off a yoke which misrule and tyranny
had rendered intolerable. False, however, as it was,

* Vindiciæ Hibernorum. p. 77.
♦ Amongst others, Clarendon.

the impression had been made, not by Rinuccini, but by
his enemies; for any such overture on his part would
have been in direct opposition to the court of Rome,
which was far more interested for the unfortunate
Charles than those who propagated the slander.

But the mod ate party was determined to conclude
with Ormond, and in order to swell the number of their
votes, they caused ex officio members to be elected to
the council. This informality, however, could not
produce the desired effect, for the clergy were determined, if they could not prevent the publication, a'
least to have it postponed.

They contended that Glamorgan's treaty was not to
be depended on, as it contained no positive guarantee
for its fulfilment. All his promises were dependent on
two contingencies; the good will of a capricious
monarch, and his ability to realize them. Moreover,
Glamorgan could not now be regarded as an agent free
to treat on behalf of his majesty, inasmuch as he was
bound to appear before the council board within thirty
days after notice, so that they knew not how soon he
might be summoned, and be obliged to leave the treaty
without the royal sanction.

On the other side it was as vehemently argued that
the Marquess of Ormond's powers to treat with the
confederates, should terminate on the first of April,
and in case they could not conclude with him, the king
might revoke his commission, and thus deprive the
country of such a valuable acquisition. They were
empowered to state, on the lord lieutenant's behalf, that
if the treaty was concluded, he would join with the
confederates in expelling the Puritans, and the Marquess
of Clanricarde would come to their aid. A more
urgent argument advanced by the Ormondist party was,
that if, instead of a peace, they only made a truce, the
soldiers who were destined to proceed to Chester, might
refuse to march, fearing that on landing they might be
treated as rebels by the royal troops.

But these arguments were strenuously combated by
the clergy. They insisted that it was easy for the
Marquess of Ormond to procure a renewal of his patent,
nor could they conceive how the royal troops could
at the Irish soldiers as rebels, without injuring the

royal cause. The three thousand who were now ready to march and embark, were but an instalment of the ten for which Glamorgan had stipulated, and it was not within the range of probabilities that they would be maltreated by the royalists, as such conduct on their part would clearly prevent the rest from setting foot in England or Wales.

Whilst these discussions were pending, an incident occurred which was calculated to confirm the clergy in their opposition to Ormond's peace. The nuncio produced letters from Rome which had been despatched early in November, informing him that a treaty was about to be concluded between the pope and the queen* of England, on behalf of the Irish Catholics. Sir Kenelm Digby, the queen's agent at the papal court, had been fully empowered to make terms for the Irish Catholics, which having received the approval of the head of the church, could not but be highly advantageous and honourable. The treaty, which was so materially to benefit them, included the English Catholics, and should of course rouse them to more strenuous efforts in the king's cause. Glamorgan, in order to give more weight to this argument, asserted that whilst he was detained in custody, Digby informed him that in case the holy see advanced an annual sum for the king's support, his majesty would extend the benefit of the pontifical treaty to the English Catholics.†

It would appear that the president of the confederates had been notified of the proceedings at Rome; but, as if attaching little or no importance to them, he did not divulge the intelligence to the council.

Muskerry and Mountgarret affected to believe that this negotiation was nothing but a fiction, and meant to delay the publication of the peace with Ormond. Ley-

---

* At this moment there was a memorial sent to the queen by Col. Fitzwilliam, praying her majesty to vouchsafe to prevail with his majesty to condescend to the just demands of his Irish subjects, the confederate Catholics, at least in private, and the colonel undertook to bring an army of 10,000 men or more into England. He required that he should be appointed commander-in-chief, &c., with a month's pay in advance for the men on their landing. The queen expressed her satisfaction, but the money was not forthcoming.—*Borlase*, 155.
† Rinuccini, 96.

burn* denounced it as non-existent, and was sharply re-
buked by the nuncio, and the general feeling of the
laity in the assembly was, that such a negotiation on the
part of the queen consort, herself unauthorized, was nu-
gatory and futile.

Notwithstanding this acrimonious controversy, the
nuncio induced the bishops to sign an agreement, by
which they bound themselves to accept no other terms
but what were stipulated in the pontifical treaty. He
at the same time caused Glamorgan to avow that he
would not any further pursue his own private treaty,
but insist on the new project as more conducive to the
king's welfare and that of the Catholics of Ireland.—
The argument of the nuncio was, that it did not become
a true son of the church to put his own peace in compe-
tition with that approved by the pope; and he therefore
should wait for the original from Rome.

On the 7th of February the nuncio addressed the
council, extolling the queen's negotiation with his holiness,
who had already contributed a considerable sum to Sir
Kenelm Digby for the maintenance of the king. He
produced the heads of the treaty which had not as yet
been signed, and expatiated on the good-will which the
pope entertained for the English Catholics, evidencing
the fact by the offer which his holiness had made of con-
tributing annually one hundred thousand crowns for the
maintenance of the royal troops, till the king, in a free
parliament, would be able to repeal all the penal laws
against the English Catholics. On the word of a prince
he assured them that the conclusion of these articles
might be hourly expected, as it was probable that Sir
Kenelm Digby was already on his way.

But nothing could abate the eagerness of Lord

---

* This Dr. Leyburn was an Englishman, and one of the queen's
chaplains. He may be said to have been the leader of a small faction
of the clergy who opposed the nuncio's views. This faction consisted
of Walsh and a few others, whom the nuncio represents as preaching
this slavish doctrine :—"The Jewish people were years without
a Temple—Our Lord instituted the eucharistic sacrifice in a private
domicile; why, therefore, should the Catholics insist on the restitution
of their temples ?" The real state of the case, however, was simply
this :—Rinuccini was determined, in due time, to enforce the monastic
rule in all its rigour, and erratic spirits like Walsh's and Caron's
dreaded the observances to which it would have bound them.—*V. Rin.*

Ormond's adherents for the peace. For fully five days
the assembly had more the appearance of a conclave
concerned with abstract speculations, than real practical
measures, and it was not till the fifteenth of the month
that Glamorgan succeeded in appointing seven of the
confederates to confer with the nuncio "for removing
mistakes and reconciling differences."

On the 18th Glamorgan signed an instrument in
which he ratified the articles between the queen and
the pope, and undertook that they should be confirmed
by the king, provided that, if the original articles of
that treaty arrived by the first of May, the said
instrument was to be void; and in the mean time to be
kept secret, unless the political articles of the peace
with the lord lieutenant should be published before.
In order to put an end to the debate, a convention
was signed on the eighteenth, between the nuncio and
the seven deputies, whereby it was stipulated "to continue the cessation till May the 1st, in expectation of
the original of the pope's treaty, and then the nuncio
should ratify what he and Glamorgan would agree on,
that there might be no further delay of an honourable
peace." But this should be no obstruction to the confederates treating with Ormond about political matters,
provided they came to no conclusion or publication of
articles, nor proceeded to any alteration of the civil
government, nor did anything to the prejudice of the
transaction between Glamorgan and the nuncio.*

Glamorgan, who was now more urgent than ever for
the immediate relief of Chester, took an oath that he
would stand by the nuncio against all opposers of the
pope's treaty, and the nuncio's measures for the good of
religion, and the service of the king—for which end he
promised to procure from France a supply of ships,
arms, and money, which were to be placed at the
disposal of the confederates. This was given under his
hand and seal the 19th of February. Two days afterwards the nuncio came to the assembly, exhorting them
to adopt vigorous measures against the parliamentarians,
and promising them a peace within two months. More
than two months had now been consumed in these

* Carte. i. 565.

debates, and it was not till the 28th of March that **the** articles of Ormond's treaty were signed by the marquess, on the king's behalf; and the Lord Muskerry, Sir Robert Talbot, John Dillon, Patrick D'Arcy, and Geoffrey Browne, on the part of the confederates. At the same time with these articles was signed a conditional obligation, whereby the confederates engaged to transport 10,000 foot into England or Wales; 6,000 by April 1st, and 4,000 by May 1st, following; and till the men were shipped, the articles were to be deposited in the hands of Clanricarde, and not to be of force or published till the 1st of May, nor then, unless upon sending of the men. And in case the above-mentioned forces were not sent (unless hindered by reasonable cause, allowed as such by the Marquess of Ormond), the articles were to be of no effect, and their counterparts returned to the respective parties.

The following is an abbreviate of the articles :—

1. " That the professors of the Roman Catholick religion in the kingdom of Ireland, or any of them, be not bound or obliged to take the oath of supremacy, expressed in the second of Queen Elizabeth, commonly called the oath of supremacy.

2. "That a parliament may be held on or before the last day of November next; and that these articles agreed on, may be transmitted into England, according to the usual form, and passed, provided that nothing may be passed to the prejudice of either Protestant or Catholick party, other than such things as upon this treaty shall be concluded.

3. " That all acts made by both or either houses of parliament, to the blemish or prejudice of his majesties Roman Catholick subjects, since the 7th of August, 1641, shall be vacated by acts of parliament.

4. " That no actions of law shall be removed before the said parliament, in case it be sooner called than the last of November; and that all impediments which may hinder the Roman Catholicks to sit in the next parliament, shall be removed before the parliament sit.

5. " That all debts do stand in state, as they were in the beginning of these troubles.

6. " That the plantation in Connaught, Kilkenny Clare, Thomond, Tipperary, Limrick, and Wicklo

may be revoked by act of parliament, and their estates secured in the next sessions.

7. "That the natives may erect one or more inns of court in or near the city of Dublin, they taking an oath; as also one or more universities, to be governed as his majesty shall appoint; as also to have schools for education of youth in the kingdom.

8. "That places of command, of forts, castles, garrisons, towns, and other places of importance, and all places of honour, profit, and trust, shall be conferred with equal indifferency upon the Catholicks, as his majesties other subjects, according to their respective merits and abilities.

9. "That £12,000 sterling be paid the king yearly, for the court of wards.

10. "That no peer may be capable of more proxies than two. And that no lords vote in parliament, unless, in five years, a lord baron purchase in Ireland £200 per annum, a viscount £400, and an earl £600, or lose their votes till they purchase. ·

11. "That the independency of the parliament of Ireland on the kingdom of England shall be decided by declaration of both houses, agreeable to the laws of the kingdom of Ireland.

12. "That the council table shall contain itself within its bounds in handling matters of state, as patents of plantations, offices, &c., and not meddle with matter betwixt party and party.

13. "That all acts concerning staple or native commodities of this kingdom shall be repealed, except wooll and woollfels; and that the commissioners, the Lord Mountgarret, and others, named in the twenty-sixth article, shall be authorized, under the great seal, to moderate and ascertain the rates of merchandize to be exported and imported.

14. "That no governor be longer resident than his majesty shall find for the good of his people, and that they make no purchase, other than by lease, for the provision of their houses.

15. "That an act of oblivion may be passed, without extending to any who will not accept of this peace.

16. "That no governor, or any other prime minister

of state in Ireland, shall be farmers of his majesties customs.

17. "That a repeal of all monopolies be passed.

18. "That commissioners be appointed to regulate the court of castle-chamber.

19. "That acts prohibiting plowing by horse tails, and burning of oats in straw, be repealed.*

20. "That course be taken against the disobedience of the cessation and peace.

21. "That such graces as were promised by his majesty in the fourth year of his reign, and sued for by a committee of both houses of parliament, and not expressed in these articles, may, in the next ensuing parliament, be desired of his majesty.

22. "That maritime causes be determined here, without appeal into England.

23 "That the increase of rents lately raised upon the commission of defective titles be repealed.

24. "That all interests of money due by way of debt, mortgage, or otherwise, and not yet satisfied since the 23d of October, 1641, to pay no more than £5 per cent.

25. "That the commissioners have power to determine all cases within their quarters, until the perfection of these articles by parliament, and raise 10,000 men for his majesty.

26. "That the Lord Mountgarret, Muskerry, Sir Daniel O'Bryan, Sir Lucas Dillon, Nicholas Plunket, Richard Bealing, Philip Mac Hugh O'Relie, Terlogh O'Neal, Thomas Flemming, Patrick Darcy, Gerald Fennel, and Jeffery Brown, or any five of them, be for the present commissioners of the peace, Oyer and Terminer, and gaol-delivery, in the present quarters of the confederate Catholicks ; with power of justise of peace, Oyer and Terminer and gaol-delivery, as in former times of peace they have usually had.

27. "That none of the Roman Catholick party, before there be a settlement by parliament, sue, implead, or arrest, or be sued, impleaded, or arrested, in any court, other than before the commissioners, or in the

---

* This article needs some explanation, as it is hard to reconcile such barbarous usages with a period so *enlightened.*

several corporations or other judicatures within their quarters.

28. "That the confederate Catholicks continue in their possessions until settlement by parliament, and to be commanded by his majesties chief governour, with the advice and consent of the commissioners, or any five of them.

29. "That all customs, from the perfection of these articles, are to be paid into his majesties receipt, and to his use; as also all rent due at Easter next, till a full settlement of parliament.

30. "That the commissioners of Oyer and Terminer, and gaol-delivery, shall have power to hear and determine all offences committed or done, or to be committed or done, from the 15th day of September, 1643, until the first day of the next parliament."

Such was the result of these negotiations by which the Catholics of Ireland were left in the strange condition of an alliance with the king through his private agent, and of suspended hostility through his lord lieutenant.

It has been asserted by Clarendon, that the nuncio consented to the treaty which was now concluded with Ormond; but that assertion is not founded on fact. He steadily opposed it; and early in February caused the bishops to sign a protest against any treaty which did not guarantee the free exercise of religion, and the restoration of the church property, as well as the appointment of a Catholic lord lieutenant to succeed Ormond. In fact, he could not, with any degree of consistency, have assented to that peace; for, of its thirty articles, the only one which touched the question of religion is the first, by which it was agreed "That the professors of the Roman Catholic religion in this kingdom of Ireland be not bound to take the oath of supremacy expressed in the second of Queen Elizabeth," whilst the vital subject was remitted to the consideration of his majesty.

The meeting of the general assembly, before breaking up, passed two resolutions, which tended much to expedite business and remove abuses. By the first it was determined, that for the future the supreme council should be reduced to nine members; that is to say, each province was to return two, who, with the secretary

made nine. This was found to be matter of great advantage, as much inconvenience was the result of the
great number who sat in their former assemblies. The
second resolution ordained that the clergy should furnish, through their own hands, two-thirds of the church
revenues for the maintenance of the war, as many frauds
had resulted from a system which, in this particular,
needed much reform.

The supreme council remained at Kilkenny, and the
nuncio, seconded by the bishops, set about remedying
the deplorable state to which the country had been reduced by armistices, and the jealousies which were fo-
mented by the contending parties. The adherents of
Ormond, more intent on sending supplies to England
than securing themselves, had sadly neglected the military affairs of Ireland. The time which they consumed
disputing in their cabals, had been turned to good account by Munroe in the north, and the parliamentary
lord president in Connaught. Rinuccini urged the supreme council to establish a military tribunal, to which
all the generals and officers commanding the confederate
troops should be amenable. Hitherto the commanders,
as well as inferior officers, had been elected by their respective provinces. Clanricarde remained neutral, and
the nuncio indulged a hope of drawing him into the
confederacy. · In fact, the neutrality of Lord Clanricarde was his reason for not presenting him with a bull
which he had brought from Rome. In the person of the
Archbishop of Tuam the confederates experienced a
great loss, and the record which the nuncio has left of
his character, cannot but be pleasing. "This prelate,"
says he, "when proceeding to Sligo took leave of his
friends, quoting some old prophecies concerning the
church over which he presided, (in sooth, the people of this country are much given to predictions,) and
stating that he was destined to return no more. When
surrounded by his enemies, he boldly declared that he
rejoiced to lay down his life for religion; and gloriously
has he closed the period of his labours, which have ere
now procured him a reward in heaven."[*]

After the bishop's death, the command devolved on

* Rinuccini Nunziatura, p. 69.

the heroic Bourke; and it was resolved that he should not be removed. Preston, who commanded in Leinster, was far from being high in the esteem of the nuncio.— Although an experienced soldier, he had not much love for the representatives of the "old Irish." He was a man of whimsical character, and full of all the prejudices which the Catholics of the Pale had ever nourished for their Celtic brethren. Alternately swayed by his attachment to Ormond and his love for the Catholic religion, he did not possess those attributes which belong to a man of bold and decided views. His hatred of Owen Roe was another cause of the nuncio's distrust; for although O'Neill and Preston had served from early youth under the same standard, there existed the most rancorous hatred between them. O'Neill despised the Leinster general, and he in return did not fail, on all occasions, to depreciate and ridicule his rival. Strange that at such a time these feelings of jealousy and mutual hatred should have existed!* The province of Ulster was overrun by the Scotch; and, as we have already stated, the rival pretensions of Owen Roe and Sir Phelim had done incalculable mischief. Indeed, nothing short of the delegated majesty of Rome could have brought about a reconciliation.†

Munster was almost entirely in the hands of Inchiquin, and the defection of Thomond aggravated the misfortunes of that province. Castlehaven, in the recent campaign, had not acted with spirit, and, in complaisance to Ormond, did not press the siege of Youghal; the fortress of Duncannon had been totally neglected : and, although it commanded the entrance to Wexford and Ross, the bickerings of the confederates did not give them time to garrison or strengthen it.

Rinuccini bitterly inveighed against this state of things, and charged the supreme council with indifference to matters of such mighty moment. But the spring had now come, and he resolved to strike a blow which was calculated to convince the Irish that they

---

* Sir Phelim O'Neill was married to Preston's daughter. Henry, the son of Owen Roe, was married to the daughter of Luke Fitzgerald, and was slain in the year 1655, in the north, after quarter given. —*Morrison's Threnodia.*

† *V.* Aiazzi, p. 136.

should place more reliance on their own swords and
energies than on the delusive promises of a king " who
had nothing of faith or generosity in him." *   Before
distributing the arms and money which he had caused
to be brought to Kilkenny, the nuncio submitted his
plan of a campaign to the council.   He inclined to make
Ulster the seat of war, for the following reasons:—
First—Its vicinity to Scotland gave easy access to the
enemy.   Secondly—The devotion of its inhabitants to
the Catholic religion was more fervent and sincere than
that of the other provinces.   It was now the granary of
Munroe, who was continually detaching parties of his
marauders into Connaught.   But the more powerful
reason was the superior generalship of Owen Roe, who
confessedly surpassed all the others in military knowledge.

Moreover, it was easy to supply the wants of the men
who were now crowding round his standard.   "The
soldiers of Ulster," says he, "and, in some parts, those
of Connaught, naturally accustomed to suffering, and
habituated to the frosts of that northern climate, have
few wishes and few wants.   Caring but little for bread,
they live upon shamrock and butter.   Their drink is
milk, and, as a great luxury, usquebaugh.   Provided
they have shoes and a few utensils, a woollen cloak
serves for their covering, more zealously careful of their
sword and musket than of their personal comfort.   They
seldom touch money, and therefore complain but little
about it." †   In the latter respect they stood in strange
contrast with the Leinster troops under Preston, for
they served for pay, which was regulated according to the
Flemish standard.

Muskerry and Mountgarret did not relish the nuncio's
partiality for the men of Ulster; nor were they roused
to a sense of the dangers which threatened that province, till the fugitives who were driven before Munroe's
bands took shelter under the walls of Kilkenny, and
foreshadowed the fate which menaced themselves, if not
speedily averted.

Moved by these considerations, the nuncio made up

---

* Lucy Hutchinson's Memoirs of her Husband, p. 66.
† Ainzzi, p. 339.   Vide *Dublin Review*, June, 1844.

his mind to give the entire of the supplies to the army under Owen Roe. But, to prevent the ill-feeling which he was told should result, he consented, however reluctantly, to bestow two-thirds of the arms, ammunition, and money on General Preston. The council, moreover, voted £3,000 to Ormond, on a proviso that he would immediately march into the east of Ulster, and operate against the Scotch.

Clanricarde, alarmed at the advance of Coote, consented to take the field in his province; and, in the absence of an enemy in Leinster, Preston was commanded to proceed and act under him. Muskerry, whose military acquirements were not of a grand order, was to proceed to Munster, and recover the castles delivered by Thomond to the parliament, and, if possible, to overwhelm Inchiquin.

The nuncio had already sent one of his retinue to report on the state of the fortress of Duncannon; and, when informed of its immediate wants, he obliged Preston to look after its defence. Many and bitter have been the reproaches cast on the head of Rinuccini; but, nevertheless, it must be admitted, that he sought to convince the Irish that they had within themselves resources which, if properly directed, might have insured success. To use his own sentiment, he found them "dazzled by the splendour of England, and chilled by the shadow of her greatness." If he failed in every other respect, does he not deserve some praise for having striven to teach the confederates that they might have obscured that glittering despotism which had so long and so fearfully ground them?

Of all these arrangements, nothing gave the nuncio greater satisfaction than the settlement of the question between Sir Phelim O'Neill and his great kinsman. "The generous reconciliation" which had been effected through him gave promise of some grand result. In a spirit savouring of the prophetic, he announced to the assembly that Ulster should soon be rid of its invaders, and the cathedral of Armagh restored to the ancient worship. There was nothing wanting to perfect these plans, but the presence of Invernizi, with the light vessels which were meant to cruise along the coast, and intercept the supplies which the parliament was sending to their adherents in the seaport towns.

Nor was the solicitude of the nuncio and the confederates for the king's relief in the least diminished by the more urgent exigencies of Ireland. By order of the supreme council 4,000 men were drawn out of the standing armies of Leinster and Munster, and 2,000 more out of the other provinces, and a day was appointed for their embarkation at Passage, in the county of Waterford. An order was issued for levying four thousand more, who were to be transported into England as soon as possible. That the troops might be sent without delay, an embargo was laid on all vessels in the river of Waterford and in the harbours of Wexford and Dungarvan.

But when everything promised fair, intelligence was brought to Glamorgan that the king had disavowed him as far back as the 29th of January; and soon after came the news of the capture of Chester by the parliament. There was now no place for the Irish to land on the coast of England, and the men returned to Clonmel and Cashel. Three hundred of them followed Lord Digby, to form a body-guard for the Prince of Wales, who was said to have taken refuge in Jersey; and a larger body sailed for Scotland, to assist Montrose, under whom they performed prodigies of valour.

Rinuccini did not conceal his feelings on this occasion; for, although he grieved over the king's losses, he was heartily rejoiced that those troops were not sent out of Ireland, where their services were so much required. Moreover, such a force could be of little avail to Charles, now that his enemies were in the ascendant; and supposing that the Irish troops had effected a landing in England or Wales, without cavalry to cover them, or strong places to receive them, their destruction must have been inevitable, for, by an act passed in October, 1644, it was ordered "that no quarter should be given to any Irishman, or papist born in Ireland."

Of the 300 men who accompanied Digby, 100 were left to garrison Scilly, and facilitate the communication between Ireland and the Continent; and it was now thought that the remainder would return with the Prince of Wales to Ireland; but the prince's advisers objecting 'o such a step, he fled to the queen at Paris, whither he was soon followed by Digby, who had left the Irish soldiers to shift for themselves. Digby was received by the queen with the most flattering assurances of regard for himself and Ormond. He exaggerated the anxiety of his colleague for the king's welfare, and deprecated the "absurd pretensions" * of the Irish Catholics, who would not accede to the lord lieutenant's terms. An active partisan of Ormond, and a virulent opponent of the just claims of the Irish Catholics, he represented them in the falsest light, and succeeded in getting from Cardinal Mazarin the sum of 10,000 pistoles, "to enable the Marquess of Ormond to satisfy his Protestant officers, and displace those whom he had cause to distrust." The queen. who was averse to the prince's landing in Ireland, promised a supply of further sums, and, at the same time, declared that she would never suffer Sir Kenelm Digby "to hearken to anything on the subject of the pontifical treaty with Ireland, as the business of that kingdom was already in those hands that were best able to manage it, and that whatsoever was sought for should not be expected from any one but the lord lieutenant." †

The promise made to the nuncio of waiting till the 1st of May for the arrival of Sir Kenelm Digby, who had not come, caused the commissioners, when they signed the peace on the 28th of March, to agree that it should lie as an *escroll* in the hands of Clanricarde, till they had sent the 10,000 men into England, and it should be thought proper to proclaim the peace ; but now that that time had elapsed, the supreme council instructed Plunket to repair to Dublin, in order to convince Ormond of the impossibility of sending the forces for which they stipulated. Mr. Plunket was charged to desire the lord lieutenant to declare his judgment of such impossibility in writing, according to the proviso in the defeasance. He was likewise instructed to declare the necessity of the union of the entire nation ; and, if the present publication of the articles of peace was necessary for that pur-

---

* Such has ever been the whining tone of men like Curry, and others, who, yielding to expediency, overlooked the grand principle of justice and right.

Carte's Orm.

pose, to show that they could not avoid publishing, at
the same time, the articles with Glamorgan, for fear of a
rupture among themselves, and to prevent the stopping
of foreign supplies; but in case his excellency did not
think the present the fitting moment to proclaim the
peace, Mr. Plunket was to beseech him to act as a peer
of the realm in the meditated attack on the Scots.

The occasion of the latter instruction was, that Sir
Charles Coote, with the Laggan forces, had penetrated
into the counties of Roscommon and Galway, with the
intention of bringing supplies into Thomond, for the
relief of Bunratty. But fearing that the attempt might
fail, the parliamentarian general contented himself with
burning the crops about Portumna and Loughrea, and
then returned to his quarters with large preys of corn
and cattle.

Irritated by the rapacity, and the wanton butchery
of Coote, Clanricarde appealed to Ormond for redress,
and called on him to proclaim Sir Charles and his
adherents traitors and rebels. There was no palliation
for their guilt, but Ormond urged that the council
would not consent to such a proposal, as the most of
them, and he in particular, were far from wishing to
offend the parliament and the faction in England.
Strange fact! The man whose exuberant loyalty
would have prompted him to proclaim the Catholics,
was squeamish and punctilious in all matters which
might lessen his fame in the eyes of Cromwell's myrmidons. He had an object to attain with the avowed
enemies of the king; and the confederates, according to
him, were not to be trusted. But the secret of Ormond's
craft and intrigue was simply this: by proclaiming
Coote he would have openly declared war against the
parliament, and obliged himself to act against the faction
in unison with the confederates, and the overthrow of
the Puritans must, of necessity, have strengthened the
hands of the Catholics, and made their demands irresistible. Ormond would perish sooner than concede,
and he well knew that the ruin of the Catholic body
should be productive of immense advantages to his own
aggrandisement.

Thus, when it was expected that Ormond would
take the field against the Scots, as he had promised,

when the federative assembly had voted him three thousand pounds for the purpose; they clearly perceived that he had no such intention, and that his real object was to delude and deceive them. He was now informed that the king had placed himself in the hands of the Scots at Newark. The intelligence reached him about the 19th of May, and he dismissed the commissioners to the committee of instruction at Limerick, with assurances that they should soon hear from him by persons whom he would send to them fully authorised and instructed for that purpose. Thus, for the present, was the publication of the peace postponed.

Ormond had played his part adroitly, and won his game. The king was now at the mercy of the Scots; "they were the greatest opposers of the Irish peace, having all along entertained hopes that Ireland should be given up to them,"[*] and come what might of the king, Ormond had done nothing to compromise himself, with his majesty's enemies. That the king was in reality desirous of a peace, is evident from his letter of the 25th of April, wherein he expressed the desire; but if proof were wanting, it is to be found in Clanricarde's communication to Ormond, telling him that his excellency was satisfied that such was his majesty's avowed wish.[†] During these negotiations the nuncio was anxiously awaiting the articles of the pontifical treaty, and had to labour hard to convince the adherents of Ormond that it might be speedily expected. He sent to Rome to remonstrate against the delay, and to his mortification, was informed by the Cardinal Barberini, that Sir K. Digby was at Paris with the queen, and that in the event of concluding with her, he would proceed to Rome instead of hastening to Ireland.[‡]

It was now determined that the cessation should continue till June, and the nuncio, accompanied by some members of the supreme council, proceeded to Limerick about the middle of May.

The troops which were to have proceeded to England under the command of Glamorgan, had been unsuccessfully employed to reduce Bunratty castle since April.

---

* Carte's Ormond, vol. iii.
† This letter is dated the 3rd of June following
‡ Rin. 123.

He had marched at the head of three thousand men from Limerick to Six-mile Bridge, where he pitched his camp, and proceeded to invest the fortress, which had been garrisoned and provisioned by the parliament forces. By a vigorous sally from the garrison, he was beaten off and driven to the walls of Limerick, and then retired on Clonmel. Rinuccini caused the Earl to be superseded by Lord Muskerry, and accompanied the army in a second assault on this stronghold, which, after a close siege of twelve days, surrendered to the confederates. This was his first essay in military tactics, and the speedy reduction of the place was mainly attributable to him. Immediately after the surrender of Bunratty he caused the captured banners to be borne in triumph to Limerick, and the effect produced by the display was to exalt him in the esteem of the popular party.

Inchiquin, maddened by the advance of the confederate army, was burning the crops and inflicting the most heart-rending barbarities on the peasantry of Munster, and the supreme council solicited Castlehaven who had been a spectator of the operations against Bunratty, to take command of their cavalry and march against him. He reluctantly accepted the command, for he was not disposed to offend Ormond who was far from being pleased with the success of the confederates, and he proceeded to Cloghnoftye, "on the mountain that runs between the counties of Cork and Limerick," and found himself at the head of one thousand horse. Mac Thomas was his second in command, and having divided their whole force into squadrons, they hung on the flanks and rear of Inchiquin, and finally prevented the destruction of the crops by compelling him to retire to his garrisons. *

Whilst the confederates were gaining these advantages in the south, Sir Charles Coote was perpetrating the most wanton barbarities in the west, and this notwithstanding the cessation. It was in vain that Clanricarde expostulated with Ormond, and required him to proclaim this sanguinary man, who under the title of lord president of Connaught, was carrying death and havoc throughout the province. But Ormond was in treaty

* Castlehaven's Mem. 65.

with Coote, "in full assurance to make advantage of it,"* and would neither proclaim the parliamentarian lord president, nor march against his colleagues in Ulster.

Preston, who ha l consented to act under Clanricarde, had entered the province at the head of about three thousand men. He calculated on exciting the peasantry against the Scotch, and recovering Sligo. But he did not receive that cordial co-operation from Clanricarde which he was led to expect, and the result of a month's campaign was the capture of the Castles of Roscommon and Clunibrun, which capitulated after he had cut to ieces 350 of their horse. But if the confederates were not crowned with success against Coote in Connaught, and Inchiquin in the south, they had reason to congratulate themselves on the victory which was won by Owen Roe in Ulster. Brilliant as was the career of the grand nephew of Hugh O'Neill on the continent, he never did so highly distinguish himself as in that province where his ancestors ruled as kings. Munroe had been supplied with monies and ammunition by the parliament commissioners, and calculated on beating O'Neill's army if it again appeared in the field, but dreadful was the retaliation which was in store for the Covenanter.

The main body of O'Neill's army had already assembled on the confines of Leinster, and having heard that Robert Munroe was marching into Tyrone, he resolved to go in quest of him. Having given orders that each soldier should carry with him provisions for sixteen days, he commenced his march, and advanced sixty miles into the interior of Ulster. On the 2nd of June, Munroe, informed of O'Neill's onward march, called a council of war and determined "to make to the fields with a month's provisions." "This movement," says Munroe, "was necessary for the preservation of our quarters." † The Scotch general had ten regiments of infantry, and fifteen companies of foot, followed by fifteen hundred waggons containing ammunition, and baggage with six fielding-pieces. Colonel Munroe was ordered to join the general (Robert) at Glasslough with three troops of horse, and 240 musquetiers, whilst Auchinbreck's troops were to follow in the rear of his columns. The English

* Carte's Orm. lii. 463.   † Munroe's Despatch.

commissioners had engaged with the Scotch general to send the Laggan forces into Connaught to intercept any supplies which might be sent from that province to the aid of the confederate troops, and maintain a communication with the Scots in Ulster. Having promised to comply with all the orders of the parliamentary commissioners, Munroe took leave of them on the second night of his march near Dromore.

On the morning of the 4th of June, he ordered seventy-two horsemen, under the command of his lieutenant, Daniel, to cross the Blackwater at Beinburb and scour the fields, and certify Colonel Munroe that he would fix his head-quarters at Glasslough. On the 5th of June, this body of cavalry fell in with a party of O'Neill's skirmishers, and took a prisoner near Armagh, from whom they learned that the confederate general had encamped the night before at Glasslough, and was marching in full force with an army of 5,000 foot and twelve troops of horse, to take up a position at Beinburb and Charlemont. Being thus informed, Munroe broke up his camp, and marched six miles further, to make a junction with Hamilton's troops, which were encamped four miles from Armagh, and at the same time ordered messengers to recall the cavalry, which he had sent to advertise Colonel Munroe of his movements.

Meanwhile O'Neill had encamped at Beinburb, between two small hills. The rear of his army was protected by a wood, and the right by the river Blackwater. He had also possessed himself of the bridge, and concealed his sharpshooters in the "scrogs and bushes."[*] Owen Roe was well informed of Munroe's plans; and in order to prevent a junction of George's forces with those of his brother, he despatched Colonels Bernard Mac Mahon and Patrick Mac Neny, with their respective regiments, to anticipate their design. This commission they executed to the satisfaction of their commander. But now, when everything that the ablest general of his day could devise to insure a glorious result had been carried into effect, there was a scene on the hill of Beinburb solemn and stern.—"The whole army, after having confessed, and the general, along with the other officers,

[*] Munroe's Derpatch, in the Thorpe Papers, R.D.S.

having received the most holy communion, the chaplain, deputed by the nuncio to the spiritual care of the army, made a brief exhortation, gave them his blessing, and, with loud cheers, they prepared for action."*

Munroe, having reconnoitred O'Neill's position, and seeing that he could not force the bridge or ford, convened his officers, to consult on what course they should adopt; whereon it was resolved to march in view of the confederate troops, and pass the Blackwater at Kinard. As they advanced they were met by Colonel Richard O'Ferral, who occupied a narrow defile through which it was necessary for the Scotch troops to pass in order to face the Irish. The fire of Munroe's guns compelled O'Neill's officer to retire. And now the two armies stood front to front; and never did two hostile hosts meet with more enthusiastic rivalry or deadly hatred. The Scots, impelled by gloomy fanaticism, beheld an army of idolaters before them—the Philistines, whom the power of Gideon was to overthrow. The confederates, animated by the love of country and their religion, and led by a chieftain whose name was a spell-word in their ranks, looked on the present as the moment to rescue their homes and altars from thraldom and disgrace. "All our army, horse and foot," says the Scotch general, "did earnestly covet fighting, which was impossible for me to gainstand without reproach of cowardice, and never did I see a greater confidence than was amongst us."

Lieutenant-Colonel Cunningham having cleared the pass for the Scotch horse, who were commanded by the Lord Viscount of Ardes, in the absence of Colonel Munroe, the whole army advanced to dislodge Owen Roe; but a shower of bullets from the " scrogs and bushes," which covered O'Neill's infantry, checked them; and then the Scotch cannon opened its fire with little effect, as owing to the admirable position of the Catholic troops only one man was struck by the shot. In vain did Munroe's cavalry charge—with the river on their right and "a marish bog" on the left, it was hopeless to think of stirring the confederates. For fully four hours did the Fabius of his country amuse the enemy with

* Rinuccini.

skirmishing. During all that time, the wind rolling the smoke of Munroe's musketry and cannon in the face of the Irish ranks, concealed the adverse lines from their sight, and the sun had shone all day in their eyes, blinding them with its dazzling glare; but that sun was now descending and producing the same effect on the Scotch, when Munroe perceived the entire of the Irish army making ready for a general assault with horse and foot.

It was the decisive moment. The Irish general, throwing himself into the midst of his men, and pointing out to them that retreat must be fatal to the enemy, ordered them to pursue vigorously, assuring them of victory. "I myself," said he, "with the aid of heaven, will lead the way: let those who fail to follow me remember that they abandon their general." This address was received with one unanimous shout by the army. The colonels threw themselves from their horses, to cut themselves off from every chance of retreat, and "charged with incredible impetuosity." *

Munroe had given orders to a squadron of his horse to break through the columns of the Irish foot as they advanced; but that squadron was panic-stricken by the terrible array of the Irish battalions, and retreated disorderly through their own foot, pursued by O'Neill's cavalry. Nevertheless Munroe's infantry stood firm, and "received the Irish, body to body, with push of pike," † till at last their cavalry reserve, being routed in a second charge, fell, pell mell, amongst his infantry, which, being now broken and disordered, had no way to retreat but over the river which lay in their front.

Terrified by the fate of their fellows, who perished under their eyes in the Blackwater, the surviving Scots vainly sought to conceal themselves in the thickets that covered the country in the vicinity of the battle-field; nor was the darkness of the night able to protect them from their victorious pursuers. Pike and skein did what the musket had left unfinished, till they were cut to pieces, and the lowest soldier of the Irish was wearied with carnage, and oppressed with plunder. Three thousand two hundred and forty-three bodies were counted on the field; the infantry was completely cut

---

* Munroe's Despatch.   † Rinuccini.

off by the straggling parties on the two following days;
and very few of the cavalry escaped.   All the guns
were taken by the Irish, together with the tents,
colours, baggage, and fifteen hundred draught horses.
Amongst the slain was found the body of Lord Blaney.
The Lord Viscount Ardes was made prisoner.   Munroe
fled to Lisnegarvy, leaving his cloak and wig on the
field, and twenty-one officers in the hands of O'Neill's
army.   Of the Irish troops only seventy were slain in
the action, and one hundred wounded, amongst whom
was a distinguished gentleman of Ulster, who served as
a volunteer.   The victorious army proclaimed that their
success was attributable to the supplies given them by
the Pope; and Sir Phelim O'Neill, on being asked for the
list of his prisoners, swore that he had not even one, as
he had given orders to his division to give no quarter
to the Scotch. *

The news of Owen Roe's victory did not reach Limerick till the 13th of June.   Father Hartegan, one of the
priests deputed to the spiritual care of the army, was
the bearer of the joyful intelligence.

On the following day (Sunday) at four o'clock, a.m.
all the troops in garrison at Limerick assembled before
the church of St. Francis, where the nuncio had
deposited thirty-two standards taken by the Irish
general from the Scotch.   These trophies were then
borne in solemn procession by the chiefs of the nobility,
followed by the nuncio, the Archbishop of Cashel, and
the bishops of Limerick, Clonfert, and Ardfert.   After
these came the supreme council, the mayor, and the
magistrates, with the entire population of the city.   The
procession moved on till it reached St. Mary's cathedral,
where the Te Deum was chanted, and on the next day
a mass of thanksgiving was offered to the Lord, " Who
fought among the valiant ones, and overthrew the
nations that were assembled against them, to destroy
the sanctuary."†

Thus, while the Irish attributed the winning of that
day to the interposition of heaven, the Scotch general,
writing from Carrickfergus, on the 11th of June, to the
parliament commissioners, ascribed his defeat to the

---

* Rinuccini, 138, 139.   † Vide Ep. Inn. P. in *Hib. Dom.*

anger of "the Lord of hosts, who had a controversy with
them, to rub shame on their faces till once they should be
humbled ; for it behooved them to taste of bitterness, as
well as others of both nations."* Yet, it does not appear
that O'Neill made that use of his victory which he might
had he commanded an army as disciplined as his people
were brave. Instead of pursuing Munroe he allowed him
to fortify himself in Carrickfergus, whence he wrote to
London for supplies, "Now that they were humbled before God, and increased in courage and resolution, and that
the enemy had not prosecuted their victory within the
Scotch quarters, being more inclined to spoil than pursue
them." His appeal was soon responded to by the parliament, and a paper was printed, and posted in the streets
of London, giving an account of "the bloody fight at
Blackwater, on the 5th of June, by the Irish rebels against
Major-General Munroe, where 5,000 Protestants were put
to the sword."† O'Neill's army now increased to upwards
of 10,000 men, as he found on the field, arms and am-
munion sufficient to equip the new levies that flocked to
him from all quarters. Rinuccini sent to congratulate
him on his victory, and transmitted decorations for his
officers, and surgeons to take charge of the wounded.
On the return of his messengers he was somewhat surprised to learn that O'Neill had determined to call
his troops the "Catholic Army," and emblazon the
cross and keys on the banners of the red hand." It
was an ill-timed testimony of his homage to the church,
for, it was calculated to create division between himself and Preston, whenever their mutual co-operation
might be required. But the phlegmatic disposition of the
Ulster general could ill brook contradiction. Yet, if
the victory at Beinburb had not all the fruits which
might have been reaped from that bloody harvest, it
secured the existence of the confederates.‡ On the

---

* Munroe's Dispatch,
  † This document, printed by Jane Coe, London, June 15th, gives
the following list :—"Taken, seven pieces of ordnance, 5,000 armes.
4,000 foot, and upwards, killed, taken, and routed. 600 horse routed.
Lord Blaney taken, and dead; Lord Montgomery and Lord Ardes
taken and dead, and almost all the officers."
  ‡ Nunziatura in Irlanda, p. 138.

person of Lord Montgomery was found the order of
march, and he himself declared that it was the intention of Munroe to penetrate to Kilkenny whilst the
confederates were employed elsewhere, and make himself master of that city; nor is it at all unlikely that
Ormond was privy to the design.

On the 2nd of June, whilst the nuncio was pressing
the siege of Bunratty, Sir George Hamilton and Colonel
Barry were sent by the lord lieutenant to Limerick, to
acquaint the confederate council that he was well
aware of the necessity of a union against the common
enemy, but that he could not join with any party not
deriving authority from his majesty; nor could anything further be done towards a union till the articles
of peace were published, about which he had not, as
yet, received his majesty's pleasure. With regard to
Glamorgan's articles, he could not, either with safety
to his conscience or honour, admit the publishing thereof,
"his majesty having already publicly disavowed any
power given by him to warrant them;" for which
reason he expected from them a declaration of their
resolution not to publish them.

It was now obvious that Muskerry and his party were
anxious to publish the political articles concluded on the
28th March, and, if possible, to publish at the same time
the articles of Glamorgan's treaty; but, when Nicholas
Plunket and Brown presented themselves to Rinuccini
to notify him of their intention of proceeding to Dublin
for that purpose, he produced the protest of the nine
bishops against any conclusion with Ormond which
did not stipulate the free exercise of religion, and the
retention of all the churches, which, up to the present
moment, were in the hands of the confederates. The
production of this protest, as it was signed without the
knowledge of the lay members of the assembly, alarmed
and confounded the commissioners. They urged that
Glamorgan's articles were sufficient to satisfy the clergy,
and that they would insist on the publication of them.
Rinuccini scouted the idea, pointing to the king's dis-
avowal of the Earl, and then warmly inveighed against
the folly of committing themselves, soul and body, to
Ormond, at a moment when they stood in the attitude

of armed men, who should enforce their rights instead of craving favours.

When the confederate commissioners received this answer, they communicated with the council, who immediately sent eight of their body, and the secretary, Belling, to induce the nuncio to consent to the publication of the political treaty. The grand argument adduced for the purpose was, that the king, as he was now in the hands of the Scotch, would be induced to make war on Ireland, than which nothing was more desired by the parliament. They sought, moreover, to convince him that the publication of the political articles should be regarded as a means to an end, rather than a definitive agreement with the lord lieutenant ; and that they themselves would be ready to take arms against Ormond, if, in progress of time, he did not cede all the advantages which they contemplated for religion.

But these arguments were unavailing. The nuncio was unbending. In a spirit which had something prophetic in it, he implored them not to rely on the promises of Ormond or the sovereign of England. He appealed to the history of the past, and dwelt at length on the tyranny and oppression exercised by the English in Ireland, and chided the pusillanimity of the men who were intent on signing an instrument which doomed them to dependence on the pleasure of a treacherous and faith-breaking monarch. Glamorgan was present on this occasion, and laboured to refute a singular argument advanced by the confederate commissioners, who asserted that the laws of England did not permit the monarch to revoke the concessions which he had once made in favor of the Catholics.[*]

But the earl put an end to the discussion by declaring that he would no longer insist on the publication of his own treaty, until he had received further powers from the king.

Nevertheless, the supreme council determined to publish the articles of Ormond's peace, and. to gratify the lord lieutenant, agreed to omit all mention of Glamorgan's concessions. These instructions were signed in

* Rinuccini, 142

the 12th of June, and Sir Nicholas Plunket and Mr. Brown were deputed to proceed forthwith to Dublin. Before leaving Limerick they waited on the nuncio, who, when informed of their intention, received them coldly, and inveighed bitterly against a proceeding which was meant to put Ormond in possession of all the garrisons and strongholds belonging to the confederates, and thus compromise their own existence. His words had such effect on Plunket that he took ill, and Brown was obliged to go without him. When he arrived in Dublin he was mortified to learn from Ormond that, by a letter from Newcastle, his majesty had ordered him " to proceed no further in the treaty of peace, nor to engage him upon conditions with the Irish after sight of those orders." This letter was sent through the English committee of Ulster to Ormond, on the 26th of June, and Brown at once returned to Limerick to receive further instructions. Alas! it is pitiful to reflect on the temporising and vacillating conduct of the Catholics of the Pale at this moment. With three armies in the field, and the people roused to enthusiasm, such as had never been witnessed, they wasted, in intrigue and diplomacy, more time than was sufficient to raise themselves to a position of independence.

Whilst the vollied thunders of Beinburb were still pealing in their ears, they were clamorous for Ormond's hollow peace. Apprehensive of losing the church property, of which many of them were proprietors, they were now jealous and distrustful of the clergy, although the nuncio was empowered to confirm the transfers, as Cardinal Pole had done in the reign of Mary. O'Neill's victory served to embitter their inveterate and deep-rooted hatred of the Ulster Irish. They were well aware that no provision had been made for "the men of the north," and that they would never consent to lay down their arms till restored to their plundered estates.

These considerations determined Muskerry and Mountgarret and the rest to place all their hopes in Ormond, who would secure them in the possession of their estates, and connive at the *toleration* of the Catholic religion. They were satisfied to live in fetters, provided they were not butchered by legal enactments against their persons and creed. Alas! how sadly did they contrast with the "old Irish," who, scorning to live as aliens in their native land, had determined to perish in the assertion of their just rights.

Tired of delay, the nuncio wrote to Rome in the middle of June, declaring that, as Sir Kenelm Digby had not come with the articles of the pontifical treaty,[*] his means of preventing the publication of the peace with Ormond were utterly exhausted. He clearly told the cardinal secretary of state that a foreign protectorate was desired by many amongst the Irish, and that O'Neill and Preston had offered to march on Dublin, and take possession of the city, as it was easy to foresee that, in case of pressure from without, Ormond would surrender it to the parliament. He, at the same time, wrote to Henrietta Maria and Cardinal Mazarin, imploring them to expedite the treaty, and thus prevent the disruption of parties and the total loss of the country.

But Sir Kenelm never came. Some imprudent expressions in Rinuccini's letters, betrayed by the nuncio at the French court to the English queen, awakened her suspicion ; and it would appear that she had determined to abandon any further negotiation with Sir Kenelm Digby and the court of Rome.

Yet, strange to say, even in his captivity the unfortunate Charles did not abandon hope of succour from Ireland. With that systematic duplicity which characterized his actions, he wrote to Glamorgan, telling him to raise money by pawning his kingdoms, which he would repay if ever he won them back. "And tell the nuncio," said he, "that if I once come into his and your hands, which ought to be wished for by you, both for the sake of England as Ireland, since all the rest despise me, I will do it ; and if I do not say this from my heart, may God never restore me to my kingdoms in this world, nor give me eternal happiness in the next." This letter he sent to Glamorgan. At the same moment he wrote to Ormond, through Lord Digby, that "he should

---

* It is now notorious that the heads of this treaty were already drawn up. Those who assert that there was no such treaty may find it either in Rinuccini's Nunziatura or in the Transactions of Glamorgan.

not proceed any further in the treaty of peace with the Irish."

Ormond was fully satisfied in his own mind that the king was desirous of peace on any terms ; but well knowing that the council in Dublin was averse to any overture which might assist the monarch, he catered to their feelings, and contented himself with saying, that he would carry out to the very letter the instructions he had received from the king at Newcastle.

Mr. Brown had not reached Limerick when George, Lord Digby, arrived in Dublin on the 4th of July. He affected surprise on learning that the articles of peace had not been perfected, as his majesty, " since his being at Newcastle, had redoubled his positive orders to the lord lieutenant for the speedy conclusion of the peace, upon dispensation with the condition of the confederate Catholics of Ireland sending the men undertaken for them."

Digby immediately wrote to Ormond that the Scots had violated all their promises to the king, depriving him of liberty, and banishing from him all who were in his confidence. He then proceeded to show that the letter dated Newcastle was either surreptitiously obtained or a manifest forgery, but in every respect most contrary to what he knew to be his majesty's free resolution and uncontrolled will." He concluded by declaring that, if the peace were any longer interrupted, "the hinderers of it would be the occasion of subverting the main foundation resolved and laid by his majesty for the recovery of his crown and posterity's rights, whether by way of accommodation or war."

On the 28th of the same month, Digby drew up and signed a declaration, wherein he offered himself to be detained a prisoner until such time as his majesty should be at liberty to express freely his unconstrained will; and then, says the declaration, " if his majesty shall not justify me to have declared it faithfully, I submit myself to suffer death; and I desire that this declaration be entered in the council-book, that I have discharged my duty, in case the mischiefs here set down shall be occasioned by deferring the peace of this kingdom upon the aforesaid letter of the 11th of June." The council at Dublin seemed to attach little importance to Digby

nor were their objections removed, till Ormond entered
another declaration on the council-book, stating "that
he was satisfied that he had full authority to conclude
the peace upon the articles deposited with the Marquess
of Clanricarde," and took upon himself to be sole judge
thereof, expecting only their assistance for causing it to
be duly observed.

The articles were finally delivered by both parties on the 29th of July: those of the confederates by
Lord Muskerry, Sir Robert Talbot, John Dillon, Patrick
D'Arcy, and Geoffry Brown, in the presence of Lords
Clanricarde, Digby and Taaffe, Daniel O'Neill, and De
Moulin, the French envoy. The council, on the same
day, ordered a proclamation to be issued ratifying the
articles of peace, and enjoining all persons to pay due
obedience to the same.

Thus did Ormond triumph. The confederation was
virtually dissolved. The grand object for which the Catholics had taken up arms was referred to the ulterior
decision of the king. The only concession in the treaty
touching the vital question of religion released the Irish
Catholics from taking the oath of supremacy. No provision was made for the plundered inhabitants of the
north, who had been ruined by the Scotch and English
undertakers; and as if to cap the climax of their folly,
it was agreed by the Lords Mountgarret and Muskerry,
that the "confederate Catholics should be commanded
by his majesty's chief governor until settlement by act
of parliament." It was a base desertion of principle,
this surrender of their rights; but, in this betrayal of
trust, do we not see something typical of that parricida,
act by which, in after times, a corrupt and venal senate
sacrificed the country to the imperialism of England?

On the 1st of August the peace was solemnly proclaimed in Dublin, although the Protestants showed the
greatest aversion to it.* On the 6th the Marquess of
Ormond sent Dr. Roberts, Ulster-king-at-arms, to proclaim it at Waterford and Kilkenny. He executed his
office at Kilkenny, Fethard, Callan, and Cashel; but
was absolutely hunted from the towns of Waterford and
Clonmel.

* Orm. vol. II. p. 10.

On the 20th the Ulster-king-at-arms arrived in Limerick, and, attended by the mayor in his regalia, proceeded to publish the peace. But so indignant were the people that they assembled at the market-cross, headed by Alderman Fanning, and Lynch the warden of Galway, and prevented the proclamation. Such was the popular feeling that they removed the mayor from office and elected Fanning in his stead.*

It would be idle to imagine that this peace gave satisfaction to the people of Ireland. On the contrary, it was soon ascertained that it gave them no guarantee for these rights which aroused them to take up arms and maintain a war of five years' duration. It was indignantly rejected by the whole province of Ulster, the cities of Waterford, Limerick, Clonmel, and Dungarvan. Twenty of the great Irish families in the province of Munster, signed a protest against it. Galway, with twelve noblemen and gentlemen, refused to receive it and in the province of Leinster it was treated with contempt by all the heads of the "old Irish."† It was a fearful moment for Ireland. The wily policy of Ormond had accomplished his designs. Divisons reigned in the council of the confederates; and the bishops and clergy, headed by the nuncio, determined to convoke a synod at Waterford, to submit the treaty, clause by clause, to their consideration. O'Neill, at the head of his victorious army, was pursuing the Scots when the intelligence of the peace reached him at Tanderagee. Preston was at Birr; and, concluding that the treaty had the approbation of all parties, caused rejoicings to be made in his camp.

But he soon found his mistake, when he learned that O'Neill's troops were marching in haste to the borders of Leinster, and thereon sent to express his regrets for the misunderstanding.

It has been constantly argued that Owen Roe was solicited by the nuncio to relinquish the prosecution of his victory after the battle of Beinburb, and move his army to protect the assembly at Waterford, and silence

* Fanning perished heroically, being taken by Ireton after the siege of Limerick, and hung for his intrepidity against the Cromwellians.
† *Vide* Hib. Dom. ad Supp. 1. 878.

all opposition to their resolutions. This, however, is
not substantially true, for O'Neill, without the order of
the confederate council, had increased his forces to
10,000 men, with more than 1000 horse, and desired
nothing so much as an opportunity of taking signal
vengeance on the adherents of Ormond, by whom he
supposed he had been excluded from the possession of
his estates in Ulster. Actuated by such feelings, he
did not await any summons from the nuncio, but
marched at the moment when he heard of the peace,
well knowing that the bishops and clergy would not
respect it. His intention was to sack Kilkenny, and he
would, doubtless, have carried his design into effect,
had he not been dissuaded by Rinuccini from shedding
innocent blood.* His troops, however, were now self-
styled "The Catholic Army," and Owen Roe proclaimed
himself the right arm of the clergy.

The synod of the bishops and clergy met at Waterford, on the 6th of August. It was composed of three
archbishops, ten bishops, five abbots, two vicars
apostolic, fourteen representatives of the religious
orders, and the provincial of the Jesuits.† They were
all unanimous in their abhorrence of the peace, and on
the 12th of the same month, they issued the following
decree "from the congregation of the secular and regular
clergy convened at Waterford on the 6th of August:"

"As to the question between us moved, and for many
days discussed, whether such as would accept of that
peace contained in the thirty articles remitted unto us
from the supreme council, are to be declared perjurious,
and consequently, whether as perjurious, they are to be
excommunicated; we having given ear to each one's
opinion and sentiment on this matter, as also having
read the writings of some doctors of divinity, it is
decreed, and by each one's vote in particular, (none
contradicting), that all and every one of the confederate
Catholics that will adhere to such a peace, and consent
to the furtherers thereof, or in any other manner or
way will embrace the same, shall be absolutely as per-

* Rinuccini, p. 224.
† The Archbishop of Cashel seems to have doubted the expediency
of Rinuccini's measures, but finally acquiesced, saying,—"In verbo
tuo lazabo rete."

jurious esteemed, chiefly inasmuch as there is no mention made in the thirty articles, nor promise for the
Catholic religion or safety thereof, nor any respect had
for the preservation of the kingdom's privileges as were
promised in the oath of association, but on the contrary, all remitted to the king's will and pleasure,
(from whom as the case stands at present with his
majesty) no certainty of benefits can be had or expected;
yet, in the mean time, all the arms, armies, fortifications, even the very supreme council of the Catholic
confederates are to be subjected to the authority and
rule of his majesty's council of state, from whom that
we might be secure we have taken that oath.

"Out of which, and several other reasons, we (moved
thereunto by conscience) would have it known, to all
and each person, as well the Irish natives as the foreign
nations, that we gave no consent, nor never will, to any
such peace, if they will not grant us further, surer, and
safer conditions for our religion, our king, and country,
according to our oath of association.

"And to the end, our flocks and all the confederate
Catholics, who in their general assemblies required our
sentence in this spiritual matter appertaining to ourselves as ecclesiastical judges, may know for certain
what is by us determined herein, and as godly and
faithful Catholics, obeying their pastors, may concur
with us, we have ordered this decree to be written, and
published everywhere in the English and Irish tongue.
Given under our hand and seal, Waterford, this 12th day
of August, 1646,—NICHOLAS FRENCH, *Chancellor*."[*]

The result of this decree may readily be imagined;
never was there a more decided reaction. The people
unanimously rejected the peace; nothing could have
given more pleasure to the general of the Ulster forces
than this declaration of the bishops; and Preston, who
had been vacillating hitherto, fearing the censures and
hating the secretary, Belling, at once declared for the
nuncio and the clergy.

Shut up in Kilkenny, whither they had gone after
the publication, Muskerry and Mountgarret, with the

---

[*] I have given this from the "Unkind Deserter," as it is probably the
transcript of the original.   I.

other councillors, prepared an appeal from the censures, and sent to Waterford to persuade the clergy to adopt some other course less objectionable to their patron Ormond. But, in this instance, they discovered their own weakness, and found out, when too late, that the power which they possessed when leagued with the hierarchy, had forsaken them. The confederate soldiers positively refused to obey them; and when the deputies returned from Waterford with word that Rinuccini and the bishops insisted on the appointment of Preston as general of the horse, and O'Neill as major-general of the army, they sent for Ormond to come to Kilkenny, in the hope that his presence might create a diversion in their favour.*

Ormond eagerly embraced the proposal, and sent some persons to treat with O'Neill, and, if possible, gain him over to the peace. But the Ulster general spurned the overtures of the lord lieutenant, and sent him back an indignant refusal. The nuncio had forwarded him at this time a sum of about £9,000 which had been borrowed from Diego della Torre, the Spanish envoy.

Ormond, however, set out from Dublin on the 28th of August, with 1,500 foot and 500 horse. He arrived at Kilkenny on the 31st of the same month, and was joyfully received by his adherents; but great was his mortification on learning that the troops which were drawn into the city after the siege of Bunratty, had gone over to the party of the nuncio and clergy at Waterford. From Kilkenny the lord lieutenant, accompanied by Clanricarde and Lord Digby, proceeded into Munster, foolishly thinking that he might conciliate Inchiquin, and prevail on him to join his forces with those of his own party against the troops of O'Neill; but in his progress through the country Ormond had ample evidence of the popular disinclination to submit to him on the terms of the Dublin treaty. Many of the towns shut their gates at his approach, and the mayor of Cashel sent to implore that he would not enter that city, as Owen O'Neill, who had encamped on the 9th of September at Roscrea, had sent to inform the magis-

* Carte, I. 579

trates, that if they received the lord lieutenant he would
storm the place. Digby's overtures were rejected by
Inchiquin, who, in answer to a letter forwarded to him,
replied, "that the peace now concluded by his majesty's
authority, to the utter ruin of all that profess the
Protestant religion, or submitted thereto, had to all the
world evidenced the just grounds of his separation from
what he (Digby) was pleased to call his duty."*

To add to Ormond's disappointment he had now
learned that Piers Fitzgerald, alias Mac Thomas, who
formerly served under Castlehaven, had collected a
strong body of cavalry and declared for the Waterford
resolutions. Indeed, the Marquess's expedition into
Munster was far from successful, and on the 11th of
September he was informed by Sir Richard Talbot, that
he should take precautions to secure the ford of Moygany,
the only place where he could cross the Barrow without
marching through the counties of Carlow and Kildare
to Munstereven. O'Neill's emissaries were already in
the county of Wicklow raising the O'Byrnes and
O'Tooles, and it was likely that they had been instructed to intercept him if he returned by their country
to Dublin.

Ormond was now apprehensive that O'Neill meditated
some design against his person, and determined to
return to the metropolis. He, therefore, sent Sir Luke
Dillon and Dr. Fennell to the prelates at Waterford,
to state "that he considered his commission for concluding a peace was determined by that which he had
already made, and that if it did not take place, there
was no possibility of renewing a treaty for another,
and was apprehensive that his return to Dublin should
put a stop to all further negotiations."

Having sent this message to Waterford, Castlehaven
came to inform him that he had not a moment to lose,
as Preston and O'Neill were rapidly advancing to cut
him off. Ormond fled to his troops, stationed at Callan,
where they were faced by 400 horse under Mac Thomas.
Thence he dispatched orders to Sir Francis Willoughby,
who was at Gowran, to march with all possible speed
and secure Leighlin Bridge. When the major-general

* Irish Tracts, R.D.S. Thorpe Papers.

came within three miles of the place he was told that Sir Walter Bagnall, with a hundred men, held the fort "at the bridge end," and he thereon sent to know if he might find that officer a friend or enemy, and received an answer, that the pass lay open to him. He crossed the bridge and left a detachment of his men to await Ormond on the Carlow side. Two hours before day the marquess, having joined these troops, fled to Kilcullen, thence to Ballymore-Eustace, and on the 13th entered Dublin, to the surprise of the citizens, who verily believed that he had been made prisoner by O'Neill and Preston. He had reason to be grateful to Bagnall, for if he held the bridge against him for half-an-hour longer he must have fallen into the hands of Owen Roe.

When Ormond was about to return to Dublin, he left Digby at Kilkenny, to learn the result of his negotiation with the bishops at Waterford; and, presuming on his powers, the latter made a proposition that, if the nuncio and three or four of the bishops would consent to the peace, and cause it to be observed by all over whom they had power, and join, under the lord lieutenant, against the common enemy, if they might privately receive a firm assurance of the repeal of the penal laws, and that the Catholic clergy should not be put out and molested in their ecclesiastical possessions before a new parliament was called, the said assurance should be procured them collaterally, severed from the articles of the peace, to which the lord lieutenant had no power to add. But this proposition was rejected, and expediency abandoned. The bishops had no guarantee for the fulfilment of the conditions offered, even were they inclined to receive them; and they feared that in the present, as well as in a former instance, Digby and Ormond could find a "starting hole" whereby the king might escape any obligation, as in the treaty with Glamorgan. When Digby received the refusal, he did not think it safe to remain any longer, and set out for France to solicit arms and monies to crush the men who were now bent on maintaining the independence of Ireland.

The destinies of the country were at this moment in the hands of the clergy and Owen O'Neill. The nuncio, elated with his temporary triumph, sent his dean to Rome, to convey to Pope Innocent the relation of affairs

and procure aids for the prosecution of what he regarded
a glorious crusade against the Puritans.   To give greater
stability to the new confederation, he determined to proceed to Kilkcuny, and establish his head-quarters there.
The way was open for him.   Owen Roe lay encamped
within three miles of the city; his army consisted of
12,000 foot, and 1,500 horse ; his troops were refreshing
themselves, after storming Roscrea Castle, on the 17th
of September.

On his approach to the city Rinuccini was joined by
Preston and Diego della Torre, at the head of the gentry.
He did not now enter as a messenger of peace ; on this
occasion he appeared as a triumphant general, surrounded
by the military, and hailed by the acclamations of the
soldiers. '' The victor of Beinburb'' on one side and
Preston on the other, he had reason to feel proud of his
escort.   But his first act was one of harshness and imprudence.   He no longer thought of conciliation ; and
yielding to the suggestions of Preston, who had a personal dislike to many of the old council, he caused them
to be committed to tne castle of Kilkenny, on the 18th,
the day of his entry.

Colonel Bagnal, who had connived at the escape of
Ormond, and Sir Robert Talbot, were likewise imprisoned ; and of the old council, D'Arcy and Plunket were
the only exceptions to this impolitic proceeding.

The nuncio and clergy now assumed the government
to themselves, and on the 26th, by a solemn decree, appointed a new council, consisting of four bishops and
eight laymen, ordering all the generals to be subject to
their orders, and investing them with the same powers
as the former council.   The unanimous voices of those
who signed the decree at Waterford appointed Rinuccini
to the presidency, intending thus to do greater honor to
the court of Rome, on whose sympathies they were now
to place all reliance.   Never did any event give greater
cause for joy to the chieftains and people of the ''old
jrish'' than this change of the confederate government.
The grand object which engrossed their cares for so many
years, they fancied was now achieved.   He who was now
the head of the government could not feel less interest
for the cause of religious independence than themselves.
Unbending and uncompromising as they knew the nuncio

to be, they no longer feared the craft and fatal influence
of Ormond. Religious as the character of the war had
been, it was now to be doubly more so ;—the moderator
of the council was a minister of the vatican, and the general of the army was the champion of the church.

The enthusiastic devotion with which the Jews honored
their leader, Maccabeus, was not more intense than that
with which the "old Irish" now regarded "Owen Roe."
He it was whose right hand was to restore the temple,
and avert the captivity of the people who had been dispersed.   Heaven, they believed, had nerved the arms of
his soldiers on the day of Beinburb; but now, when they
saw the cross and the keys interwoven on the banners of
the red-hand, they looked on him with a feeling of vene-
ration.

"This age," wrote the nuncio to Pope Innocent X.,
"has never seen so unexpected a change.   I should com-
pare it to the most famous successes in Europe.   The
clergy of Ireland, so much despised by the Ormondists,
were, in the twinkling of an eye, masters of the kingdom.   Generals, officers, and soldiers, strove who should
fight for them; and, at last, the supreme council, deprived of all power, was confounded with amazement to
see all authority devolve on the clergy." *

Muskerry being now removed from the command of
the confederate troops in Munster, Glamorgan was appointed in his stead, and the nuncio wrote to Rome in-
timating that as soon as Ormond was driven out of
Dublin it was the intention of the new council to create
the former lord lieutenant.   The reasons assigned for the
appointment of Glamorgan were the high consideration
in which he was held by the Catholics, and his unflinch-
ing fidelity to Rinuccini's views; moreover, the nuncio
never relinquished his design of sending troops to England, and he thought that he could not commit the
leadership in this affair to any one more seriously concerned for the interests of the king.   The idea of appointing an Irishman to that high post was fraught with
danger, inasmuch as it would have created jealousies
and rivalry, which it was the object of all to avoid, that
the great cause might not sustain any injury from the

* Nunziatura in Irlanda.

conflict of parties. But a stronger reason was founded
on the king's letter from Newcastle, in which he insinuated that he contemplated coming to Ireland and
placing himself in the hands of Glamorgan and the
nuncio.

The new council was to continue in existence till the
next general assembly, and orders were immediately issued for levying troops and raising monies for the maintenance of three armies. For these purposes there was no
lack of compulsory enactments; where the arm of the
flesh failed the spiritual weapon was in readiness;
but neither was required to awaken the energies and
hatred of the Catholic population against Ormond.
The grand object was to seize Dublin, and secure
it against the parliament. It was well known that
Ormond was in concert with them, and anxious to surrender the government to any but the confederates.—
And so desirous was he to secure the city against O'Neill
and Preston, that, on his return from Kilkenny, he set
about repairing the fortifications "from the College to
St. Keven's, and so to St. James's Gate."* The Marchioness of Ormond, with several ladies of quality,
might be seen carrying baskets of earth to the workmen
on the ramparts.†

In fact there could not have been any doubt of Ormond's intentions. By letters published early in September, it was currently stated that the lord lieutenant
"was incensed against the Irish rebels," and that he
had offered to capitulate with the king's enemies. So
sensible was he of the necessity of giving Dublin to
them, and of prosecuting the war in connexion with the
parliament, against the Irish, that Captain Willoughby,
and Captain Wood, two sea captains with whom he
had some overtures, had very good reason to believe that
he would deliver Dublin to them both, and cause to be
delivered the rest of the garrisons in Ireland in his power
to the use of the parliament.

"There are already come from Dublin, and are with
us," says the parliamentarian correspondence, "Quarter-Master Willoughby, Sir Gerald Lowther, and Sir
Jobe Davis, sufficient pledges of the reality of this truth,

* Irish Tracts, R. D. S.　　　　† Carte's Orm.

that the Marquess of Ormond doth really intend to comply with the parliament against the rebels. That he desired fifty barrels of powder to be sent to Dublin to secure it against the Irish, and satisfaction being given by the said gentlemen coming to, and remaining with us, there are twenty barrels sent, and thirty barrels more are to be sent afterwards. It is desired that the supplies of soldiers from Liverpool and Bristol be sent over to Dublin and other parts possessed by Ormond and his party to secure them for the parliament."*

Nor were the confederates ignorant of Ormond's intrigues with the parliamentarians. They knew that Dublin was ill provided against a combined attack. The Wicklow clans were well inclined to swoop down on the city from the south side, and only waited the presence of O'Neill and Preston on the north bank of the Liffey. Within the walls the lord lieutenant could not muster more than 6,000 men, so that to make it tenable against the confederates, with his customary duplicity he invoked the aid of those who were at war with the king to crush the men whom he had the hardihood to designate rebels.

When the confederates were made aware of Ormond's designs, they concluded that further delay was fraught with danger, and they determined to march at once, and if possible save the city before the arrival of the supplies from England. But the rivalry and mutual hatred of Preston and O'Neill, caused them to pause before the armies were marched from their camps. The nuncio had reason to doubt Preston's sincerity. His conduct, whilst acting under Clanricarde in Connaught, was calculated to awaken suspicion in the minds of those who were the avowed enemies of Ormond. A considerable sum, part of the monies brought by Lord Digby from France, had been given to Preston, and this circumstance was of itself sufficient to create fears for the fidelity of the Leinster general.

When, however, it was debated in the council whether Preston should have any share in the siege of Dublin, French, bishop of Ferns, argued that it would not be

---

* Irish Tracts, R.D.S. Extracts of Letters from Chester, and published by order of the Parliament.

politic to exclude the Leinster general from the command of his troops in his own province, and that he should co-operate with O'Neill in the enterprise. Finally, It was concluded that the two generals should have joint command; and the nuncio, who never forgave Preston's rejoicings on the publication of the peace. made him take an oath that he would act faithfully and sincerely in the operations against the city. Preston's heart was not in the cause, and he positively refused to take the oath till the following clause was added, namely, that they would not attack the city without first having sought more ample concessions from the lord lieutenant, and that all their movements should be regulated by his declaration. Long before either of the two armies moved from their cantonments, the Leinster general asserted that he feared O'Neill's design was to attack him, and destroy his troops. The nuncio's partiality for Owen Roe was a cause of perpetual disquiet to him, and if anything were required to confirm it, it was the unequal distribution of the monies, for Rinuccini on the 22nd of December, bestowed 8,000 dollars on O'Neill's forces, when the sum which he gave Preston was only about £150.

The two armies marched from their respective quarters at the end of October. The united forces amounted to 16,000 foot and 1,600 horse. O'Neill's troops took Maryborough, Stradbally, Grange, Mellan, and all the strong places in the Queen's County, till he came. to Athy, where he crossed the Barrow, and was joined by the nuncio. Preston, whose route lay through the county Carlow, declined storming the castle of the town, though feebly garrisoned, and lingered on his way to the capital. He complained bitterly that the troops under the command of O'Neill were garrisoning the various strong places which they had seized in the province of Leinster, and gave out that the attempt on Dublin was all but justifiable. From Harristown they continued their march to Nass, and on the 9th of November encamped at Lucan, in order to arrange their plans. There it was agreed that Preston's head quarters should be at Leixlip, and O'Neill's at Newcastle. The winter had set in with unusual rigour, and all the country, for miles around, presented the appearance of a dreary waste. Ormond,

terrified by their approach, at the suggestion of Castlehaven caused the mills to be burned and the crops destroyed. The citizens were dreadfully alarmed, and the
exaggerated reports of the ferocity of O'Neill's creaghts,
determined many of them to embark for England. To
quiet their apprehensions, the lord lieutenant had written to Munroe, in Ulster, to send him aid, and the powder sent by the parliament was looked on as an earnest
of their good feeling to the inhabitants of Dublin. Such
was the weak condition of the defences about the city,
that the inhabitants wondered that the two armies did
not advance and seize it in the broad day; but their
wonder grew more strong, when they beheld from the
battlements of Christ Church, and the high ground
about the castle, two hundred watch-fires blazing in the
night time on the other side of the Liffey.

Where the confederate armies fancied they would find
an abundance of provisions, they now discovered that
the foresight of Ormond had ruined their hopes. A
flood in the Liffey, swollen by the heavy rains, had carried away the bridges, and thus prevented the supplies
from being brought from the county Wicklow. The
rains were succeeded by snow and frost; and from
twenty to thirty of the soldiers, night after night,
perished at their posts.* Indeed, nothing sustained
them, save the hope of good quarters in Dublin, which
they now regarded as in their grasp. But there was a
more deadly enemy within their camps than the storm
which raged without—dissension and fear of each other.
They sent to Ormond, demanding admission of Catholic
troops into Drogheda and Dublin, and a free and public
exercise of the Catholic religion, such as Catholics enjoyed in other countries. Their proposition being regarded as "too scandalous," did not get even a reply
from the lord lieutenant. When they should be up and
stirring against him, the two confederate generals were
taking precautions against each other. O'Neill accused
Preston of intriguing with the lord lieutenant, and meditating a plan which would have put him in a position
to be attacked by Ormond from the city and the Leinster general from his camp. Preston, on the other

* Phìlopater Iræn.

hand, affirmed that he believed O'Neill's design was to
destroy him and cut off his army. The nuncio clearly
saw the impossibility of reconciling the two generals,
and summoned the council to consult whether it was not
best to seize and imprison Preston. The opinions
varied. Some thought it best to inflict that punishment, as all they held dear was jeopardized by the
vacillating conduct of the Leinster general. But, at
an unfortunate moment, it was decided, contrary to the
nuncio's sentiment, that such a course would be fatal.
Under such circumstances, the nuncio deemed it his duty
to prevent bloodshed between the two armies, wisely concluding that the loss of Dublin was inconsiderable, when
compared to the result of a conflict between O'Neill and
Preston. It was a strange sight to see the president of
the council going from camp to camp of the confederate
armies, endeavouring to effect a union between the
respective leaders. But if the fact moves us to pity,
and excites our contempt for the temporizing Preston,
it conveys to us a moral, never too often repeated, that
in union there is hope, and in everything beside reverse
and ruin.

On the 11th of November Clanricarde came to Preston's quarters, and laboured to persuade the nuncio and
council, through him, to sign a peace with Ormond. He
engaged to obtain a repeal of all the penal enactments,
and that the queen and prince should confirm the articles until the king would be at liberty to declare his assent in a free parliament; but the fear of committing
himself to such uncertain conditions, induced the nuncio to withhold his consent. It was evident that Ormond feared the loss of Dublin, else he would not have
commissioned Clanricarde to negotiate with the nuncio,
and the former knew well that every delay on the part
of the confederates added to his chances of holding the
city against them. Contrary to Owen Roe's avowed request, Rinuccini, accompanied by Heber Mac Mahon and
the Bishop of Ferns, visited Preston in his tent, and
vainly sought to induce him to lay aside his apprehensions of O'Neill's good will and sincerity; but the nuncio, perceiving that he could not succeed, charged the
Leinster general with having formed a design to seize
his person, and commit him and the Bishop of Clogher

to the custody of Ormond. Preston did not deny the charge, but merely asserted that he never would consent to the arrest.

They were now fully twelve days before Dublin without having made any attempt on it. Provisions were every day becoming more scarce; and the council was once more summoned to suggest some decisive step. The two generals were present; and one day, while the council was urging an advance, and all were assembled to discuss it, some one knocked at the door of the chamber, and Preston rose suddenly to open it; having heard three or four words from the person without, he returned in a fright, and said the English were already in Dublin. In a moment Owen Roe and the others sprang up from their seats, as if a serpent had stung them,* and, thinking each man of himself, departed from his companions. The generals signalled by cannon fire that every man was to return to his post; and O'Neill having made a bridge of trees and house timber over the Liffey at Leixlip, returned with his troops into Meath, and thence into the Queen's County. This occurrence took place on the 16th, and the next morning the members of the council fled to Kilkenny in the utmost alarm.

The nuncio remained three days at Lucan after the departure of O'Neill; during that time the Marquess of Clanricarde made several propositions, and informed him of the falsehood of the report of any English having landed. The only concession which Ormond authorized Clanricarde to make, was the admission of Preston's troops to garrison Dublin, on condition that they would unite with the troops under Ormond, and compel the council to accept the peace, with the addition of Clanricarde's engagement. The nuncio, however, proposed the free exercise of religion as an indispensable condition, but as Ormond was opposed to the insertion of any such agreement, the negotiation ended in smoke. Preston had accepted Ormond's proposal, and according to his agreement with Clanricarde, a day was appointed on which he was to unite his troops with a detachment led by the latter from the gates of Dublin. But in the mean time the nuncio had expostulated with the

* Nunziatura in Irlanda.

Minster general, who expressed his sorrow for having made such terms, so that Clanricarde, on the day appointed for the rendezvous, found a letter of excuses instead of an army of allies, and with loud indignation returned disappointed to Dublin.

Rinuccini soon afterwards followed the council to Kilkenny, where he caused O'Neill and Preston to sign a mutual agreement, by which they bound themselves to forget all past dissensions, and whether acting singly or collectively for the future, to have but one object present to their eyes — the independence of their religion, and the deliverance of their common country.

Nothing could have given greater joy to the members of the old council imprisoned at Kilkenny, than the failure of the siege of Dublin. Whenever they received news of any disaster to the confederate arms, they drank to their losses in beakers of beer. They naturally concluded that their liberation was nigh, and as the government, in the hands of the clergy, was only temporary and provisional, they calculated on a crisis which would again restore them to the power which they had lost.

It was now resolved to call a general assembly of the kingdom, as it was urged that such a proceeding would give greater satisfaction to the people who were anxious for the formation of a government in which the representatives were not elected solely by the clergy. Contrary to the wishes of the nuncio, the members of the old council were now released from imprisonment. Belling entered on a defence of his own conduct and that of his colleagues in the matter of the peace concluded with Ormond, and published in August. He asserted that in signing the peace he had done nothing more than what was sanctioned by Pope Innocent, who, in the presence of Luke Wadding, cautioned the delegates* of the confederates against seeking more than his majesty was able to concede in his difficulties. This was an assertion which required more than the word of Belling for its confirmation, and the nuncio denied that his holiness had ever made any such statement, as it was totally irreconcilable with the instructions he had

* Philop. Iren.

received from Rome, which charged him not to abate a single tittle of the just demands of the Catholics.

In the meantime Ormond was carrying on a negotiation with the parliament commissioners, Clotworthy, Meredith, King, and Salway, who had anchored in the bay of Dublin on the 13th of November. At the prayer of the citizens he invited them to land on the 14th, and fixed their quarters at Ringsend and Baggotrath, and on the day following opened a treaty with them which was carried on till the 23rd of the month. The terms which they proposed not being agreeable to the lord lieutenant, they embarked a few days afterwards, and carried their supplies to the Scots in Ulster, who, in the absence of O'Neill, had sent 700 men from Lisnegarvy, and ravaged the counties of Cavan, Monaghan and Louth, and amongst other places, demolished Carrickmacross.

The result of the negotiation with the parliament commissioners was prejudicial to the lord lieutenant; it sowed such seeds of jealousy and discontent* that the citizens of Dublin refused to contribute further to the payment of his troops, so that he was forced, in the cold and wet winter, to draw out his half-starved and half-naked army and march into the county Westmeath, to procure provisions. The defection of Preston, who, in his excuse for not adopting Ormond's offer, asserted that his troops were not "excommunication proof," was a sore blow to him. His object was to act with the Scots in Ulster, and having gained over the unsteady Preston, to annihilate O'Neill, and thus force the observance of the peace. In his present circumstances one incident saved him from the army of Owen Roe. While he was keeping "a melancholy Christmas"† at Trim, a short cessation, proposed by Muskerry, was agreed to, else "the half-starved and half-naked" army of Dublin must have made a sorry figure before the Ulster general.

Thwarted in his scheme, he did not despair for a moment, and the assurance sent him by his kinsman Muskerry, "that in the approaching general assembly matters should be arranged agreeably to his pleasure," consoled him for the uneasiness and trouble he experienced in the vicinity of O'Neill's army.

* Borlase.   † Cox.

Nor was Preston's vacillation useless to the lord lieutenant; on the contrary, Ormond had strong reasons for calculating on the sympathies of the Leinster general. His enmity to O'Neill, however it might have been masked, must sooner or later develope itself, and as he had but little feeling for the "old Irish," he knew that the nuncio would eventually distrust him. One thing was certain, and that certainty could not but be grateful to Ormond: the two generals who had quarrelled under the walls of Dublin, were so divided by the antagonism of class that their cordial co-operation could not be looked for. On leaving Dublin the lord lieutenant had been induced to believe that by making an attack on Athlone, he might get possession of that important fortress. It had been surprised early in September, and taken by one of O'Neill's officers from Lord Dillon, who held it for Ormond. Dillon had made his profession of faith on the 6th of December, and was received into the Catholic church by the nuncio, who entreated Owen Roe to reinstate him in the command. But, so determined was the Ulster general, that he could not be induced to comply, and sent Richard O'Ferrall and Roger Maguire, with positive orders to hold the place against Ormond and every one else.

The day of the general assembly was now at hand, and on the result of the meeting the fate of Ireland depended. The subject which had hitherto divided the council of the confederates was that of religion ; and, as if anticipating the decision of the majority, Ormond wrote to Digby, who was setting out for Paris, that the commands to be forwarded to him by the queen and the Prince of Wales, touching that vital question, "should not thwart the grounds he had laid to himself."

"For, in that matter," ran the instruction of the lord lieutenant, "I shall obey by suffering, and particularly that there be no concession to the Papists to perpetuate churches or church livings ;" but, as far as regarded the quiet exercise of their religion, it might be free for his majesty to tolerate it, if he could see anything in them but 'Irish rebels.'"

Thus the sum of all they had struggled for was to be the toleration of their creed. The blood and sweat of five years were to be rewarded by a connivance at the practice of their conscientious convictions, in the rude hut and "up in the mountain solitudes." At the fitting time the cathedrals and the ecclesiastical revenues were to be given back to the Protestant clergy, who had already petitioned Ormond for stipend till they were restored to their benefices. Out of these sacred edifices, which the piety of their forefathers had erected, the Catholic clergy were to be expelled, to propitiate the lord lieutenant. The craven-hearted Catholics of the Pale seconded his views, and as they were his adherents and sycophantic clients, he looked on them as his most useful instruments in creating division and disunion. But they were destined to discover their error when it was irremediable, and find that the man on whom they placed such hopes and confidence was "an inconstant friend and an unforgiving enemy."[*]

CHAPTER VII.

NEVER did that city seated on the "stubborn Nore" contain within its walls a more august or brilliant assemblage than on the 10th of January, 1647. The morning of that memorable day beheld the representatives of the confederate Catholics assisting at high mass in the cathedral of St. Canice. It was a solemn scene, such as memory loves to dwell on. David, Bishop of Ossory, was the officiating priest, and a choir of Italians sung the responses. On the left of the grand altar sat the nuncio on a lofty throne, arrayed in glittering cope and jewelled mitre; around him sat eleven bishops, with the primate, Hugh O'Reilly, at their head. Immediately behind the bishops, sat the temporal peers, attended by their esquires. Diego della Torre and Du Moulins, the envoys from the Spanish and French courts, had distinguished places near them. Two hundred and twenty-four gentlemen,

------

* "Amicus levissimus, inimicus gravissimus."— *Proverb quoted in the Unkind Deserter.*

representing the Commons of Ireland, occupied the remaining space about the richly ornamented altar. The cheering ray of the winter sun shone feebly through the great eastern window,* whose brilliant tints had excited the artistic cupidity of Rinuccini The piety and chivalry of the land were represented within the sacred edifice, and above the heads of that glorious assemblage, were suspended the torn banners of Beinburb, for they had not as yet been sent as votive offerings to the holy see.

There they knelt around that altar which they had sworn to uphold. Many an illustrious name has been preserved to us of those who were on that day invoking blessings on the cause of their religion and country. M'Carthy Riagh and O'Sullivan More, from the south; O'Donnell and M'Gennis, from the north; O'Conor Don and O'Conor Sligo, from the west; Preston and Talbot from the plains of Leinster, with the descendant of Pheagh Mac-Hugh O'Byrne, from his fortalice of Bally-nacorr, in the Wicklow mountains. The "ite missa est," pronounced at the conclusion of that day's solemnity, sent them forth to struggle for their homes and altars on their own soil, and on almost all the battled-fields of the continent. But of all who were now kneeling beneath the roof of St. Canice, one† alone was destined to find a grave within its precints. Little did they then think of that fearful storm which was soon to sweep their native land and desolate their homesteads; but if they could have anticipated how fondly aftertimes should cherish the recollection of their virtues and heroism, it might have consoled them for the bitter trials and heart-burnings they had to endure. Sir Phelim O'Neill perishing on the scaffold, a martyr to 'ruth,‡ and Terence Albert O'Bryan, the Bishop of

---

* This window was the gift of Bishop Ledred; and Grose in his Antiquities states that Rinuccini offered 700l. for it, in order to send it to Rome. It were better he had succeeded in purchasing it, for it would have been preserved though at a distance from us. When Axtel was governor of Kilkenny in Cromwell s time, his savages smashed it, in a fit of holy indignation against popish saints and pictures.

† Mountgarret, who died in 1651.   *Vide* Hib. Dom

Emly, in sight of the gibbet, pronouncing in the ears
of Ireton, the prophecy of his death by pestilence, are
facts which cannot be forgotten.   Irish genius has yet
to make them glow on canvass in the temple of
nationality; nor shall distinction of creed prevent us
doing honor to the men whose love of fatherland must
endear them to the recollection of all.

But the scene is changed, and the bishops, nobles, and
commons are assembled in the great gallery of Kilkenny
castle.

The nuncio was the first to address the assembly.
Adverting to the congregation of the prelates and clergy
at Waterford, he solemnly declared that necessity alone
had compelled him and the bishops to adopt that course,
which was indubitably agreeable to the people at large,
however otherwise it might have been to the adherents
of Lord Ormond.   Much contrary to his own wish he
had been induced to take the conspicuous and onerous
part of president of the congregation, which he was now
ready to resign, in order to bring about an indissoluble
union of parties.   In terms which were any thing but
flattering to the commissioners engaged in the late negotiations with Ormond, he repudiated the articles of the
peace which they had concluded.   They had done this,
he affirmed, without the consent of the prelacy and people of Ireland; but as it was now evident that laity and
clergy longed for repose, he exhorted them to proceed to
the conclusion of an honorable peace, which fully guaranteed the independence of their religion. "So anxious,"
he continued, "is Pope Innocent for the security of your
religion and country, that he has recently sent from
Rome the Dean of Fermo, with supplies of money and
paternal assurances of his good will towards you.   The
benevolence of the holy father is only commensurate with
the joy he has experienced on receiving news of your
victories; and if proof be wanting, see it here in the request which I am commissioned to convey to you, that
you will send the standards* captured from your enemies,

* " These standards," writes the nuncio to Cardinal Paufilio, "were
so torn in the death-struggle at Beinburb and elsewhere, that he was
obliged to remove some of them from the staffs in order to forward them
to Rome."—*Rinuccini.*

that they may be hung up in the basilicas of Rome, to record your devotion to the holy see, and the indomitable bravery of the Irish people."

He concluded his address by assuring them that his feelings were all opposed to any position which would impose on him the burden of temporal concerns, as his solicitude was for the weal of that religion for which they had taken up arms. Yet, if any thing in the history of the events which had transpired remained to console him, it was the timely victory won by the men of Ulster; "for," said he, with marked emphasis, "if heaven had not fought on the side of O'Neill, on the memorable day of Beinburb, the representatives of the Catholic confederates would not be to-day assembled in this goodly city. The churches must have been desecrated—the priesthood scattered—and the peers temporal and spiritual who now listen to my voice, either sacrificed by the swords of the Puritans or languishing in prison."

The address concluded, and received with acclamation, a most important point was now to be discussed before entering on the consideration of other matters. There was, indeed, a unanimous desire amongst all parties for the conclusion of peace; but the conditions on which it was to be drawn up constituted the stumbling-block between the clergy, and Muskerry and Mountgarret, who thought of nothing so much as catering to Ormond.

Smarting under the blow inflicted by the edict of Waterford, which denounced them as perjurers, the commissioners now sought to justify their proceedings in the matter of the treaty, and disprove the crime which the declaration of the prelates meant to attach. In this discussion three weeks were consumed, and the heat of the contending parties was near bringing about the most disastrous consequences to the entire body. The demon of discord was amongst them, and when it was moved by the Bishop of Ferns that Preston should be impeached, as conniving with the adherents of Ormond, swords and daggers were near being drawn on both sides. * In this matter it required the joint influence of the prelates, and Plunket, the chairman, to suppress a most unseemly tumult.

* Philop. Iren. 41.

Day after day was the unhappy question of the Water.
ford declaration raised and discussed ;—the commissioners, on the one side, vindicating their conduct in the
transaction with Ormond, and the prelates, on the other,
defending the course they had adopted.   In self-defence
it was argued by the commissioners that their consent to
the thirty articles was founded on the secret concessions
of Glamorgan, and therefore the charge of perjury was
not sustainable.   This assertion was far from satisfactory
to the prelates, who maintained that when the commissioners were subscribing the treaty they must have
known that Glamorgan had been disavowed.   In order,
however, to terminate such rancorous recriminations,
the commissioners now agreed to condemn the peace ;
and, for that purpose, an instrument was drawn up
which embraced both points—the evacuation of the
peace and the vindication of their own conduct.   The
resolution, published the 2nd of February, set forth that
the commissioners had acted honestly, and pursuant to
their instructions, in making the peace, and that the
clergy had acted conscientiously in rejecting it.   It is
hard to reconcile such contradiction, but as the commissioners could not be induced to reject the peace on any
other terms, the resolution was agreed to.   It was now
necessary that the assembly should advertise Ormond of
what they had done by a public manifesto, and on the
same day it was almost unanimously resolved, that "they
would not accept that peace, and therefore they protested against it as invalid and of no force, and that the
nation would accept of no peace not containing a sufficient security for the religion, lives, and estates of the
confederate Catholics."

This resolution was published two or three days after
Lord Taaffe and Colonel Barry had got a safe conduct to
come into the confederate quarters.   They brought a
letter from Ormond to the chairman of the assembly,
urging the necessity of adhering to the peace concluded
in August, and asking £1,000 per month for the subsistence of the king's troops; but before the deputies were
granted an audience they learned that, out of three hundred, twelve alone were for Ormond's peace, and they
consequently declined presenting the lord lieutenant's

It was now moved, that a new oath should be admi
nistered to all persons for the continuance of their union
till all the propositions which were annexed to it should
be obtained and secured. The nuncio successfully
pressed the matter, and it was finally subscribed by the
peers, spiritual and temporal, and all the commons,
without dissent. The propositions annexed were pre-
cisely those which had been drawn up by the prelates
in the assembly of Waterford, and of which no mention
was made in the thirty articles of Ormond. They were
as follows :—

1. "That the Roman Catholic clergy and laity have
and enjoy the free and public exercise of the Roman
Catholic religion throughout the kingdom, as it was ir
the reign of Henry VII. or any other Catholic king, his
predecessors.

2. "That the secular clergy of Ireland, viz., primates, archbishops, bishops, ordinaries, deans, chapters,
archdeacons, and other dignitaries ;_vicars, and all other
pastors of the secular clergy, and their respective suc-·
cessors, shall have and enjoy, all and every of them, all
manner of jurisdiction, privileges, and immunities, in as
full and ample manner as the Roman Catholic clergy
had or enjoyed within this realm at any time during the
reign of the late king, Henry VII., king of England
and lord of Ireland, any declaration of law, laws, statutes, power, or any other authority to the contrary notwithstanding.

3. "That all laws and statutes made since the time of
King Henry VIII., whereby any restraint, penalty,
mulct, or incapacity, or other restriction whatsoever, is
or may be laid upon any of the Roman Catholics, either
of the clergy or laity, for the said exercise of the Roman Catholic religion within this kingdom, and of their
several functions, jurisdictions, and privileges, may be
repealed, revoked, and declared void in the next parliament, by one or more acts of parliament to be passed
therein.

4. "That the primates, bishops, ordinaries, deans, and
chapters, archdeacons, chancellors, treasurers, chanters,
guardians of collegiate churches, prebendaries, and
other dignitaries, shall have, hold, and enjoy all the
churches and church-livings in as large and ample man-

ner as the late Protestant clergy respectively enjoyed the same on the 1st day of September, 1641, together with all their rights, profits, emoluments, perquisites, liberties to their respective sees and churches belonging, as well in all places now in possession of the confederate Catholics, as also in all other places that shall be recovered by them from the adverse party within this kingdom, saving to the Roman Catholic laity and their respective rights, according to the laws of this kingdom."

Such were the conditions on which peace with Ormond was to be sought. Henceforth they were solemnly sworn to preserve their allegiance to the king intact, but never to lay down their arms till the aforesaid articles were fully ratified. A proclamation, enjoining all Catholics to contend for these their chartered rights, was published by order of the general assembly on the 8th of March, and all who refused to take the oath with the annexed conditions, were denounced as traitors to their God and country.

But if any proof were wanting of the overweening loyalty of those men who were denounced by Ormond as Irish rebels, it is to be found in the history of the transactions of the confederates during this meeting at Kilkenny. Amongst other questions there discussed, was that of the appointment of the bishops to Irish sees. The Catholic lawyers, amongst the most conspicuous of whom was Mr. D'Arcy, contended that the right of patronage was vested in the crown, and that the choice of bishops and incumbents should be made in a settled form between the supreme council (who acted at present in the king's right) and the metropolitans and chapters.* The novelty of the doctrine startled the nuncio, who imagined at first that it was a scheme on the part of the Ormondist party to introduce into the vacant sees their own clients and adherents; but he was soon made aware that the four lawyers who advanced the proposition, vesting the right of nomination in the crown, were really sincere in their opinion. Taking away that right, they contended, would amount to a breach of their allegiance, as they had sworn to main-

* Hib. Dom. Unkind Deserter.   † Rin. p. 200.

tain inviolate all his majesty's just prerogatives, rights, and jurisdiction. Another argument insisted on was, that they had no other means left them of preventing Protestants being appointed to the vacant secs, if it was not admitted that the *jus patronatus*, or power of appointing, was actually vested in the crown. Conceding that power to the Pope, they said nothing could be expected from a Protestant monarch or executive. In vain did Rinuccini endeavour to convince them that no such power belonged of right to the crown. Granting that at any point of time such privilege belonged to it, that privilege must have been granted from the Holy See; and now that the King of England professed no longer the doctrines of Rome, the power of nominating, if it ever granted such, must naturally have reverted to the fountain head.

The nuncio repudiated their pernicious dogmas, and after times has put the seal on his decision. But yet "so stiff" were the lawyers in their opinion, that he was forced to move the article might be set aside till he had consulted the court of Rome on the subject. But it was a foregone conclusion, and having satisfied the importunity of these over loyal men, whose temporizing failed in this instance, he assured them that any recommendation emanating from the supreme council should be treated with marked respect by the Holy See, which, however, would not acknowledge the right of election vested in any other than the representative of the "Fisherman."

Having settled this point, the other debates turned on the obligation of the oath recently taken; in regard of which it was moved—"That though the propositions of the clergy were ratified and approved by the assembly, and annexed to the oath, yet the assembly should not by any of these propositions be excluded from assenting to any medium to be agreed to by vote of that body, and inserted by them in their instructions about churches or ecclesiastical lands, in parts and places possessed by the Protestants, at the conclusion of any peace or accommodation to be made with the lord lieutenant, or any other person empowered by his majesty."*

* Rin. p. 201; Carte Orm. p. 597.

The assembly now set about considering the propositions submitted by Barry on behalf of Ormond. The peace was pronounced as of no force, but they consented to a cessation for three weeks, till March the 13th, and soon after to a month longer, allowing the lord lieutenant to enlarge his quarters in the county of Dublin in lieu of the money which he demanded for the maintenance of his troops.

As soon as the cessation was concluded, a proposal was made in the general assembly to treat the question of a peace, as it was now no longer doubtful that Ormond had written on the 6th of February to the parliament commissioners, offering to deliver the towns and garrisons to such as they should depute to receive them. For this purpose Geoffry Brown and Dr. Fennel were ordered to proceed to Dublin to propose a conjunction of the confederate forces with those of Ormond, on the distinct understanding that both armies should act independently of each other, and under their respective leaders. The propositions annexed to the oath were to be an indispensable condition to this arrangement, and the confederate troops were to be admitted into the king's garrisons, or to have the towns put into their hands. Ormond, who was willing to lend a ready ear to any accommodation with the parliament, scouted the proposals of the confederate deputies; nor did he condescend to give them a formal answer till the assembly sent Theobald Butler to press him on the subject, when he declared that he would not assent to the propositions.

Thus, when all hopes of a peace were entirely frustrated, the assembly turned their attention to the re-appointment of the generals who were to command their troops in the various provinces. The treasury was empty, and the crops wasted, and a solitary chance was left to console them in the anticipation of many evils. The Dean of Fermo had not yet appeared with the monies which had been given by the Holy See, and collected by the indefatigable industry of Luke Wadding. His coming was hourly looked for, and the assurances given by Mazarin led the confederates to think that the Queen of England was interested in their cause, and consequently would not fail to succour them, now that they stood in arms against the parliament.—

Conflicting and various were the communications from the court of the English queen; at one moment it was rumoured that she designed coming with the Prince of Wales, and that she inclined to the demands of the Catholics in the matter of their recent treaty with the lord lieutenant, and that the latter, far from negotiating with the rebels in England, was determined to hold Dublin for her majesty and the prince. But the more energetic of the council clearly perceived that it was to be a death struggle between them and the parliament, and took their precautions accordingly. It was now referred to a select committee of the confederate council to devise means for the support of their troops, till the supplies which they were expecting had arrived. The exigency was promptly met, and a resolution of the committee determined that, along with the ordinary contributions, a tenth of all fruits and chattels should be given by the laity, and an eighth by the bishops and clergy, secular and regular. Everything that could tend to replenish their exhausted coffers was readily effected, and the chalices and church furniture were turned into money.

At the same time it was resolved that "Owen Roe" should have the command of the Connaught, as well as the Ulster forces. Preston, feared and distrusted by the nuncio and clegy, was re-appointed to command in Leinster; and, much to the annoyance of Muskerry and his party, Glamorgan was to head the troops of Munster.

Never did the confederates apprehend greater danger of their existence than at this moment. The storm which so long lowered was about to burst on the land; nor did it need the wit of a seer to foretell the havoc and ruin which were suspended above their heads. The blow which was struck by O'Neill in Ulster had only stunned the Covenanters; the supplies sent by the parliament had recruited Munroe's strength, and he now burned for revenge. From the south there came disastrous news. Inchiquin was up again, merciless and infuriated; and the Marquess of Ormond, falsely stating that the "insolent demands of the Catholics" had compelled him to treat with the king's enemies, was about to open the gates of Dublin to that ruthless faction.

At such a moment, and when so much lay at stake,

no practicable alternative was adopted by the nuncio or the lord lieutenant. The former was not a man for the doctrines of expediency; or, in other words, he was too much the statesman of principle. He did not care to bring about a union between the Catholic and Protestant aristocracy, but devoted all his energies to realize an imaginary project. Yet he might have perceived that in the council of the confederates there were fatal jealousies and false friends, and that the bond of their common religion alone kept them for the while together. Were it not for this, into how many sections must they not have been divided? Nevertheless, let us not throw the blame on the confederates, or stigmatise them as the cause of all the evils which came on their native land. The fatal policy of Ormond was not less culpable than that of Rinuccini. The assembly had continued their meetings ten weeks longer than at any other period, in the hope of inducing him to forego his coquetry with the parliament, but all in vain. He hated the Catholics with an intense hate, and would rather have seen the crescent flying from the Castle of Dublin than the standard of the confederates. He higgled too long, says his eulogist O'Connor, and allowed the seasonable opportunity for action to elapse. Had he thrown the weight of his influence into the scale against the Puritans as against the nuncio, Preston and O'Neill would have joined him against the Scots. The nobility and gentry would have been with him to a man, and the monarchy would have been saved.*

All other resources failing, it was now determined by the confederates to have recourse to the sword. Freedom of conscience, and the restoration of the churches and the plundered estates of the Catholic nobility and gentry, were the objects which banded them together. The exhortations of their clergy cheered them to the struggle, and the poor but faithful peasantry flocked around their standard wherever it was raised.

The last act of Ormond cleared away all doubt as to his intentions towards the parliament. His second son, Lord Richard Butler, with the Earl of Roscommon, and

Sir James Ware, had been sent as hostages for his performance of the articles, in consideration of which, he was to surrender Dublin to the English rebels.[*] The assembly resolved, therefore, to break up in the beginning of April, and before adjourning they appointed their next meeting to take place on the 12th of November following. A new supreme council of twenty-four was now elected; all of whom, with the exception of Muskerry and three others, were inflexibly opposed to the Marquess of Ormond.

The hostages had scarcely arrived in England when 1,000 foot and 400 horse were marched from Ulster, and received by Ormond into the garrisons of Drogheda and Dublin, where they were allowed their own form of worship, and had churches assigned to them as well as ministers. Colonel Castle had already been admitted to the city with his regiment which had lately arrived from England, and the letters forwarded by Ware and the Earl of Roscommon gave Ormond to understand that he would soon receive reinforcements from the traitors on the other side of the channel.

Yet, such was the inclination of the Irish Catholics for peace, and their zeal for his majesty's service, that they gladly availed themselves of an incident which they thought was calculated to promote it. Indeed, any honourable peace could not be too dearly purchased by them, for their treasury was empty, and the country reduced to a state approaching sterility.

The truce with Ormond expired on the 10th of April, and Preston marched his forces into the county Carlow, and sat down before the castle, which he took by storm. It was evidently the intention of the confederates to march on Dublin, and repair the errors that had been committed there in the last winter. Their object was to take the city out of the hands of Ormond, and prevent the landing of the parliamentary troops. Indeed the lord lieutenant would freely have ceded it to any power save the confederates, and was now begging the intervention of the terrible Inchiquin, who had an army of 5,000 foot and 1,500 horse at his command, with the

---

[*] Notwithstanding the king's command, "not to submit to them on any terms."

promise of supplies from England. He had **already**
taken Dromana, Cappoquin, and Dungarvan, which were
but feebly. garrisoned by the confederates. In order,
therefore, to oppose him, it was settled that Preston,
instead of carrying the war into the quarters of the
lord lieutenant in Leinster, should at once proceed to
Munster and act with the troops under the command of
Glamorgan. The incident which favoured this design
was the arrival of Dr. Leyburn, who, under the assumed
name of Winter Grant, had recently come from the
court of the English queen with instructions for the
lord lieutenant; it was, therefore, resolved, on the 10th
of May, that the confederates should embrace the
opportunity of Grant's coming, and renew their overtures for an accommodation.

Lord Digby, who was at Leixlip on May the 12th,
wrote to Ormond, advertising him of Grant's arrival,
with despatches from the queen of an urgent nature.
Grant immediately afterwards presented himself in
Dublin, and having consigned the despatches to the lord
lieutenant, assured him, that the queen and prince had
such unbounded confidence in him, that not even the
reports which were hourly reaching them of his negotiations with the parliament, could shake or diminish.
The notion of delivering Dublin to the king's enemies
was farthest from their suspicions. But Leyburn, who
had so much confidence in Ormond's integrity, was
soon undeceived, for he did not scruple to inform him
" that if there were necessity, he would rather give up
the city and the places under his command to the
English, than to the Irish rebels."[*]

Leyburn, who affected to believe that Ormond
would never submit to the parliament, and that a successful negotiation might induce him to join the
confederate troops, was now commissioned to procure a
cessation between the lord lieutenant and the Catholics.
Ormond freely consented to a cessation for three weeks,
well knowing that, ere that time had elapsed, the
additional reinforcements and troops should have arrived
from England.   His object was to gain time, and when
Leyburn was about proceeding to Kilkenny, " he desired

* Leyb. Mem.

to know from his excellency what he should say in case
it was objected by the confederates, that he consented
to so short a cessation only that he might gain time to
receive more forces from the parliament." To which
he got an answer, "that he should receive orders on the
way, if, on consideration, there was cause." Accordingly,
on the next day, a courier overtook him with a letter
from the lord lieutenant, which empowered him " to
undertake to the confederates that if a cessation should
be agreed upon, he would not receive into the garrisons
under his command, forces from the parliament during
three weeks; but M. Leyburn was to use his utmost
endeavours to procure a cessation without that condition, or at least that it should be kept private; which
last he was to engage them in before he consented to
the said condition."

But on the arrival of Leyburn in the confederate
quarters,.he was astonished at finding that they were
already aware that Ormond was in treaty with the
parliament, and that he had upwards of three thousand
of their men long since admitted into the city and
other garrisons where his orthodoxy did not exclude
them from the free exercise of their religion. The
confederates soon perceived that this manœuvre on the
part of Ormond was of a piece with his accustomed
duplicity, and they forthwith objected to so short a
cessation; but at the same time proposed to lengthen it
to six months, provided his lordship would, in the
meantime, admit no more of the parliament forces into
his garrisons. But Herod and Pilate were now friends.
The extermination of the confederates was Ormond's
ambition, and he positively refused to accede to their
requests.

Nor can it be said that Rinuccini exercised any
influence in this negotiation carried on by Leyburn,
on behalf of Ormond, with the confederates. He had
been absent during that eventful period, and solely
occupied with ecclesiastical affairs in Wexford and
other towns. When the final answer of Ormond
reached the supreme council resident in Kilkenny, he
hastened thither, only to learn that Leyburn, as well
as the queen, had formed an exaggerated notion
of Ormond's loyalty and sincerity. The terms on

which the confederates insisted, were in his eyes
utterly impracticable.   The propositions regarding
religion and settlement of a peace, which would enable
him to act with the truly loyal Catholics against the
parliament, he heartily despised; and all negotiation
was put an end to when he declared that their proposals
were fitter to be treated on in a league offensive and
defensive, between neighbouring princes, than between
his majesty's governor of a kingdom, and his subjects
of the same, declined from their obedience.*

It has been asserted, though no mention of the fact
occurs in Rinuccini's despatches, that Ormond was at
this time carrying on a negotiation with O'Neill, on
whose honour he placed great reliance.   But it is
difficult to understand how this could have been the
case, as there was no provision made for the restoration
of the forfeited lands in Ulster : moreover, the Ulster
general had too much reason to dread Preston, to place
himself, as it were, between two fires, as he must have
done had he marched into Leinster, and taken up a
position between Preston and the city.   However the
case may be, Rinuccini is charged with having detained
the Ulster general's nephew at Kilkenny, when he was
sent by Owen Roe to persuade the council to an
accommodation. †

Every expedient had now been tried which was calculated to preserve Ireland from the English rebels ; but
Ormond was in their confidence, and clearly saw that
the king's circumstances were irretrievable.   For awhile
it had been argued that the advent of the Queen and
Prince of Wales might have created a salutary reaction, and brought about a union of parties, which
would throw difficulties in the way of the parliamentarians.   But that hope was soon abandoned.   The
capital was in the hands of the enemy.   Ormond was,
in reality, at their mercy ; and it is stated, on the authority of many, that he sought to dissuade the queen from
such an enterprise, if she ever really meditated it,
urging that the step would render her husband's enemies still more implacable.

All hope of taking Dublin out of Ormond's hands had

* Carte.   † Philip. Irsa

now vanished. O'Neill asserted that fifteen days would have been sufficient to seize it; but the reluctance of the people of Leinster to receive his army, and the want of money and provisions, determined him to make no attempt. Fifty thousand dollars, forwarded by the Holy See for the confederate armies, were still on the coast of France. The parliamentary cruisers stood in the way, and these succours, so desirable at this moment, awaited a favourable opportunity of being brought to their desti. nation.

In the beginning of June, the supreme council pro. ceeded into Munster, and made their head-quarters at Clonmel. Inchiquin was dealing death and devastation along the sea coast, almost into the county Cork. The jealousies of the confederate generals had given him time and opportunity to place one-half the province under contribution. Glamorgan awaited orders to act, as well as money to pay his troops; and a great portion of the army reluctantly obeyed a general who had su- perseded Lord Muskerry. Several regiments mutinied, demanding that he should be re-appointed, whilst others threatened to take his life. At the very doors of the council-chamber these clamours were kept up, till, on the 12th of the month, as they were debating on the best way of suppressing the insubordination, Muskerry went out, and getting on horseback, as if he were going to take the air, proceeded to the camp; in an hour's time the whole of the army declared for him, and turned Glamorgan out of the command. The next day he en- tered Clonmel, attended by a guard, and Glamorgan, by way of reparation to his honour, was reinstated for a few days, and then ceded the command to Muskerry. The latter immediately resigned in favour of Lord Taaffe, a creature of Ormond, without any character for military achievements.

Thus was Muskerry enabled to give his whole atten- tion to political affairs in the supreme council; and the troops in Munster were completely at the beck of his de- pendant, who was in the interest of the unsteady Pres- ton and the faithless Ormond. The nuncio soon after- wards proceeded into the province of Connaught, to concert with Owen Roe whatever measures were most necessary against the perils which they knew must fol-

low the surrender of Dublin. Nor had they long to wait
for that base and perfidious act, which was, in a great
measure, the cause of the death of the unfortunate
Charles; and, what is far more to be lamented, the undeniable cause of all those horrors which subsequently
came upon unhappy Ireland. But Ormond, in the spirit
of a well-known distich, would rather see the loyal and
faithful Catholics exterminated by the swords of the
Puritans, than admitted to hold the city against those
men whom he subsequently pronounced to have been
the murderers of the king's person, usurpers of his
rights, and destroyers of the Irish nation; by whom
the nobility and gentry of it were massacred at home,
and led into slavery or driven into beggary abroad."*

And yet this very man had already entered into terms
with the ruthless faction, which he thus characterized;
for, on the 7th of June, their commissioners came into
the bay of Dublin with 600 horse and 1,400 foot. At
this moment, Ormond was well aware that the king's
person had been sold to the parliament by the Scotch,
and still he did not hesitate to sign and conclude a treaty
with his enemies on the 19th, by which he obliged himself to surrender the sword on the 28th of the following
month, or sooner, upon four days' notice. An incident,
which is worthy of being recorded, occurred at the
time. Smith, who was then lord mayor, and at the
venerable age of four score years, waited on Ormond,
when he heard that he was about to deliver the city into
the hands of the parliamentarians, and sternly informed
him that he held the king's sword, and would never resign it to rebels. Whereon Ormond checked him,
and ordered him to withdraw. The patriotic mayor was
subsequently sent for, and Ormond, never at a loss for
stratagem, read a letter from the king, artfully suppressing the date and circumstances under which it was written, and thus imposed on the credulity of the old man
who would have died to sustain his country and sove
reign.

Digby and Preston remonstrated in vain. The latter
was ready to make a junction with the forces in Munster
under Taaffe, and hold the city against the invaders;

* Carte's Orm. Appendix, p. 19.

but all to no purpose. Ormond declined all overtures which might have averted the pending destruction; "because, forsooth, he held it by no means safe." He was greedy of gain, and knew that he could not expect anything from the king, who was now in imminent danger of his life. He could not serve two masters, and therefore bowed to mammon. On the 16th of July, he got notice to remove with his family from the castle, and deliver the regalia within four days; but, as the messenger, who was commissioned to give him £5,000 for his treachery, had not yet arrived, he did not depart for a few days. The messenger finally came, and having got his reward, and a promise from the parliament of £2,000 per annum, he sailed from the city on the 28th of July.

It is recorded of him that he indulged in a histrionic performance before the Irish coast had "failed his sight," likening himself to Hannibal when recalled to Carthage, and predicting to those around him that he would one day return in power to that city which he had basely and treacherously surrendered; but, alas! ere his ship had reached the mid channel, Jones, with his myrmidons, were in Dublin, and the fate of Ireland was sealed. Yet, this baseness of Ormond did not open the eyes of his dupes and adherents. They were fascinated by him;— they hoped in him and swore by him. Nor did his kinsman, Muskerry, discover the duplicity and heartlessness of the viceroy till, when stretched in the last agonies on his death-bed, he declared to those about him that "the heaviest fear that possessed his soul, then going into eternity, was his having confided so much in his grace, who had deceived them all, and ruined his poor country and countrymen." *

Indignation and alarm seized the minds of the people when the news of Ormond's conduct travelled through the land. Hitherto they had warred and struggled for their religion, but now, when the swords of the parliamentarians were at their throats, they began to learn that they were to fight for their very existence.

In vain was Clanricarde importuned to take his place in their ranks. His influence was great, but his sympa-

* Unkin l Deserter.

thy with Ormond was greater still. He did not hesitate to impute to the confederates the crime which any un-prejudiced man must have thrown on the lord lieute-nant, and he determined to preserve a strict neutrality.

Owing to the imbecility of the gasconading Taaffe, who had command of the Munster forces, Inchiquin, with a small army, thinned by disease, was destroying by fire whatever he could not reach with the sword. Owen Roe was in the heart of Connaught, without money; and such was the feeling created by Muskerry against him in the south, that the inhabitants of Mun-ster would more willingly have received the troops of the grand seignor into their province than those he com-manded.*

An effort, however, was to be made to recover the ca-pital, and the faction who had adhered to Ormond de-clared that it should be regained with as much ease as it had been lost. The undertaking was committed to the hasty and rash Preston, who fancied that he would eclipse the military genius of his rival by capturing Dublin. Nor could the success of his enterprise be separated from the anticipation of O'Neill's destruction. Muskerry urged him to advance without delay on the city, and promised that he should be immediately joined by the troops under Taaffe, and that their combined forces should then proceed to attack O'Neill,—the grand obstacle to the project which they now contemplated, the recall of Ormond.

Jones had scarcely established himself in Dublin, when he sent orders to the north to Coote and Conway to put their troops in motion, and join him in Leinster. The forces under his command did not amount to more than 4,000 foot, two regiments of horse, with two demi-cul-verins, "one saker, and four sakaruts." He marched from Dublin on the 1st of August, and took up his quar-ters in the village of Swords. On the next day he con-tinued his march through Hollywood to the Naul, and thence to Garretstown, where he got notice that the forces from the north were *en route* to join him. On the 4th he pitched his camp on the hill of Skreene, where he was met by Colonel Moore with the Dundalk troops, and

* Carte.

soon afterwards by Titchbourne, with those of Drogheda, and Conway, with a party of the old British,—making altogether 700 horse and 12,000 foot, with two pieces of ordnance.

Here they held a council of war, and whilst they were debating, Cadogan and Graham came from Trim to inform them that Preston had on that morning raised his camp, and marched with his entire force, consisting of 7,000 foot and 1,000 horse, to a place called Portlester, five miles west of Trim. On the same day Jones put his troops in motion, and advanced to the hill of Tara, where he reviewed the army, and on the next day proceeded to Skurlockstown, within a mile of Trim, where he quartered for the night.

Next day he resumed his march and advanced on Trimleston, where Preston had left a feeble garrison, and the parliamentarian general having surrounded it in hopes of drawing Preston to a fight, sent out a party of fifty horse to ascertain his movements. They soon brought back word that the confederate general had broken up his camp at an early hour, and was crossing the country towards Kilcock, with the intention of throwing himself between Dublin and Jones's army.

The march was immediately sounded, and before the parliamentarian columns crossed the Boyne, the garrison of Trimleston surrendered. Great was their joy, and on they went singing hymns to the Lord of Hosts, till they reached Lynch's Knock. * Preston was strongly fortified on Dungan Hill, not more than a mile from their position. This was on the 8th of August, and the sanguine hopes of Preston and the adherents of

---

* Lynch's Knock, with its ruined castle, may be seen within the beautiful demesne of Summerhill. The property was given some time after the action here narrated to the brother of Colonel Jones, who was appointed Bishop of Meath. There are some traditionary stories concerning the battle preserved in the neighbourhood; and the peasantry point out a grave on the brow of the hill, which they call Colkitto's burial-place. It is evidently that of some distinguished man of Preston's army, but not of the chivalrous Alexander. Were it not for a neat little volume, published by Dr. Butler, Protestant rector of Trim, it might be difficult to identify the locality, which is in the townland of Drumlargin. Trimleston Castle is a most interesting ruin, and might be easily restored, were such the wish of its lord.

Ormond, who calculated on triumph, were soon to be completely frustrated. A steady general, such as O'Neill, would have harassed the parliamentary troops; but Preston was the Marcellus, choleric and mercurial, and the Fabius was not where he should have been.

Jones advanced in full force to the foot of the hill, but Preston's guns being badly pointed, did little execution. The action commenced at ten o'clock, a.m., and at twelve, when the confederate general grew weary of skirmishing, he determined to charge down the hill and overwhelm the phalanxes that were forming at its base. His infantry were met with undaunted bravery, and, notwithstanding the exertions of Alexander Mac Donnell, surnamed Colkitto, were thrown into confusion, and driven back to their former position. Again and again did they come to the charge, and as often were they broken. Preston's cavalry, which was badly placed, their horses being fetlock-deep in the marshy ground, spurred to protect the foot, but they were encountered by Jones's cavalry, when the whole force was driven into an adjacent bog. They were now surrounded by the entire strength of Jones, Moore, Conway, and Titchbourne, and a withering fire from their guns and musketry, literally mowed down the devoted men to whom no quarter was given. With a desperate effort some of the confederate foot forced their way out of the bog, but they were hacked to pieces by Jones's dragoons; and Preston, seeing all hope vanished, fled precipitately from the scene of slaughter, leaving his carriage and papers in the hands of the enemy. On the field and about the hill were reckoned of the confederates killed about 5,470, of whom 400 were the "redshanks" belonging to the brave Mac Donnell of the Isles.

In his retreat, followed by about five hundred foot, the wreck of his army, Preston burned Naas, Harristown, and Moyglare. He did not even make an effort to recover his four guns, "each carrying a twelve-pound shot," and sixty-four fair oxen, which attended his train. The parliamentarians had only twenty killed in the action, and very few wounded. Immediately afterwards Jones retired to Dublin with his prisoners, colours, and baggage; "nor would he allow the standards taken from the confederates to be brought in triumph to the city, for that would be attributing to man the work which was due to the Lord alone."[*]

On his arrival in the city he was met with good news from the parliament; they had forwarded him £1,500 for the temporary sustenance of his forces, and £1,000 as a reward of his good services against the rebels.

Disastrous as was this blow, the confederates did not despair; many a man, who had hitherto shrunk from the contest, was now ready to gird on the sword; but if anything could make us look with contempt on the followers of Ormond who had calculated upon signal success, it is the expression of obsequious respect with which they now turned to Owen Roe. Indeed he had had melancholy proof of his rival's inferiority, and bitterly remarked, when the news of Preston's defeat reached him, that he acted without judgment, and needlessly sacrificed his troops. But all hope was not lost while O'Neill had an army; nor has the poet exaggerated the esteem in which the descendant of a hundred kings was held at this moment by his countrymen.[†] Yet, sad it is to be obliged to say that the destruction of Preston's army was the salvation of O'Neill's. Yes, the Fabius of Ireland still lived, and had he commanded at Dungan's-hill, the "red hand" must have floated from the Castle of Dublin.

The craven-hearted crew who had hitherto affected to despise him, now sent to implore his protection and aid. The army of Leinster was annihilated; they had no longer a single garrison between Dublin and Kilkenny, and well might they tremble for their safety. A few months before Muskerry and the Butlers were loud in their denunciations of O'Neill. The cruelty and the rapacity of his soldiers were their constant theme; and when a few women had been plundered in the vicinity of Kilkenny by some marauders, they came to the council-room to represent their grievances to Muskerry, who ordered them to proceed to the residence of the nuncio,

---

[*] Irish Tracts, R. D. S.
[†] " Sagest in the council was he, kindest in the hall,
Sure we never won a battle—'twas Owen won them all."
Spirit of the Nation, 4to ed. p. 5.

and inform him of the unbridled licentiousness of his
favourite general. But all this was now forgotten in their
hour of need. Flushed with victory, Jones was once more
in the field, and no one knew at what moment he would
be thundering at the gates of Kilkenny. In this state
of things the Bishop of Ferns was despatched to Owen
Roe, who was about to besiege the Castle of Enniskillen
and force his way into the heart of Ulster, and solicited
him to advance immediately and intercept Jones. The
suggestion was cheerfully adopted, and the Ulster general, at the head of 12,000 men, came with lightning
speed and pitched his camp on the ground where Preston
had been defeated. It was the salvation of the confederates; for, as Rinuccini remarks, the Fabius of his
country, in the midst of bogs and marshes, kept Jones in
such check by the rapidity of his movements, that for
four entire months he was obliged to confine himself to
his quarters, nor dared he meet the invincible chieftain.[*]
Fearing a surprise which might utterly destroy him,
Jones retired into Dublin, and Owen Roe's light troops
advanced even as far as Castleknock, getting plunder
and provisions *go leor*, and reducing the English within
the city to the direst distress. [†]

Never was there a more unfortunate appointment than
that of Taaffe to the command of the Munster troops.
He was totally unfit for it, and in every respect inferior
to Preston. When Glamorgan, who was really a chivalrous man, was removed from the command, he consigned
a fine army to Taaffe, consisting of 12,000 foot and 800
horse, with an excellent park of artillery. He was
keeping up a correspondence with Ormond, who had
gone to France and remained utterly inactive, whilst
Inchiquin was destroying every thing about him. But
he was doing the work of Ormond, who meditated coming back at no distant period, and calculated on finding
Taaffe's troops ready to march with him and second his
views.

Inchiquin, after having put the counties of Limerick
and Clare under contribution, entered Tipperary on the
3rd of September. He had no artillery with him, and
his soldiers had no more provisions than they could

* Rinuccini, 336.   † O'Neill's Journal, in the Desid. Cur. Hib.

carry in their haversacks. He stormed ten or twelve small castles, and then crossed the river Suir near Cahir, a fortress deemed impregnable by the English as well as Irish troops. But an accident led to the capture of it. One of Inchiquin's foragers had been hurt under its walls, and was permitted, at his own request, to send for a surgeon to dress his wounds. One Hippsley, an ingenious man, who knew something of the healing art, assumed a disguise, and was admitted to the interior of the fortress, where the wounded man lay. But, being better skilled in the science of fortification than surgery, he observed a point in the outward bawn where the castle was assaultable, and when he returned reported the fact. It was thereon agreed that he should lead an attack; and the pusillanimity of the Munster guards was such that, on seeing the outworks and some turrets taken, the governor appointed by Taaffe surrendered the whole place in a few hours after. Thus was reduced a castle which, in 1599, held out for two months against the Earl of Essex and an army of 20,000 men—thus was the most important fortress in all Munster lost, by the want of discrimination in the hot-headed fool who now was to oppose Inchiquin. Had there been at the time a well-organized system of military affairs in Ireland, he should have been shot, to prevent greater disasters.

Inchiquin, having fortified himself in Cahir, began to make continual incursions into the surrounding country. His soldiers, who a short time before had nothing but roots to subsist on, were now abundantly supplied with every necessary; the finest county in Ireland lay open to them; and in a very short time they destroyed £20,000 worth of corn. It may not have been the case—yet it would appear that there was a bloody collusion between the arrogant Taaffe and the inhuman Inchiquin. Whenever the latter advanced, the former fled; nor did he fire a shot while the ferocious Murrogh was butchering the peasantry, and burning their crops.

There is not on record a more appalling tragedy than that of Cashel, and the guilt is to be thrown on Taaffe as well as Inchiquin. Towards the end of September, when the confederate general heard of his approach, he fled, leaving a feeble garrison in the city of King Cormac. Soon after, Inchiquin sat down before its gates.

and sent to the municipal authorities, to state, that if he
did not get £3,000 and a month's pay for his troops, he
would take the place by storm. The messenger brought
back word, that the authorities would 'not accept his
terms ; Inchiquin opened a fire on the crumbling
wall, and then dashed into the town. Short was the
struggle, but, oh ! it was revolting and bloody. The feeble
garrison laid down their arms, and were butchered in
cold blood. Those who remained in their houses were
dragged out by Murrogh's soldiers, and basely murdered at their own doors. In the midst of the carnage
a multitude fled to the cathedral on the rock. As they
hurried to the sanctuary, their feet plashed in the blood
of their relatives and friends; but they thought that the
sanctity of the place might protect them, and they
grouped around the altars and concealed themselves in
the crypts. On came the savage Inchiquin : supplica-
tions and cries for mercy were unavailing : the banditti
who followed at his heels took possession of the doors
and windows; volley after volley was poured into the
church; and when the ringing of the musketry and the
groans of agony had ceased, in went the murderers, and
dragged forth from their hiding-places the few who
survived. The old man stricken in years was hacked to
pieces on the floor : the tender girl and the venerable
matron shared the same fate. Twenty priests, who
were concealed under the altars, were pierced by the
pikes of these savages, and when the work of slaughter
was done they fired the town. Three thousand human
beings had ceased to live, and this bloody deed was done
by an Irishman who had been brought up in the " *school
of wards*," and had every germ of humanity and nationality plucked from his heart by the anti-popish education which he received.

Oh ! if on that fatal night when the cruel Murrogh
retired, some wayfarer, attracted by the fitful glare of
the burning roof-tree half quenched in blood, had
entered the city, he must have concluded that it had
been visited, not by the wrath of man, but that of God,
for some dire outrage against his majesty.

On went this destroying demon, unopposed by Taaffe.
Ere he reached Fethard, the townspeople had heard
of the butchering in Cashel : they dared not resist,

CONFEDERATION OF KILKENNY.

and they surrendered at discretion. Clonmel was yet to be taken—but there was within its walls as gallant a heart as ever throbbed beneath the plaid—that man was Alexander Mac Donnell of the Isles. He had escaped from the slaughter at Dungan-hill, and with a single regiment of his followers, he closed the gates, and dared Inchiquin to the contest. But "Murrogh of the burnings," well knowing the stubborn foe he had to deal with, retired from before the town. Oh! shame and degradation. This gallant chieftain, with a small body of troops, was able to scare away Murrogh, whilst the Quixotic Connaught general was retreating with 7,000 men. But Inchiquin was glutted with blood, and retired to Cahir; and Taaffe continued his march into the county Cork.

The parliament was well satisfied with the achievements of their proselyte; and as he had complained that Lord Lisle was about to supplant him in the presidency of Munster, they dreaded to displease him, and thereon refused to renew Lord Lisle's commission. Inchiquin was, therefore, proclaimed president, and he had scarce retired from Clonmel, when he received large supplies of men and money from England.*

It was a moment of dreadful suspense for the confederates. Jones was cooped up in Dublin by the watchful vigilance of O'Neill, who was encamped at Trim. But they knew not the hour when Inchiquin would take the field again and march straight upon Kilkenny.

Taaffe was the only hope they had in Munster, and now that the time for the next general assembly was fast approaching, that general received orders towards the middle of October, to watch Inchiquin's movements, and if possible to destroy his army. It was warmly argued in the council at Kilkenny, that the season was too far advanced to resume hostilities, but the party which was ever doubting the sincerity of Ormond's adherents, prevailed, and orders were immediately issued, commanding Taaffe to attack Inchiquin if any favourable opportunity presented itself. Early in November the latter took the field. He advanced

* Ludlow's Mem.

towards Mallow, and lay encamped there till the 12th
of the month.   Taaffe had no alternative, and he
determined to fight. His army consisted of 6,000 foot
and 1,200 horse.   Inchiquin's troops did not amount to
more than 5,000 foot and 1,200 horse, with an excellent
train of artillery.   Taaffe quitted his quarters at
Kanturk, and on the 12th, encamped on the hill of
Knockninoss, commonly called Knock-na-gaoll, or
Englishman's Hill, a few miles west of Mallow.   There
was an old prophecy connected with this spot which
induced him to pitch his camp on it.   The prophecy
ran, that the representative of the Mac Donagh should
win a battle there and recover his patrimony.   Now it so
happened that Taaffe's grandfather had got all the
possessions of the Mac Donaghs "as the reward of his
services against the rebels in the late wars," and by a
strange sort of logic, he concluded that he was the
representative of the clan Mac Donagh in a far more
agreeable sense than that of lineage.   The vain man
regarded this as the prestige of victory, and therefore
strongly entrenched himself on the hill.   He had with
him Lieutenant-General Purcell and the brave Colkitto:
irrespective of the prophecy, his position was a good
one, and a better general would have held it against
twice the number which Inchiquin brought into action.

Inchiquin was but little disposed to risk a battle under
such disadvantages; but, at the instance of Colonel
Semple and some other officers recently come from
England, he was prevailed on to march against the
confederates. Both armies were in view of each other
at one o'clock on the 13th.   Inchiquin seeing the
danger of attacking his enemy on the hill, encamped
at a place called Garryduff, and sent this characteristic
note to Taaffe :—

"MY LORD—There is a very fair piece of ground
betwixt your lordship's army and ours, on this side the
brook, whither if you please to advance, we will do
the like.   We do not so much doubt the gallantry of
your resolution, as to doubt you will not come; but do
give you this notice to the end, you may see we do
stand upon no advantage of ground, and are willing to
dispute our quarrel upon indifferent terms, being con

fident that the justness of our cause will be, this day,
made manifest by the Lord, and that your lordship's
judgment will be rectified concerning your lordship's
humble servant,

                                   "INCHIQUIN.
    "Garryduff, Nov. 13th, 1647."

As no answer was sent to this communication,
Inchiquin determined to advance and take a position
on the right of the hill, where he brought up his guns
and opened a heavy fire on 3,000 Scotch and Irish,
commanded by Mac Donnell, and two regiments of
horse, led by Purcell; Taaffe himself being on the
left with 4,000 infantry and two regiments of cavalry
as a reserve. The troops under Mac Donnell, after a
few vollies, dashed impetuously down the slopes, and
throwing away their muskets, slew the artillerymen
with their broad swords, and seized the guns, and then
attacked the left of Inchiquin's position, which they
chased off the field for a distance of three miles, killing
2,000 of them while they lost but five. Lord Castle-
connell's regiment now advanced from its position on
the hill to attack Inchiquin in front, but they were so
vigorously met by the latter, that after a few vollies
they broke and fled, and were immediately followed by
the rest of the Munster troops. In vain did Taaffe call
on them to rally: with his own hand he killed many of
the fugitives, but they were panic-stricken and could
not be brought back. The cavalry, under Purcell,
followed the infantry, and Inchiquin turned his whole
force on the few brave men who had seized his guns.
So sure were those brave fellows that Inchiquin was in
full retreat, that they were resting on the ground and
had not time to load when they were shot down and
piked. The heroic Alexander, who was now returning
to his men, was met by fourteen of Inchiquin's
cavalry, and having killed four of them with his own
hand, was treacherously assassinated while parleying
with an officer. It was a disgraceful flight, and only
to be remembered as a stain upon the national character.
The loss to the confederates amounted to 1,500 men,
not to mention officers and the materiel; whilst that of
Inchiquin was comparatively trifling, if we take into

consideration the booty that was found on the field. It was a lamentable day for the confederates, for it cost them the life of the ardent and chivalrous Colkitto, to whose valour Inchiquin did not fail to do honour;* for in his letter to Lenthal, the speaker of the House of Commons, he states "that none truly fought but the regiments commanded by Alexander Mac Donnell, the rest having fled to Liscarroll and New Market."†

Gratefully was the news of this victory received in England. Every reverse which the confederate arms sustained, was hailed with the most frantic plaudits. The fanatics from their pulpits, and the dictaters in the parliament, bore testimony to the heroic prowess of Murrogh the burner, whom they regarded as fighting the battle of the Lord, against the unrighteous; and they soon after sent him £10,000 for his army, and a present of £1,000 for his own good services.

CHAPTER VIII.

The defeat at Knockninoss was communicated in a few days afterwards by Taaffe to the general assembly, which had met at Kilkenny on the 12th of November.

Pending the election of the representatives, every nerve was strained by the Ormondist party to return members who were favourable to their views: nor were they disappointed. They had toiled with incredible activity to carry their point, and they could now command a majority in the federative assembly. Ulster, which used to send sixty-three members, now sent only nine; the state of the country interfered with the election, and the nine demanded to have sixty-three voices. The other provinces, for the same reason, were also defective, but not in an equal degree; and the demand of the Ulster mem-

* There is, says Smith, (Hist. of Cork) a very odd kind of music well known in Munster by the name of Mac Allisdrum's march, being a wild rhapsody made in honour of this commander, to this day much esteemed by the Irish, and played at all their feasts.
† Irish Tracts, R. D. Society.

bers was silenced, on the plea that the other provinces
might insist on a similar privilege. The Ulster members
were opposed to peace, and, although they sat in the
assembly, they declared that their province would
regard the decisions of the council as invalid, and of no
force.

The only opposition which was now dreaded by the
Ormondist party was that of the bishops elect. The
bulls from the holy see had already arrived, nominating
to eleven vacancies. The new prelates, with the exception of John * of Tuam, were all in the interest of the
nuncio; for he was a De Burgho, and warmly attached
to the policy of Clanricarde. The new bishops, however, were an important addition to the nuncio's party ;
and much did the Ormondists dread the influence they
were likely to command. They were admitted to the assembly, in right of their sees; but Muskerry objected
to the bishop of Ross, whom he declared not qualified to
take his place amongst the spiritual peers, as he had not
been recommended by the supreme council; but, circumstanced as the confederates were at that moment
(for they were meditating a negotiation with Rome), the
objection was not pressed, and the bishop elect was admitted to his place.

Never before did the council of the confederates meet
under more gloomy auspices. Wailing and lamentation
might be heard throughout the length and breadth of
the land. Within four months they had lost two armies,
and the ravages of war were such that the country remained untilled, and looked as if it had been struck
with the curse of sterility. One gallant heart was yet
undismayed, and beat high with hope. From the rock
of Dunamase to the northern bank of the Liffey did
his faithful clansmen carry his standard. That man
was Owen Roe. Inchiquin, flushed with recent victory,
might have marched on Kilkenny, if he did not dread
the celerity of movement and the masterly ..tics of
O'Neill. Jones dared not to cross the Liffey, or he
would have driven him back with slaughter;—and yet
there was in this new council many a man who sighed
for O'Neill's ruin as the only hope for Ireland. Natu-

---

* He was the very antipodes of his predecessor Malachy.

rally enough, the first question submitted to the consideration of the assembly was the unhappy state of Ireland, almost brought to ruin by the dissensions and misfortunes of her own children. With a feeling of devotion as intense as that with which the sun-worshipper turns to his god, the Ormond party now looked to England, in the vain hope of effecting some accommodation with the king. But the project of sending deputies to the royal person was soon abandoned, when the news reached them of his captivity in Carisbrooke Castle. The immediate effect which this astounding intelligence produced, was the publication of an edict from the assembly, calling the people to arms, and offering, to all officers who would desert Inchiquin's standard, the same grade which they held in their former employment, provided they declared for the confederates. A strong inclination for peace pervaded the assembly, and the Ormondist faction would have openly avowed it, could they have hoped to gain any thing like reasonable terms from the parliament; but their undeniable loyalty to the king, which far exceeded their devotion to their country, removed all hope in that regard.

As the means for protracting the war were now totally exhausted, the question of a foreign protectorate was openly mooted in the assembly. In the selection of foreign princes who were deemed as most eligible, the pope was the first whose name was introduced. Nor were the agents from the French and Spanish courts inactive whilst the question was being discussed. These two courts had a serious interest in that subject, and both put forward rival claims. Indeed Ireland was, for both, the nursery of soldiers; and a singular instance of their mutual jealousies on the subject is recorded as having taken place early in this year. M. Tallon and Diego della Torre* had enlisted several regiments for the two crowns, and sailed from Waterford with the levies; but they had not cleared the Irish coast when Tallon attacked Torre's ships, and carried all the soldiers to France. Thus the French envoy pressed the claim of the French crown, as more likely to be beneficial to Ireland in case a foreign protectorate was determined on,

* Carte's Orm.

to the exclusion of Spain, which he represented as intriguing with the English parliament. But the rival pretensions did not meet much encouragement from the assembly.

As to the pope, no matter how earnestly Rinuccini might have wished to have him proclaimed protector, his inability to furnish means would have been sufficient reason for negativing such an appointment. But, along with this consideration, the distance between Ireland and Rome, would have rendered such an expedient perfectly useless. The instructions which the nuncio had received from his court were satisfactory on the subject ; for he had been already warned, "not to let that point ever come into consultation, as a protectorate at such a distance could be of no use to the Irish, who could expect but little succour from the pope ; moreover, it would expose the Papal See to the jealousy of princes, and exhaust its exchequer, beside a thousand other reasons which forbade any thoughts of that nature."*

But these discussions were introduced into the assembly by the Ormondist faction, without any real view to their practicability. Their grand object was to restore Ormond to power. The nuncio and prelates had thought that the queen would have appointed Glamorgan, now Earl of Worcester, to the viceroyalty of Ireland. But Ormond who had been at St. Germains long before, succeeded in depreciating the earl, and lessening him in the eyes of her majesty In the last interview which Ormond had with the king, he received a positive assurance that he should one day return to Ireland invested with the plenitude of power. And the queen, caught by his obsequious flattery and magniloquent promises, confirmed the determination of her consort.

A curious circumstance transpired during these debates. A book, entitled "An Apologetic Discussion," written by an Irish Jesuit, invalidating the title of England to the sovereignty of the sister country, and exhorting the Irish to elect a king from among themselves, had been brought into the country, and widely circulated. It was immediately concluded by the partizans of Ormond, that the Irish meant to place the crown on O'Neill's

* Carte. p 2.

head, and thus renounce their allegiance to their rightful sovereign. The book was, thereupon, condemned and ordered to be burned by the executioner ; and the author, who had struck hard at English misrule, was consigned to all the pains and penalties of high treason, should he ever venture into the country.*

But the Ormondist party had now made up their minds to adopt a more practicable course to realize their darling project. By an act of the assembly it was resolved to send agents to the Queen and Prince of Wales, and also to the Pope and King of Spain.

The agents who were to proceed on these missions were soon named. French, bishop of Ferns, and Nicholas Plunket were to proceed to Rome. Muskerry, Brown, and Heber MacMahon were appointed to the French court.

Nor was this scheme without its hidden treachery. It was the object of Ormond's partisans to remove from the assembly all whom they knew to be hostile to their designs. French and Plunket were in the interest of the nuncio and clergy, and MacMahon. Bishop of Clogher, was O'Neill's second in command, and most useful to that gallant chieftain.

When the nomination took place, MacMahon rose in the assembly and declared that he would not leave the kingdom. Loud murmurs of disapprobation followed the announcement. A majority of fifty had already determined the question, when the patriotic bishop addressed them in Latin:—" My lords and gentlemen, hence I will not go. My character and motives have been misrepresented in your English and French courts; my life, therefore, would be endangered ; and, setting this consideration aside, my ignorance of the French and Sassenagh languages must incapacitate me from taking part in the negotiations you contemplate." The Ormondists were thunderstruck when they heard this. Many of them cried out that the confederation was dissolved and utterly ruined by the dissensions of the prelates. Preston rushed out to collect his troops, for the bishop was guilty of contempt, and it was likely he would be committed to prison. The gates of Kilkenny were

* *Vide* Hardiman's Hist. of Galway.

closed, and a messenger proceeded to O'Neill's head-
quarters to inform him of the occurrence. When Owen
Roe heard the treatment which his friend experienced,
he sent back word that he would not act very leniently
with the assembly if the slightest indignity were offered
to the prelate.

When the assembly received notice of O'Neill's intentions, they dropped the question, and the Marquess of
Antrim was appointed in place of the bishop. Nor are
we to be surprised at the indignation of Owen Roe at
this moment. MacMahon was his confidant and friend ;
they loved each other with the tenderest affection. On
the morning of Beinburb the bishop shrived his chief,
and in that evening's ever-memorable sunset he was
charging at his side. MacMahon knew nothing of court
chicane and wily intrigue. The crozier was not any
longer useful to him in protecting his flock, and he
therefore had girt on the sword. He was to O'Neill
what Daiberto, Bishop of Pisa, was to Godfrey,* in
the days of the crusaders, and he would not be separated from him. What business had that stern old bishop
in the saloons of St. Germains, when his people were in
arms for their lives, their altars, and homesteads ?

At no former period was there a greater want of
energy on the part of these Ormondists than at the present moment. They were now paralysed by the effects
of their own imprudence. The prejudice which they
had excited against O'Neill was the cause of all the disasters in the south; and even now, when he was ready
to march, at the head of 12,000 foot and 1,500 horse,
they lacked the spirit which was required. But they
dreaded O'Neill, as if he meant to exterminate them,
root and branch; and they hated the nuncio, as though
he were in concert with him to wrest the ecclesiastical
revenues out of their possession. When energetic action
was required they preferred going a-begging beyond
seas, and they consoled themselves with the hope of
being beneficial to the country by soliciting alms
from despots, when they should have been usefully
engaged in hunting them out at home. View it as we
will, the remnant of nationality was at this moment

* De Rossi " Il conte Ugolino."　　o

in the hearts of O'Neill and the clergy, for they alone were ready and willing to sacrifice all to it.

Those craven cowards, who could fight with "courtly words," were now determined to bring over the Prince of Wales; and if they did not succeed in their designs, they were to insist on the immediate recall of Lord Ormond.

After a month's discussion, a draft of the instructions to be given to the respective agents, was submitted to the supreme council, and corrected by the bishops. When corrected, they were signed by nine prelates and six lay peers. The Roman agents were directed to assure the pope, that they would insist upon such terms as would secure the free and public exercise of the Catholic religion, on having a Catholic lord lieutenant, and publishing the religious articles at the same time with the civil. They were then to solicit aids; and, in case a satisfactory settlement could not be had, they were to implore the holy father to take on himself the protectorate of Ireland.

Those destined to France and Spain were charged to solicit arms and money, and assistance to procure them a happy peace; and if they found such a peace could not be had, and that the pope would decline the protectorship, they were to inform themselves where it could be placed most for the advantage of the nation, and manage it accordingly.

Such were the instructions; but an important point remained to be settled before the departure of the deputies—the appointment of members who were to govern in the assembly whilst they awaited answers to their negotiation. The Ormondists proposed the very men who had been instrumental in concluding the former peace, and the clergy objected to them. A medium was therefore agreed upon, that an equal number of both should be chosen; but Muskerry had made an arrangement early in the session, which in a great measure sadly discomfited the party which was opposed to his views.

As members might be absent on an occasion when it would be necessary to sign or issue orders, he proposed that supernumeraries should be appointed to fill their places; and the result was, that forty-eight were ap-

pointed who were all devoted to the interests of Ormond and Muskerry. In vain did the prelates protest
against this arrangement; and the bishop of Ferns, see-
:ng that his absence was a trick devised by the anti-
clerical body, would fain withdraw from the embassy;
but the Ormondists were now in a majority—masters of
the assembly; and the council were, almost to a man, in
favour of their views.

The prelates knew well that Ormond would never
consent to any peace which would leave the Catholics in
possession of the churches, and the public exercise of
religion with all its splendour; and they accordingly
drew up a document which they signed, pledging themselves that they would never consent that the queen or
prince of Wales should be invited over till the religious
articles should be secured, or that any peace should be
made which would tend to lessen the public exercise of
their religion.

French and Plunket sailed from Waterford on the 10th
of February; but, meeting with storms, were forced to
put back, and sailed again on the 17th. They brought
with them a strange document, signed by Owen O'Neill
and eight bishops, entreating the pope to raise Rinuccini
to the dignity of cardinal. Muskerry and Brown sailed
soon after;—nor should it be forgotten that there was a
strict understanding between the nuncio and Muskerry,
that a special provision should be made for restoring the
"old Irish" to their plundered estates in Ulster. But
Muskerry was not sincere when he acquiesced in this
matter, for he had no notion that such justice should be
done the kinsmen and abettors of the man who had been
a thorn in the side of Ormond. Yet it is not honourable
to his memory that he left an impression on Rinuccini's
mind that O'Neill would be restored, at the very moment when he was cordially opposed to such an ad-
justment. *

The Earl of Antrim, whose services in the king's caus
entitled him to a much higher place in the royal esteem
sailed before his colleagues; and he thought he woul
have been immediately appointed lord lieutenant. B

* Carte, ii. 20.

he was a Catholic; and he had soon reason enough to
find himself undeceived. Could the urgent instance of
the nuncio and the Irish bishops have carried this point,
a great good would have been effected; but Glamorgan
was refused; and such was the fatal leaning to the bi-
fronted Ormond, that all hopes of the queen and prince
were centred in him.

They landed at St. Malo on the 14th of March, and
soon afterwards waited on the queen at St. Germains.—
Taaffe and Preston, who were humbled by their recent
defeat, were now siding with the Ormond party in the
cry for peace, and forwarded private instructions to
Ormond, assuring him of their devotion to his interests,
but, above all, of their hatred of the nuncio, O'Neill,
and the prelates, whom they represented as plotting the
introduction of some foreign power. They expressed
the most ardent desire for the advent of the Prince of
Wales, and only wanted assistance to march against
O'Neill, who was the only obstacle they dreaded. But
in case the prince would decline coming into Ireland,
they entreated to be furnished with such instructions as
should guide them in all things conformable to the royal
feelings.

On the question of religion, however, they were pro-
foundly silent. As it had been agreed that this point
should not be touched till some communication came
from the deputies who had gone to Rome. The chief
and grand subjects which engaged their negotiation regarded temporal concessions, which were calculated to
secure to them their estates; nor did they get a final
answer from the queen till the 13th of May.

That answer rated them on their rebellious conduct
in rejecting the former peace; and to this fruitful source
were ascribed all the misfortunes of Ireland and of the
king himself. Adverting, then, to the question of religion, she assured the Marquess of Antrim in parti-
.cular, "that, under existing circumstances, there was
no giving them a final and conclusive answer; but she
assured them, that she would soon give them some such
as she should think fit to receive in Ireland more particular and full propositions from the Irish confederates;
and that the person thus authorized should be instructed

in whatever was consistent with justice and his majesty's honour."*

Such was the queen's reply. Much like every other royal speech dictated by the minister, and far more full of promise than good intentions. Ormond dictated it—Queen Maria pronounced it. The person to be authorized to restore peace to Ireland was the Marquess of Ormond, and his adherents hastened back to prepare for his advent.

Ormond, who had been secretly treating with Inchiquin before the surrender of Dublin, still kept up a correspondence with him; and he had no reason to be disappointed. Inchiquin was to the parliament what Preston was to the confederates, fond of changing sides, and actuated more by private resentments than a sense of public duty to their respective parties. The vacillation of both these men was of great use to Ormond; and he could not but be rejoiced when he learned that "Murrogh of the burnings" had once more declared for the king. The monies which had been advanced to him by the parliament, he declared were insufficient for the payment and maintenance of his troops; and, after a short repose, he took the field again, and threatened to re-enact the tragedy of Cashel in the city of Waterford. The vigilance of the garrison, however, compelled him to abandon his deadly intentions, and he marched into the county Kilkenny, murdering the peasantry, and exacting contributions. Jones, whose army was reduced to great straits in Dublin, finding that O'Neill's troops had retired on Kilkenny, now marched out of the city, and secured provisions, having reduced Maynooth Castle, which was but feebly garrisoned; and the simultaneous movements of Inchiquin and the parliament-governor of Dublin led many to think that it was a preconcerted design between them both.†

The presence of O'Neill saved Kilkenny at this moment, for Inchiquin had not the ability or the force to meet him. All the mischief which Murrogh had committed up to the present did not amount to more than mere border raids, and the supreme council held a meeting at Clonmel, where Rinuccini made an offer,

* Carte. † Rinuccini, p. 296.

on the part of Owen Roe, to advance into Munster, and
quarter his army in the very cantonments occupied
by Inchiquin's troops. But all these overtures were
rejected by the Ormondists, who had rather see O'Neill
extinguished than Inchiquin suffer the least molestation.

Exasperated by this determined opposition, which led
him to think that he was to be victimized, to the implacable resentment of Muskerry and his partizans,
O'Neill sent word to the council that he would imme-
diatly retire into the north, and leave them to shift for
themselves. But such was the nuncio's influence with
him, that he was induced to protract his stay in Leinster,
to keep watch and ward over the faction which was
secretly plotting his ruin. An event had lately transpired which added to the hatred already conceived for
Owen Roe by the Ormondists. Whilst Rinuccini was
eagerly expecting the arrival of the Dean of Fermo,
with the supplies of money from Rome, the ship so
long expected was signalled from the ramparts of Duncannon, and the Dean Massari landed at Waterford on
the 23rd of March. Along with the money there came
a letter from the pope to Owen Roe, extolling his love
for the religion of his fathers, and his chivalrous devotion to his native land. The sword of the Earl of
Tyrone, "which had rifted the field like lightning at
Beal-an-atha-Buidhe," had been carefully preserved by
Father Luke Wadding ; and the hand of the pontiff
blessed the blade, and ordered it to be given to him
who well could wield it. This simple circumstance,
taken in connexion with O'Mahony's book, was the
signal for an outcry. O'Neill was to be a king; the
book was the declaration of his sovereignty, and that
sword was the emblem of royalty. Henceforth no
matter on what side he stood, as long as a man could be
found to oppose him, O'Neill was doomed to ruin and
destruction.*

But the real intentions of Ormond's abettors did not
transpire till about the beginning of April, when Colonel
John Barry, the companion of Ormond in his flight from
London, landed in Ireland. He immediately gave out

Gall. of Irish Writers, p. 98.

that the marquess had a secret commission from the king to treat with Inchiquin, and having been furnished with a safe conduct by the supreme council, he hastened to notify them of the fact. The Scotch who were cooped up in the seaport towns in Ulster, were anxious to change sides, and nothing now remained but the coming of Ormond to unite all parties in a determined league against Jones in Dublin and all those who were in the interest of the parliament.

The supreme council gladly seized the opportunity of writing to Murrogh, proposing a truce; but, affecting to disregard them, his answer was addressed to Dr. Fennell, one of Ormond's creatures, demanding 4,000 dollars per month as the price of his adhesion. This was gladly accepted, and the men who would not give a fraction to O'Neill, readily accepted the offer of him whose hands were stained with the blood shed at Cashel. Two months before the supreme council had resolved to raise an army of 7,000 infantry and 700 horse, but now that Ormond was to come, the project was abandoned, for he, forsooth, was a host in himself, and nothing but his presence was required.

A proclamation, calling a meeting of the confederates at Kilkenny on the 20th of April, was now circulated throughout the land, and many and various were the anticipations to which it gave rise. The question which was to fix attention, was a treaty or truce with Inchiquin. The Ormondists hailed it as the consummation of their hopes, for it would restore their idol to power. But, alas! there were many who could easily foresee that in the coming session the prophetic warning, too often disregarded in Ireland, was to be fulfilled to the very letter :—" Every kingdom divided shall be made desolate."

Owen Roe was at Dunamase, girt by his faithful followers, while the confederates were assembling in the city of Kilkenny. Sad and anxious were the moments which the gallant chieftain spent in the ancient halls of the O'Moores, waiting the result of the deliberations of his friends and foes. Oh! how the lordly soul of the Ulster general must have burned with indignation, when he reflected that the destinies of his country were now to be poised by the descendants of those Norman barons who had secretly sworn to destroy him and his. And all this, to propitiate Ormond and Murrogh O'Brien! The craven slaves had tied up his hands, when he was ready to strike a blow which might have saved the country; and they were now ready to purchase the friendship of a blood-stained wretch, even at the price of his extinction. What wonder, if he let loose the creaghts whom these pusillanimous temporizers so much dreaded? But the influence of the nuncio withheld him. The dean of Fermo had come from the Vatican, to convey to him the blessing of the holy father. A considerable sum of money, from the same source, and by the same agency, was placed at his disposal; and from the ramparts of that stronghold he often turned his looks in the direction of Kilkenny, awaiting the signal which was to call him forth to battle again for the land of his sires. But, alas! division and dissensions have ever been the bane of Ireland. Such were the causes which brought the Norman to our shores; and now the same spirit of discord was destined to work our ruin again :—

> " Ex illo fluere, ac retro sublapsa referri
> Spes Danaum, fractæ vires, aversa Dei mens."

Rinuccini was at Waterford when a letter from the supreme council, now packed with the adherents of Ormond, summoned him to attend the assembly. An intercepted despatch from Inchiquin, which revealed a conspiracy against the life of O'Neill, had fallen into his hands; and some dark hints about an attempt to be made on his own person caused him to pause.

Before he ventured amongst them, he addressed a reply to their summons, which set forth that, as they were unable to carry on the war against Jones in Dublin and Inchiquin in Munster, it was deemed expedient to treat with the latter, and thus leave them free to march against Jones, and make themselves masters of the metropolis.

But Rinuccini knew that it was a foregone conclusion, and that they had determined to carry their point against all opposition. He therefore wrote to the council, to dissuade them, if possible, from making any truce with Murrogh O'Brien. He besought them, above all

things, to consider well the character of the man whose
hand they were now ready to grasp. That hand was
red with the blood so wantonly shed at Cashel; and, but
a few days before, he who was now meditating an alliance
with them was anxious to take their lives, even at the
very walls of Kilkenny. "What!" wrote the nuncio,
"are you now going to bestow on Inchiquin those
monies which, if properly allocated, would send O'Neill's
army into the south, and utterly destroy those bandits
who, being disregarded by the parliament, are driven by
necessity to court your friendship? Europe is shocked
at the atrocities of this man, and will you parley with
him when you ought to avenge your brethren, sacrilegiously murdered and plundered by his brigands. Cessations and truces have been the ruin of the country, and are you to make terms with a man who, if he
were not driven out by the famishing state of
his troops, would not dare to take the field?

"Let me supplicate you to do something worthy of
yourselves and the confederacy. You have an army
ready to march,—send it into Munster, and leave me
free to inform the holy father that you have restored religion, and rescued the peasantry from the cruel and ex-
orbitant taxation imposed by a man on whose sincerity
you can place no reliance. I will attend your summons,
but before I come I have thought it well to put you in
possession of my sentiments."[*]

His epistle met a prompt and argumentative reply.
Inchiquin was fortified in almost all the strong places in
the south. It was not now the time to undertake sieges,
even though they had the means; "and granting that
O'Neill's army could be sent into Munster, are we to
suppose," said the Ormondists, "that Jones and the other
parliamentarian generals will remain inactive? What
terms can we expect from the queen and Prince of Wales,
if, instead of making war against their avowed enemies,
we reject the overtures of a man who is willing to fight
with us under the same standard and for the same cause?
The churches which he has desecrated we will restore,
and our care will be to see the plundered peasantry in-
demnified for their losses. Let us not then reject the

* Philop. Iræn.

overtures of the man whom our refusal will exasperate, and drive back to the ranks of the parliament, and finally induce him to give Cork, Youghal, and Kinsale into their hands. What doubts could be obtained of his fidelity to the new cause since he had imprisoned those who refused to sign for the king? And as to his rapacity and sacrileges, which the Christian world must execrate, remember that our own countrymen are at this moment spoiling the peasantry almost under the walls of Dublin. Write, therefore, to Rome—supplicate the holy father to send us aid through Plunket and the Bishop of Ferns ; and now that we are no longer apprehensive of Inchiquin, let us make a stern struggle for the cause of that king to whom our oath of association conscientiously binds us."

An additional argument was borrowed from the supposition that he sanctioned a truce which O'Neill was about to negotiate with the Scotch, as if to convict him of factious inconsistency. But these arguments were unavailing. Rinuccini was firm in his resolve to oppose the truce with Inchiquin. He dictated a letter in reply to this, arguing that the parliamentarians in Dublin were as badly off as the troops of Inchiquin in the south, and that immediate action against one and the other was more necessary than truces and diplomacy. He treated the assumed inability of the confederates to carry on the war as the result of pusillanimity, and concluded by denying that he ever was concerned in any truce between O'Neill and the Scotch.

But the object of this correspondence was to induce the nuncio to proceed to Kilkenny, on the assurance that nothing should be done "without his entire satisfaction ;" but, in fact, it was not for the purpose of gaining his concurrence, but rather to secure a portion of the money which had been recently sent from Rome.

He proceeded, however, and the session commenced on the 20th of April;—it was doomed to be the last in which he was ever to take part.

The question which now fixed the attention of Ireland was that which had already formed the subject of the correspondence between the nuncio and the supreme council. The long catalogue of the reverses sustained by the confederate arms, and the difficulties to which

Ireland was reduced, furnished ample matter for the eloquence as well as intrigue of both parties.

The enemy, said the Ormondists, is almost at your
doors. Jones, aided by the rebel parliament of England,
is only waiting his opportunity to march against you,
and Inchiquin in the south will soon be in a condition to
operate with him, if you reject the truce which he offers.
Under such circumstances, you cannot pause a moment
to conclude with him. We are destitute of means, and
cannot oppose him. The political articles which he pro-
poses are unobjectionable, and the two which regard religion must prove satisfactory in our present disastrous
condition.

The articles touching that most important subject
stipulated that no confederate Catholic should suffer any
injury in the free exercise of his religion, so long as the
said cessation should be observed; that the property in
the actual possession of the clergy as well as of the
laity shall remain in the same undisturbed state as it
had been when the cessation commenced.*

Such were the conditions made by Inchiquin in the
matter of religion; and be it observed, that it was resolved that the Catholic religion should not be exercised
in his quarters or garrisons. The enlightened policy of
Europe at the present day will not tolerate the persecution of the Christian of any denomination in Turkey;
and are we to wonder that an enlightened Italian, in the
year 1648, would not sign his consent to such terms on
behalf of the Catholics of Ireland?

He took, however, the real view of the case, and rejected the terms, as far from consonant to the spirit of
the oath by which the confederates had bound them-

---

* The following are the articles of Inchiquin's treaty:—

"It is agreed and resolved, that none professing the Catholic religion, cleric or laic, suffer any molestation or detriment from 'he Lord
Inchiquin, or any of his adherents, on account of the free exercise of
religion, and the performance of its functions, during the continuance
of this truce, always excepting that it be not practised or exercised in
the garrisons or quarters of the said Lord Inchiquin.

"2ndly. It is agreed and resolved, that the property pertaining to
laics and clerics, now in their possession, be secured to them respectively, and continue to them, without any detriment, from the day on
which the truce commenced, with the same advantages as before, provided that they submit to this agreement, and do not decline to pay
the taxes and afford their contributions to the public cause."

selves, and manfully scorned the truce on such disho-
nourable proposals.

But the Ormondists in the council gladly acquiesced,
and, in a true sense, may be said to have preferred their
monarch and the possession of their revenues to their
God and religion.

"Make no truce with this man," said the nuncio,
"he has thrice times changed sides. If the massacre at
Cashel has left no trace on your memories, recollect that
a month ago he pillaged the town of Carrick, and slew
the inhabitants, who were Catholics, palliating the atro-
city by asserting he could not restrain his soldiers. Remember, too, that he has driven the Catholic clergy out
of the cathedral of Callan, and introduced those who do
not profess your religion. Talk not of your inability to
carry war into his quarters. The army under Jones has
been worn out watching O'Neill during the summer, and
does not amount to more than 3,000 men. Preston,
with the troops recently levied in Leinster, ought to be
able to meet him. Inchiquin has not more than 3,000
men in Munster; they are naked and hungry, and you
fear him when you ought to despise him. In Connaught
and Ulster, the Scotch are able to do little more than
commit robberies for their sustenance. At the present
moment Owen O'Neill has an army of more than 6,000
men. He is ready to act against Inchiquin in the south,
and I will supply monies to pay his troops, and thus rid
you of these scruples with which the ravages of his
soldiers have so long afflicted you. I exhort you to
union of heart and purpose; and remember that your
rulers of England have never treated you, Catholics,
with respect, except when you stood in a united and formidable league."* The energetic remonstrance of the
nuncio produced an instantaneous effect. John, Archbishop of Tuam, whose political tendencies were on the
side of Clanricarde, and consequently of Ormond,
seized a pen, and signed the condemnation of the truce,
and the same course was immediately adopted by thirteen of the bishops. But the truce had been already
concluded between the Ormondists and Inchiquin a
Dungarvan.

* Rin. pp 312, 420

It had scarcely been signed when the Ormondists proclaimed through the country that peace was restored, and that they were soon to march on Dublin, and drive Jones from the metropolis. Mountgarret, at the head of 300 horse, entered Kilkenny, to intimidate the refractory and enforce obedience. But there was a terrible weapon still in reserve. The sword of Aodh O'Neill was not potent to carry out the nuncio's views, and he determined to have recourse to another, which, if it did not pierce the flesh, effectually contributed to divide the spirit.

Inchiquin's designs against O'Neill were now developed. Preston and Murrogh united their forces. They had pledged themselves to see the truce observed, and to resort to violence when it might be deemed necessary Heavens! that the petty feeling of jealousy could instigate the scion of the house of Gormanstown to grasp the bloody hand of Inchiquin, and pledge himself to destroy the gallant O'Neill. Yet such was the case. All who did not obey that fatal truce were to be pursued as rebels. Fourteen bishops, the majority of the clergy, and the popular feeling, were opposed to it. O'Neill was still the unshaken friend of the hierarchy, and was involved in the same condemnation. Far better for Preston that he had nobly fallen under the walls of Louvain, when his laurels were fresh, than live to conspire against the braver and the nobler soldier; but he represented in his own person the deadly hatred of his class for the "old Irish" nobility. Taaffe, that braggart who found that the prophecy of Knock-na-gaoll was not to be realized in his person, was also in arms, hectoring and vapouring over the new alliance. Clanricarde, who worshipped England and everything English, hailed the dark storm which lowered over the land; for it only concealed from his view for a moment the messiah of his political faith. That messiah was Ormond. Clanricarde, therefore, abandoned his neutrality, and 3,000 men assembled round him, to march against O'Neill. Is it for this that

"Glory guards Clanricarde's grave"?

Seven days after the publication of the truce, a crowd

was attracted to St. Canice's cathedral by a strange
document affixed to the gate. It was a sentence of
comminatory excommunication against all who would
respect the truce. On that same day, the Dean of
Fermo, by order of Rinuccini, took down the comminatory sentence and substituted another, *latæ senten-
tice*, against all abettors of it, and an interdict against
all cities, towns, and villages in which it should be
received or observed.

Oh! it was a fearful expedient, and there is but one
consideration which can reconcile a true Irish heart to
this hasty proceeding — that is, the preservation of
O'Neill—for was not his life immeasurably more
valuable than a host of such men as Preston, Clanricarde, or Muskerry? Alas! no other reflection
remains to palliate the cruelty of such a measure as
that of an interdict. Harsh and heartless we would
not hesitate to pronounce Rinuccini, if this act were
not meant to throw the ægis of his spiritual authority
round the man who fought for the church of his
fathers. But, view it as we will, it was impolitic to
bar the gates which lead from earth to heaven, and
refuse the consolations of religion to the afflicted and
sorrowing spirit. Was it for this that brave hearts
sighed and toiled? Or could the men who rose for
their religion in the year 1641 have anticipated that ere
seven years a dignitary of their own church would
have quenched the lamp, and forbidden the celebration
of the mass on those very altars for which they fought,
and bled, and died.

But, where is Rinuccini? At day break on the
morning of the 27th he scaled the garden wall of his
house, and accompanied by two attendants, proceeded
through an unfrequented gate to Maryborough, where
Owen Roe lay encamped. The gallant chief was
ignorant of the doings at Kilkenny, and when he heard
of the truce he began to think of his personal safety.
His army had not been collected—700 true hearts were
all the protection which now surrounded him, and when
he learned that it was the nuncio's intention to quit
the country, tongue cannot tell the pathetic grief of
the noble chieftain. Messengers were soon despatched

from Kilkenny with overtures to Rinuccini, inviting him to return, and offering to cancel the truce if he would advance £10,000; but the die was cast. O'Neill and the bishops sent back a draft of some propositions to the supreme council, which, after a lapse of twelve days, were returned with such modifications as were not acceptable. The delay in the transmission was to give Preston an opportunity of collecting all his forces, and surprising O'Neill. On the twelfth day after his arrival in Maryborough, a messenger rushed breathless into the apartment where Owen Roe and the nuncio were conversing, stating that Preston with ten thousand men were marching on Birr, four miles distant from the camp. "At the announcement," says the nuncio, "O'Neill's features underwent an extraordinary change: astonishment was the first emotion, and then a sudden palor shadowed his visage." But Preston did not advance, and ignorance of O'Neill's numerical inferiority saved him for the moment.

But the censures and the excommunication were doing well. Preston's troops began to mutiny. Unlike their chief they were not all "excommunication proof," and 2,000 of them deserted to O'Neill—happily for the latter; for when the nuncio sent his confessor to Preston, in the vain hope of winning him over, he declared that either he or Owen Roe should speedily perish, and that the opinion of eight bishops was against the validity of the censures.

O'Neill and the nuncio bade an eternal adieu to each other. The former broke up his camp; and now that the supreme council had dared to brand him as a rebel, he hastened to collect his troops. Ten thousand foot, and fifteen hundred horse soon rallied round the standard of the "red hand." But let it be the work of him who has written the Life of Aodh O'Neill to tell how his gallant descendant vindicated the honour of his name; how he scared Preston on the broad plains of Leinster, and baffled five generals at the pass of Ballaghmore. The nuncio retired to Galway, and the din of arms gave place for a while to theological controversy.

Walsh was the corriphæus of those who impugned the

validity of the censures.* Four bishops who had sanctioned the condemnation of the truce, now declared
themselves satisfied with some modifications which had
been introduced, and protested against the nuncio. The
supreme council issued a circular cautioning all ecclesiastical authorities against interfering with their subjects
on account of the censures or interdict.

Scandal and division were the natural results, and a
deputation proceeded to Galway, warning Rinuccini
that an appeal had been made to Rome against his "un-
canonical proceedings." A scene ensued which it would
be needless to record. Suffice it to say, that priest was
armed against priest; secular and regular were alternately
engaged in the most acrimonious conflict of controversy;
nor did greater excitement prevail in the days of Savo-
narola.

In vain did the nuncio endeavour to convoke a national
synod. He issued a summons to the bishops on the 13th
of July, to meet him on the 15th. Clanricarde's troops
blocked up every pass. O'Neill, who was now on the
borders of Leitrim, sent two regiments to facilitate the
approach of the bishops who yet remained on his side,
and Colonel Maguire lost his life in storming the Castle
of Drumruisk.

But all too late. The synod never met, and Rinuccini
hastened to retire from that fated land, where, to use his
own sentiment, "he had never seen the sun." The
schemes and the hopes of his enemies were fully realized.
Ormond landed at Cork on the 29th of September, 1648.
He then proceeded to Carrick-on-Suir, where he was met
by the bishops and members of the supreme council, and
thence marched to Kilkenny. The life of Charles I. terminated almost simultaneously with the existence of the
confederation, and a new era began to dawn on Ireland,
remarkable for its fidelity to that house of Stuart, which,
alas! but ill requited her unhappy and misgoverned
children.

In the month of February, Rinuccini sailed from Galway and proceeded to Rome. The state of his own

* The gross aspersions cast upon the Jesuits, the champions of the
cross and literature, by this disobedient friar, are as foul as any that
their modern maligners have penned.

principality demanded his immediate attention, but it
was necessary that he should give Innocent X. an account of his luckless nunciature. Some fatality seems to
have been attached to that office. Nicholas Sanders, an
Englishman, sent by Gregory XIII., died of starvation
under a tree in the mountains of Kerry. Owen O'Hagan,
Bishop of Ross, who had been appointed by Clement
VIII., perished in the wars of Tirowen with a sword in
one hand and a rosary in the other.* Could his predecessors have been called from their graves to meet Rinuccini on his return, what a similarity of incident must
they not have narrated?

Yet, let us do justice to the memory of the man. It
has been asserted, on the authority of Walsh and
the disappointed Callaghan,† that he was met with re-
buke on his return to Rome. "*Temerarie te gessisti*,
are the words which Innocent X. is said to have applied
to him. But any charge from such men as Walsh or
Callaghan should be cautiously received. The former
stands convicted of maligning many an illustrious name,
and echoed the cry of Ormond's pack, who denounced
the men of 1641 as "bloody rebels." The sycophant of
Ormond could entertain no kindly feeling for Rinuccini,
who laboured to reconcile him to the observance of the
monastic rules, which he boldly disregarded. Aiazzi,
Rinuccini's biographer, informs us that he was offered a
high place of dignity in the pontifical court, which he
modestly declined, preferring his pastoral charge at
Fermo.

Nor let it be said that he was a bigot; whoever would
make the charge ought to reflect under what circumstances Rinuccini had to act. Had he not to contend
with men who were the avowed and unrelenting enemies
of the Irish Catholics; and would he not have deserved
to be branded as untrue to his charge, if he did not urge
them on to win their own again? Did he do aught that

* Walsh's Hist. of the Rem. p. 34.
† The author of the Vindiciæ Hib. thought to become Bishop of
Cork, but was disappointed by the Nuncio's veto. He subsequently
produced his scurrilous work in reply to a book from the pen of the
Rev. Paul King, a pious and patriotic Franciscan friar. *V.* Bishop
Talbot's "Friar Disciplined."

was irreconcilable with enlightened policy, in insisting on freedom of conscience and the untrammelled exercise of that religion of which he was a minister?

Will any one blame him for so far interfering in temporal concerns, as to aid the plundered Catholics of Ulster in wresting their property from the robber gripe of the undertakers? Yes: he had an incontrovertible right to enforce these just demands; and, when argument failed, he was justified in resorting to the sword. Scotland had won religious independence by this weapon, and why should not Ireland have tried it? Let those who would condemn him on the score of bigotry, reflect that he was acting against men who had sworn the extirpation of the "idolatrous papists," and then ask themselves how can they justify their assertion? His notions, it is true, were purely Italian: he did not think Catholicity could flourish where it was unaccompanied by all the pomp and splendour which he was accustomed to in his own sunny clime. Catholicity in Ireland appeared to him like a leafless branch of the mighty tree, and he fain would see it in full flower. Perhaps, in this particular, he erred; but, according to the rigid laws of justice, he had a right to insist on the restoration of the cathedrals and the ecclesiastical revenues to the Catholic clergy; and who will blame him if he sighed for the day when he might hear Catholic psalmody pealing in all the temples of the land? No, he deserves not the name of bigot; nor can the charge be sustained.

But a graver accusation is brought against him,—he is charged with having divided the confederates. This is an assumption: it supposes that they were united before his advent. But it is false. Failure was the result of their divisions, and he vainly sought to convince them that they had within themselves all the elements of strength and power if they combined. Under the walls of Dublin, was it his fault if O'Neill and Preston fell on each other, and gave Ormond the satisfaction of witnessing the two armies in deadly strife? Were not Muskerry and Preston, and Belling and Clanricarde, the sworn friends of Ormond, and the avowed enemies of the Ulster Irish and their glorious chief? But enough: the censures were inexpedient, but in one sense they were useful. The man who stood by his creed had a right to be protected by it. He loved Ireland, and would have died for her independence; but he lived to learn that Cromwell triumphed, and shed the blood of her noblest sons. Amongst those, many were of that party which clung to Rinuccini. They were faithful to the last, and lion-hearted when others shuddered at their doom. General Purcell fainted when Ireton pronounced his death sentence:* and Terence Albert O'Brien, the bishop of Emly, scorned Ireton to his teeth, and foretold that he should soon meet him at the tribunal of God;—and this was the case; for the blood of the bishop was not congealed on the block before Ireton died of the plague.

Heber Mac Mahon, bishop of Clogher, died nobly for fatherland; but in another place will the record be longer and more minute. On the list of martyrs to religion and country, you will nowhere find more illustrious names than those, and they were all of Rinuccini's party and sentiments. I dare not contrast with them the Ormondists who survived these virtuous and patriotic men. The storm swept harmlessly over their heads. Ormond got more by the revolution than his Norman ancestors won by the sword: his fortunes, and those of his adherents, were created out of the ruin of the Catholics; for they were scattered to the four winds of heaven.

But it is time to record one proof of Rinuccini's love of Ireland. On his return he caused frescoes to be painted in the archiepiscopal palace at Fermo, of the actions which had been fought during his nunciature; the bad taste of one of his successors caused them to be destroyed. It is to be regretted, for they would have thrown a light on this period of our history. How gladly would the pilgrim turn from the tomb of Hugh O'Neill to the pictures of Bunratty, Beinburb, and Ballaghmore! But all that now remains, in that old city, to recall the memory of the man, is the monumental inscription.

The summary of an eventful life may be collected from a single line engraved upon it:—

"Ad fœderatos Catholicos Hiberniæ pontificia legatione functo."

* Hib. Dom.

Above that tomb many of our exiled chieftains have trod and wept. Many a prayer, too, has been offered within the cathedral of Fermo for " the dear old land !" Oh ! may she soon arise from thraldom and provincialism, to take her place amid the nations !

APPENDIX.

—

TABLE OF THE LEVIES ORDERED BY THE SUPREME COUNCIL IN THE YEAR 1642.

Referred to at page 52.

Counties.	Infantry.	Cavalry.
Westmeath	3000	50
Meath	3000	50
Kildare	3000	50
Wexford	3000	50
King's County	2800	50
Queen's County	2400	40
Wicklow	2400	40
Dublin	2000	50
Kilkenny City and County	3000	50
Louth	1700	20
Longford	3000	50
Carlow	2400	50
Total	31,700	550

I HAVE thought it advisable to insert the following letter, referred to at page 120. It has been regarded by some as evidence of a collusion between Glamorgan and Lord Ormond :—

"LORD HERBERT (PRETENDED EARLE OF GLAMORGAN) HIS LETTER TO HIS LADY.

" MY dearest heart, I hope these will prevent any newes shal come unto you of me, since my comittment to the Castle of Dublin. To which I assure thee I went as cheerefully and as willingly as they could wish, whosoever they were by whose meanes it was procured, and should as unwillingly goe foorth, were the gates both of the Castle and Town open unto me, until I were cleered, as they are willing to make me unserviceable to the King, and lay me aside, who have procured for me this restraint; When I consider thee a Woman, as I thinke, I know you are, I feare least you should be apprehensive: but when I reflect that you are of the House of Thomond, and that you were once pleased to say these words unto me, That I should never, in tendernesse of you, desist from doing, what in honour I was obliged to doe, I grow confident, that in this you will now shew your magnanimity, and by it the greatest testimony of affection, that you can possibly afford me; and am also confident, that you know me so well, that I need not tell you how cleare I am, and void of feare, the only effect of a good con- science, and that I am guilty of nothing, that may tes- tifie one thought of disloyalty to his Majestie, or of what may staine the honour of the family I come of, or set a Brand upon my future posteritie. Courage (my heart) were I amongst the King's Enemies you might feare; but being only a prisoner amongst his Friends and faith- ful Subjects, you need doubt nothing, but that this cloud will be soone dissipated, by the Sunne-shine of the King my Master, and did you but know how well and merry I am, you would bee as little troubled as my selfe, who have nothing that can afflict me, but lest your apprehen- sion might hurt you, especially since all the while I could get no opportunity of sending, nor yet by any certaine probable meanes, but by my Cousin Bruertons, Master Mannerings, our Cousin Constable of the Castle, and my Lord Lieutenant's leave: and I hope you and I shall live to acknowledge our obligation to them, there being nothing in this world that I desire more, then you should at least heare from me; And believe it (sweet heart) were I before the Parliament in London, I could justify, both the King and my selfe in what I have done, And so I pray acquaint my Father, who I know so cau- tious, that he would hardly accept a Letter from me, but yet I presume most humbly to ask his blessing, and as heartily as I send mine to pretty Mall, and I hope this day or to morrow will set a period to my businesse.

to the shame of those who have been occasioners of it: but I must needs say from my Lord Lieutenant, and the Privie Councell here, I have received as much justice, nobleness and favour, as I could possibly expect: the Circumstances of these proceedings are too long to write unto you, but I am confident all will prove to my greater honour; And my Right Honourable accuser, my Lord George Digby, will be at last rectified and confirmed in the good which he is pleased to say he ever had of me hitherto, as the greatest affliction that he ever had, did doe what his conscience enforced him unto, and indeed did wrap up the bitter pill of the Impeachment of suspition of high Treason in so good words, as that I swallowed it, with the greatest ease in the world, and it hath hither had no other operation. then that it hath purged Melancholy: for as I was not at the present not any way dismayed, so have I not since been any way at all disheartened. So I pray let not any of my friends that's there, believe any thing, untill ye have the perfect relation of it from my selfe. And this request I chiefly make unto you, to whom I remaine a most faithfull, and most passionately devoted Husband and servant, "GLAMORGAN.

"Remember my service to my Brother, my cosin Browne, and the rest of my good friends."

"London: Printed for Edward Husband, Printer to the Honorable House of Commons. March 17, 1645."

THIS document, preserved in the original at Rome, has been translated in that great organ of Catholicity, the *Dublin Review:* March 1845. It may be regarded as a perfect picture of that portion of Ireland which came immediately under the notice of the Italian writer, who is thought to have been Father Arcamoni, the nuncio's confessor. This letter must have been written immediately after the arrival of the nuncio.—

"The courtesy of the poor people among whom my lord the nuncio took up his quarters, was unexampled.

A fat bullock, two sheep, and a porker, were instantly slaughtered, and an immense supply of beer, butter, and milk, was brought to him; and even we, who were still on board, experienced the kindness of the poor fishermen, who sent us presents of excellent fish and oysters of most prodigious size in the utmost abundance. While we were creeping along in the frigate, in the track of the nuncio, I observed a harbour about half-a-mile in length, and a pistol-shot in breadth, so very beautiful, that curiosity led me to take the boat and go on shore, for the purpose of examining the wonders of the place. In a short time I was surrounded by an immense multitude of men, women, and boys, who had come running down from different places in the mountains to see me; and some of them happening to observe the crucifix which I wore on my breast, they all made a circle round me, and kissed it one after another. After this, they made signs of the greatest affection and friendship to me, and conducted me, almost perforce, to one of the nearest huts, where I was seated on a cushion stuffed with feathers; and the mistress of the house, a venerable old dame, sat down beside me along with her daughters, and offered to kiss me, according to the usage of the country; and had I not explained by signs, that this would not be becoming in one who bore Christ crucified on his breast, and who accompanied the nuncio as priest, I think they would have been offended. The old dame then brought me in a wooden vessel, a great draught of most delicious milk, expressing the utmost anxiety that I should drink it. As it was of a most excellent flavour I drank copiously of it, and was quite revived by the draught. They all endeavoured to stand as close to me as possible, and those who were able to touch me, considered themselves happy; so that it was with difficulty I could disengage myself from them, in order to return to the frigate: on the contrary, they wished to escort me to the very water edge, and some of the young men wished to accompany me altogether. What is most remarkable, is, that in these wild and mountainous places, and among a poor people who are reduced to absolute misery, by the devastations of the heretic enemy, I found, notwithstanding, the noble influence of our holy Catholic faith, for there was not

one, man, woman, or child, however small, who could
not repeat, the Our Father, the Hail Mary, the Creed,
and the commandments of the Holy Church.

"The country through which we have passed, though
mountainous, is agreeable; and, being entirely pasture-
land, is most abundantly stocked with cattle of every
kind. Occasionally one meets a long tract of valley,
interspersed with woods and groves; which, as they are
neither high nor densely planted, partake more of the
agreeable than of the gloomy. For seventy miles the
country which we met was almost all of this character;
but having once crossed the mountains, we entered
upon an immense plain, occasionally diversified with
hills and valleys, highly cultivated, and enriched with
an infinite number of cattle, especially oxen and sheep;
from the latter of which is obtained the very finest of
what is called English wool.

"The men are fine-looking and of incredible strength;
they are stout runners, and bear every sort of hard-
ship with indescribable cheerfulness. They are all
devoted to arms, and especially now that they are at
war. Those who apply themselves to the study of literature are most learned; and you meet persons of every
profession and science among them.

"The women are remarkably tall and beautiful, and
display a charming union of gracefulness with modesty
and devotion. Their manners are marked by extreme
simplicity; and they freely mix in conversation everywhere, without suspicion or jealousy. Their costume
is different from ours, and somewhat resembles the
French; except that they wear, besides, a long cloak
and profuse locks of hair, and go without any head-
dress, contenting themselves with a kind of handker-
chief, almost after the Greek fashion, which displays
their natural beauty to great advantage. They are extremely prolific, and almost all the women who marry
have large families. There are some who have as many
as thirty children alive; and the number of those who
have from fifteen to twenty is immense; and they all
are handsome, tall, and robust, the majority being light-
haired, and of a clear white and red complexion.

"They give most superb entertainments both of flesh
and fish, for they have both in the greatest abundance

They are perpetually pledging healths, the usual drink being Spanish wines, French claret, most delicious beer, and most excellent milk. Butter is used on all occasions, and there is no species of provisions which is not found in the greatest abundance. As yet we have all accommodated ourselves to the usages of the country. [A line is here effaced.] They also eat fruit, as apples, pears, plums, artichokes ; and all eatables are cheap. A fat ox costs a pistole, a sheep thirty bajocchi, a pair of capons or fowls, a paul, eggs a farthing a-piece, and so on for the rest in proportion. You can have a large fish for a soldo. But game is so abundant that they make no account of it at all. Birds may almost be killed with sticks, and especially thrushes, blackbirds, and chaffinches. Both the salt and fresh water fish are most exquisite, and so abundant, that for three pauls we bought one hundred and fifty pounds of excellent fish; as pike, salmon, herring, trout, &c., and all of excellent quality. We got a thousand pilchards and oysters for twenty-five bajocchi.

"The horses are very plenty, stout, handsome, swift, and cheap; so that for twenty crowns you might buy a nag, which in Italy would be worth a hundred gold pieces."

FINIS.

www.ingramcontent.com/pod-product-compliance
Lightning Source LLC
Chambersburg PA
CBHW030734280326
41926CB00086B/1357